Granddad's Mondays

94 More Stories for My Grandchildren about the Reiss Family and Farm which dates from 1838 in St. Clair County, Illinois. Stories span to 1930s to present

by Stephen W. Reiss

Granddad's Monday
Copyright © 2024 by Stephen W. Reiss

ISBN: 979-8894790466 (hc)
ISBN: 979-8894790442 (sc)
ISBN: 979-8894790459 (e)

The Reading Glass
BOOKS

The Reading Glass Books
(888) 420-3050
www.readingglassbooks.com
fulfillment@readingglassbooks.com

Dedication to the Past

Three wonderful women married into the Reiss family and quickly became dynamic matriarchs for the family, the farm, and their respective generations.

Margaret Basler Reiss Ebert

Anna Sybilla Feder Reiss

Catherine Luetzelschwab Reiss

Dedication to the Future

We are blessed with four terrific grandchildren, ages 1 to 6. Two are in Chicago and two are in Springfield. Our home near Peoria is almost midway between them. My wife's name is Diane but our grandchildren call her Grand DD. They call me Granddad.

William Stephen Reiss

Kayla Marie Reiss

Ava Brooke Reiss

Blake Saber Reiss

Inspiration

Tradition means giving votes to the most obscure of all classes, our ancestors. It is the democracy of the dead. Tradition refuses to submit to the self-important living who merely happen to be walking around.

> G. K. Chesterton
> British author, philosopher

In family and faith, a knowledge of roots older than yourself is the key to fruit that will outlast you.

> Rev. Bob Phillips
> First Methodist Church of Peoria, IL

Before you knock over an ancient landmark, learn why it was put there.

> Proverbs 22:28

Ask now about the former days, long before your time.

> Deuteronomy 4:32

To forget one's ancestors is to be a brook without a source, a tree without a root.

> Chinese proverb

Why waste your money looking up your family tree, just go into politics and your opponents will do it for you.

> Mark Twain

Introduction – 94 More Stories

April 1, 2012 was Palm Sunday. I was in the balcony at the First United Methodist Church of Peoria, Illinois. My mind wandered during several hymns. It struck me that I was more than 65 years older than our two grandchildren born in 2010 and 2011. Sadly, I concluded that I would probably never have comprehensive adult conversations with our grandchildren about important family history, significant experiences, family vacation travels, and heavy philosophical subjects. Consequently, I resolved that Sunday morning to write two stories on such subjects to our grandchildren every Monday. They would be called Granddad's Mondays (GMs) and they would go as email attachments to their parents who are our two sons and their wives. My wife would get a copy and there would occasional blind copies to special relatives and friends. A third grandchild arrived in December 2013 and a fourth in January 2015. Now I'm more than 70 years older than the last two grandchildren.

Initially I found these stories very easy to write in less than an hour as one page including a photo. Within a month however my stories lengthened to two or three pages with more photos which required two or more hours to complete. I was having fun and often downloaded a paragraph from the Internet and an occasional aerial photo. That extra researching taught me more about those GM subjects. I was having great fun and took pride in each story being self- explanatory, informative, and entertaining. I have privately published annual volumes of stories at PIP Printing here in Peoria as Granddad's Mondays for 2012, then 2013, and on through 2023. The grandchildren and I appear on each book cover. Each grandchild and their parents receive an autographed book for Christmas. Even though our grandchildren might not read these books for another 20 years or more, at least my stories are in weekly emails and annual print such that they will outlast me. There have been 1,516 stories so far through mid-2024.

I have 780 family letters which my great great grandmother Margaret saved from her siblings, children, grandchildren, and friends from 1852 to 1888. That's 36 years including the Civil War and parts of three generations. Most were written in "old" German and had to be translated. The fun ones were written in phonetic English with thousands of misspellings. All of these letters were published in 2009 by Author House in a book titled It Takes A Matriarch. This was such a fun and fact-filled exercise that I'm looking forward to meeting those people in heaven, if that's the way it works!!!

I have 1,000 daily letters that my parents exchanged for 1.5 years during World War II. Dad was in Burma and India. Mom was in California with newborn me. In transcribing those letters, I got to meet and appreciate my parents when they were in their mid-twenties which is otherwise impossible. Those letters were published by Author House in a book titled From Burma With Love. My wife and I visited Burma, now called Myanmar, for ten days in 2013. That was very special.

I have two of my grandmother Katie's five-year daily diaries beginning in 1944 and 1949 while my grandparents owned and operated the family farm south of Belleville, Illinois in St. Clair County. I transcribed those diaries, added a few explanatory paragraphs in italics, added lots of old photographs, and published them with Author House as Quilter, Granger, Grandma, Matriarch and as Granger, Quilter, Grandma, Matriarch.

I have 150 stories which my dad wrote for the Sullivan Daily Times in Sullivan, Indiana from 1984 to 2004. I also have a dozen professional speeches he made on the subject of reclaiming strip-mined coal lands back into productive farming. He was president of the farming subsidiary for a large Midwestern coal company. All of his writings are in another book by Author House called Family, Farming and Freedom.

I have 85 poems and almost that many milk bottles from the Reiss Dairy in Sikeston, Missouri. Those poems were composed by local citizen/customers from 1938 to about 1952, printed on new orders of milk bottles, and are now popular items on eBay. All that history is in another book by Author House called Reiss Dairy, Famous for Milk Bottles with Poems.

I have 40 years of my Uncle Frank's daily diaries. He was a professor in the Agriculture Department at the University of Illinois for 43 years. I read all 4.2 million of his words and transcribed 96,000 of them into a book titled Highlights of 40 Years of Frank Reiss Diaries. It was published by PIP Printing in Peoria and distributed only to family members. Frank was born and raised on the family farm and helped his parents manage it for another 20 years. I digitized 26,000 old family slides from 1943 onward. That project took over 100 hours in 40 sittings using a magic electronic black box. Those photos and the flexibility to Photoshop are now a major resource for more stories.

All of my seven non-GM books involved compiling, editing, and developing transitions so everything flowed well with 1.22 million words on 2,584 total pages. Now all those books, old photos, my 40 years working for Caterpillar in Peoria and Asia, and thousands of my personal memories are very fertile resource soil for planting and cultivating special stories for our special grandchildren. There have been 584 GM stories through 2016. Some 179 of them appear in this and a companion volume published by Pip Printing. First title is 85 Stories for My Grandchildren About the Reiss Family and Farm in St. Clair County, Illinois – 1830 to 1930. This second title is 94 More Stories for My Grandchildren About the Reiss Family and Farm in St. Clair County, Illinois – 1930 to Present.

Most of my GM stories are about other people but with my spin on who they were and what transpired. Even though I'm officially writing to our four young grandchildren, I'm really writing to our sons, Adam and Grant, and to their wives, Heather and Hany, with occasional bcc's to relatives. I can and do discretely plant seeds, coach, educate, encourage, and document history for the future benefit of all generations. If I forget to send stories on an occasional Monday, my sons call with a reminder. That's a compliment.

I'm having an absolute ball because all these books and stories will survive my cremation!!!

Stephen W. Reiss

Dunlap, Illinois

Table of Contents

Decade of the 1930s   **1**

1. Pop's first farm truck   2
2. Frank Reiss' valedictory speech   6
3. Reiss Dairy   9
4. Rhode Island Reds   16
5. Reiss reflects on the night before he left for college   19

Decade of the 1940s   **21**

6. A new house on the Reiss farm in 1940   22
7. Dad's letter in 1941 from Fort Benning, Georgia   26
8. The Japanese attack Pearl Harbor   30
9. Camp Roberts   36
10. War bond   42
11. Dog tags   45
12. Irv and Mary Reiss wedding   47
13. Cedar Row Farm Gazette   54
14. Learning Chinese at Yale University   58
15. Fruitcake for Christmas   63
16. B. J. Elder   66
17. CBI boots for Stevie   70
18. I'm coming home   73
19. Irv Reiss medals from World War II   75
20. Saving war letters   78
21. DC electricity comes to the Reiss farm in 1940   82
22. AC electricity comes to the Reiss farm on November 17, 1945   85
23. A new water well in 1944   88
24. Growing potatoes in 1944   89
25. Aerial photo of Reiss farm   91
26. Raising chickens and eggs in 1944   94
27. Growing corn and raising hogs in 1944   101
28. Grandma and Pop's trip in 1946   107
29. The Floraville Grange   110
30. Pop's pine woods   117
31. Quilter, Granger, Grandma, Matriarch   120
32. Croquet and Ayrshire   127
33. Wall telephones   129

Decade of the 1950s   **133**

34. Grandma's flower and vegetable gardens   134
35. Grandma's stove   138

36. Grandma's sausage and eggs 140
37. Grandma's custard fruit pies 144
38. Grandma's apron 147
39. The Indian mound 151
40. Brooder houses 154
41. Clay marbles 158
42. Smithton Sportsmen's Club 161
43. Round slingshots 169
44. Adam Reiss log cabin demolished in 1957 171
45. Feather blankets 174
46. The old corn crib 176
47. Pop's grindstone sharpening wheel 178
48. St. Louis Cardinals baseball games 180
49. Our grapevine swing 182
50. Indian ball 185
51. Cedar Christmas tree 186
52. Cisterns and Saturday night baths 188
53. Pop's farm scale 190
54. Pop's bucksaw 192
55. St. Paul United Church of Christ in Floraville 194

Decade of the 1960s **197**

56. Pop's hands 198
57. Richard's letter to Grandma of 2/6/1968 201
58. Painting grandma's house, kitchen, and living room 204

Decade of the 1970s **207**

59. Franklin Reiss testimony in Washington, DC in 1979 208
60. History of Floraville, Illinois 213
61. St. Michael's Catholic Church in Paderborn 218

Decade of the 1980s **227**

62. Reiss sesquicentennial reunion 1984 228
63. Irv Reiss reflects on one Sunday down on the farm 232
64. Golden weddings 234
65. Reiss farm history by Franklin Reiss 238

Decade of the 1990s **241**

66. Reiss Family Bible 242
67. Family streets and roads 245
68. Belleville, Illinois 249
69. Frank Reiss – My Story 251

Decade of the 2000s   **257**

70. Hunting on the Reiss family farm   258
71. Reiss dodransbicentennial reunion 2009   261
72. Illinois farm provides a good beginning to life   264
73. Irv Reiss' last story   266
74. Reiss family farm residents   267
75. Lang family tenant history   270
76. Dedication of the World War II Memorial   276
77. Irv Reiss funeral, eulogy, and obituary   278

Decade of the 2010s   **285**

78. Serendipities from It Takes A Matriarch   286
79. Two Reiss weddings   288
80. My best birthday gift ever   292
81. Reiss family farm eclipsed on August 21, 2017   294
82. Generativity   296
83. What your heirs really want   297
84. Reiss and Basler graves in St. Clair County   302
85. Book donations   308
86. This is not a box   312
87. Larry Brinker   316
88. Thanks, Katy   320
89. Broad Hollow Grange   323
90. George Basler at the Battle of Stones River   326
91. My dear son   333
92. The old barn is demolished   334
93. The old barn garden   338
94. The old barn is recycled   341

1930 – 1939

1930 Population of St. Clair County is 157,775.

1930 States total 48, national population is 123.08 million.

1930 President is Herbert Hoover. Franklin Roosevelt is inaugurated in 1933.

1930 Clarence Birdseye invents frozen food with his quick-freezing process and patents the concept.

1931 The Star-Spangled Banner is approved by President Hoover and Congress as the national anthem.

1931 The state of Nevada legalizes gambling.

1931 Construction is completed on the Empire State Building in New York City.

1932 Olan Mills started portrait photography and church directory businesses in Chattanooga, Tennessee. He was my grandfather Andrew Stephenson's first cousin. No discounts.

1935 The Social Security Act is passed by Congress. Workers began contributing into the system at a rate of 2% of the first $3,000 in earnings, half paid by the employee and half paid by the employer.

1936 Gone with the Wind is published by Margaret Mitchell.

1937 The Golden Gate Bridge opened in San Francisco.

1938 The National Minimum Wage was signed into law at $.25 per hour plus time and a half for overtime.

1838 Father/son John and Alex McCullough developed a soft-serve ice cream formula and convinced Sherb Noble to offer it in his ice cream store in Kankakee, Illinois. The three went into business in 1940 as Dairy Queen in Joliet, Illinois. There are now over 6,400 stores in 25 countries.

1939 The Baseball Hall of Fame opened in Cooperstown, New York.

1939 Albert Einstein alerted President Roosevelt to an atomic bomb opportunity, which led to the creation of the Manhattan Project.

Pop's First Farm Truck

Dear Will, Kayla, Ava, and Blake,   March 30, 2015

My grandparents bought their first truck in 1937. Here's the receipt from Smithton Garage showing that it was a **1929 Model A pickup**. The number 77,133 was written in pencil on the backside and is probably the mileage showing eight years of usage by previous owners. We don't have any photos but just bear with me for a minute.

Here are entries from Grandma's diaries which mention this truck, nothing very dramatic.

August 1944

Tues 15 – We went to Bill & Anita's to get our truck, also got fertilizer.

October 1944

Thurs 19 – We were at Millstadt to have truck tested.

November 1944

Thurs 9 – We were at Millstadt to have truck fixed and tested.

December 1944

Tues 27 – Geo got stuck with the truck in orchard while spreading fertilizer.

August 1951

Sat 25 – We were at the Quirin sale, had a flat tire on truck.

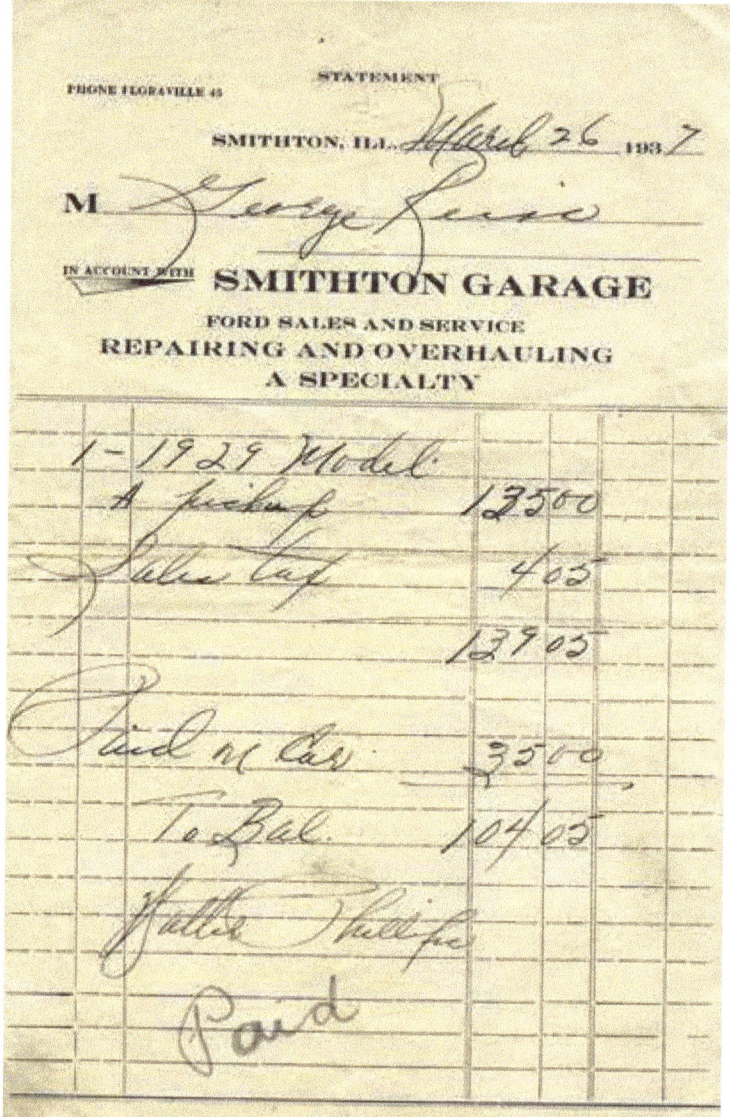

The Ford Model A of 1928–1931 was the second huge success for the Ford Motor Company, after its predecessor, the Model T. First produced on October 20, 1927, but not sold until December 2, the Model A replaced the venerable Model T, which had been produced for 18 years and 15,000,000 units. This new Model A was designated as a 1928 model and was available in four standard colors.

By 2/4/1929, one million Model As had been sold, and by 7/24/1929, two million. The range of body styles ran from a pickup truck, to the Tudor at $500, to the Town Car with a dual cowl at

$1200. In March 1930, Model A sales hit three million, and there were nine body styles available. The Model A was produced through 1931. When production ended in March 1932, there were 4,849,340 Model As made in all styles. Its successor was the Model B.

In 1929 Ford made 156,433 pickup trucks which was 9.1% of total production of 1,715,100 vehicles. In 1931 Ford made 103,561 pickup trucks which was 16.5% of total production of 626,579 vehicles. Total 1931 production was only 36.5% of the peak Model A year of 1929 due to impact of the Great Depression and increased competition from other manufacturers.

For pickup buyers the only Model A pickup available, at least at first, was an Open Cab type. It featured a new styled body provided to Ford by Briggs Manufacturing. It also used a soft top

that was non-retractable that used side curtains of canvas and mica to keep out the elements. Though these cabs were the new, pickup boxes used were a carryover from the Model T. Briggs also offered other boxes including some made of wood.

The trucks featured a new body, new engine, new transmission, new frames, and new wheels compared to the Model T. Their new 4-cylinder engine displaced 200 cubic inches and produced 40 horsepower at 2200 RPM.

Our Associate Pastor, Eric Swanson, restored a 1931 Model A truck over the last two years while he lived in Peoria. He was recently transferred to his own church in Leroy, IL so Grand DD and I took him to lunch recently in return for driving and photographing his pickup. There are few differences between what Pop's 1929 pickup and what Eric's 1931 pickup looks like. Eric's has a wooden bed which he fabricated from original plans.

Here I am driving Eric's truck. All the cab levers and pedals were identical to Pop's truck so I felt connected to family history. I enjoyed the ah-ooo-gah horn that you see on the front bumper. Eric often drives his truck in parades and festivals in Leroy partly as an icebreaker to invite folks to his Methodist Church.

Here's Eric's engine compartment which is mostly air. It's radically simpler than engine compartments in today's cars and trucks where you don't dare work on them yourself. Will, Kayla, Ava, and Blake, that's my family truck history lesson for today. I'll add that Uncle Ken and I spent many hours disassembling Pop's 1929 truck in 1955 which had expired a few years earlier. It looked a lot worse than the one on the next page.

Love, Granddad

Franklin Reiss – 10th Year Valedictory Speech (1930)

Dear Will and Kayla,   August 13, 2012

One of the smartest men in our family was your great great uncle Franklin J. Reiss. He was my dad's next older brother. He was born on Halloween Day in 1915 which was October 31. Like his two brothers he went to this one-room school in Floraville, Illinois for the first eight years of public education. His father George Reiss was on the school board back then and very much knew the value of a good education because he had only four years himself. Frank's mother Katie had about six years of public education.

In 1929 and 1930 Frank went to high school in Millstadt, Illinois which was just a two-year program from 1914 to 1943. Classes were held on the top floor of the elementary school building which was demolished in 1954. If students wanted a four-year high school diploma, they had to transfer to a larger school like Belleville Township High School which is what Frank eventually did.

Like I said, your uncle Frank was a smart guy. Below is the valedictory speech he gave in June 1930 as the top of 6 students in his sophomore graduating class at Millstadt High School. He gave this speech at age 14 and a half. The whole thing was published in the local newspaper 82 years ago. Pretty impressive, don't you think?

Uncle Frank transferred to BTHS for his last two years of high school. Then he laid out for four years to save money for college by working on his dad's and various neighbor farms. Frank went to the University of Illinois where he earned a BS, MS, and PhD in Agricultural Economics. He was employed by that university for 40 years from 1940 to 1980 as a professor in the Ag Econ Department. So Uncle Frank had three college degrees, his wife Gerry had two, his son George has two, and his son Richard had two plus parts of two more. I'm glad we're all related to such smart people.

The newspaper report starts with this opener – The following is the text of the valedictory address delivered by Franklin Reiss, member of the tenth year graduating class of 1930, at the commencement exercises last week.

Dear parents, teachers, and friends. I am indeed glad and proud of the honor of appearing before you tonight as the valedictorian of the Class of 1930 of the Millstadt High School.

Since we now have reached that stage of life where we much push out into the wide world, seek our own path, and choose for ourselves; I have thought it appropriate to confine my remarks to that topic which is so vitally important to us, who, soon will be the masters of our own destinies: that of MAKING OUR FIRST DECISION.

The question or problem that demands our first decision after we leave this hall tonight is: "Shall we continue in high school for two more years and then become four year high school graduates; or shall we forevermore sever our relations with school after these exercises?"

We fully realize that if we quit school and secure employment, we shall be able to earn our own living and be dependent no longer on our parents. The various luxuries of the 20th Century such as automobiles, radios, stylish clothes, amusements, and entertainment shall in a short time come into our possession. No longer need we give up good times, parties, social affairs, and make other sacrifices in order to prepare our lessons. No longer need we be extremely careful about our manners, habits, and speech. But, we must be satisfied with long, tiresome working hours and drudgery. We must be contended with a very minimum wage and our earnings will be small. Advancement will be slow and small, and we shall never know what the morrow will bring. And, we can't sit down and whine when the trained boy or girl, who once was our equal in school, passes us up and achieves remarkable success.

We will know that if we continue in high school, we shall be able to choose a profession or life's work, study it in college, and then take our place among the well-trained, financially independent and progressive members of society. The dawn of a new day is here which places a premium on well-trained and educated young people, offers them untold opportunities and gives them a golden chance to become highly successful and enjoy the comforts of life. Forty or fifty years ago, four, five, or six years of public education was considered sufficient for any boy or girl. Ten or fifteen years ago, the boy or girl who finished the 8th grade was spoken of, what we say in German, as being "learned out." Today the young man or woman who finishes high school, realizes that his or her schooling and training has just begun. Without a high school diploma, no one can study for medicine, dentistry, law, pharmacy, nursing, engineering, public school teaching, the ministry, and other professions. Already, the business world demands a high school training for its bookkeepers, stenographers, newspaper reporters, office boys and girls, salesmen and saleswomen, drug store clerks, mail clerks, farm managers, telephone operators, factory managers, and superintendents and other numerous occupations.

Many of us say that father and mother got along all right and quite well in this world, and they did not have much schooling. Yes, but how much greater father and mother's possibilities for success would have been, and how much happier their lives would have been had they enjoyed more schooling. There have been many men and women who have made great successes of life without much schooling, yet very few of them would claim that their lack of schooling was a factor in their success. It is expected of us to become more successful than our parents because the rest of the world moves forward and we must move with it or be overshadowed, stepped upon and trodden down. And thus we have come to a crossroad where we must choose one way from the other. Regardless of what path we follow, may we set a standard and decide to reach it. Without a goal, we are certain to drift and waste through life.

Will and Kayla, you can see that a good education and lots of personal extra effort can open many doors in your lives. Kayla, your mom is another perfect example. Her extra efforts to study and succeed in school in Malaysia earned her a scholarship to the University of Michigan where she continued to excel. Long story short – your mom's smarts are why you were born in Chicago and why you have me for a grandfather. I think your dad is pretty smart too for choosing your mom as his wife. It just doesn't get any better than that.

Love, Granddad

Reiss Dairy

Dear Will and Kayla,   October 15, 2012

You may not remember this but shortly after each of you was born and your moms were supplying all your milk, each referred to themselves as "The Reiss Dairy." Pretty clever, don't you think? But it was 74 years ago this past Saturday on October 13, 1938 that the following advertisement appeared in "The Sikeston (Missouri) Herald" newspaper that eventually made the original Reiss Dairy very famous. Here's the history.

Are You A DITTLER or a DOODLER?

In case you don't already know, a dittler is a writer of ditties, and a doodler is a person who, during spare time, draws objects of art, geometric figures, artistic representations, etc.

You may wonder where lies the connection between Reiss Dairy and Dittlers and Doodlers— Here it is:

Reiss Dairy will pay $1.00 each for ditties to be put on the reverse side of our milk bottles. You are already acquainted with Old King Cole, Yankee Doodle, Little Miss Muffett and others.

Write your ditty on a sheet of paper and you may accompany it with a suitable doodle (drawing) if you wish, then hand same to a Reiss Dairy salesman or mail direct to ReissDairy.

The best ditties and doodles will be put on the reverse side of Reiss Dairy milk bottles with the name of the author below.

REISS DAIRY

Sikeston is located just north of the boot-heel of southeast Missouri or about halfway between St. Louis and Memphis. The city was founded in 1860 and named for John Sikes. Current population is 16,500.

In 1926 your great great great uncle John Reiss started his own dairy business on his farm just northeast of Sikeston. He was milking 10 cows and called his business Reiss Farm Dairy. His milk bottles had raised or embosd letters and were not painted. He bottled and sold milk from other farmers as his business grew.

In 1935 he built

a new processing building in Sikeston, brought his son-in-law Lonnie Standley into the business, and renamed it Reiss Dairy. They soon changed away from embossed milk bottles to smooth painted milk bottles. At different times over the next two decades they also sold ice cream, dairy bars, eggs, whipping cream, cottage cheese, and related items.

They had a lunch counter called the Cow Bell where sundaes and other treats were created for customers. I remember enjoying a marshmallow sundae at this counter in August 1961, and it was free! They chose Jo-Kay as the name for their ice cream after Lonnie's two daughters, Jo Ellen and Kay. Neat idea, don't you think? It would be like naming our home made applesauce Will-Kay after the two of you. Here are two more newspaper articles:

"The Sikeston Herald" October 20, 1938

"Dittlers and Doodlers Abound in Sikeston"

Seemingly a large number of Sikestonians answered "yes" to the question asked by the Reiss Dairy in last week's Herald – "Are You a Dittler or a Doodler?" Approximately 75 persons responded to the advertisement with suggested "ditties" and "doodles" to be put on the reverse side of Reiss Dairy milk bottles. The best ones submitted will be put on the bottles with the author's name below, and will also win the writer a prize of $1.00.

The contest will continue this week. Details are to be found in the advertisement of the Reiss Dairy published elsewhere in this issue of The Herald.

"The Sikeston Herald" December 1, 1938

"Reiss Dairy Begins Use of Ditties and Sketches Submitted by Customers"

The Reiss Dairy has this week begun to use a number of ditties and sketches submitted by customers and other citizens of the territory served by this enterprising business firm.

In response to an advertisement published exclusively by The Herald a few weeks ago, approximately 250 ditties concerning the use of milk were submitted and according to officials of the Dairy, ditties are still being presented. Also about fifty drawings of the objects and scenes suggestive of the proper use of milk were submitted. The preponderance of ditties over the drawings submitted indicated that most folks can write better than they can draw.

Of the many drawings and ditties submitted, five were etched onto the sides of 14,000 milk bottles received this week by the Dairy for use in Sikeston and the many other Southeast Missouri towns served by it. The etchings are in red making them very noticeable when the bottles are filled.

One group of bottles is etched with a ditty and drawing submitted by Carol Headlee, a 16-year-old high school girl of Morehouse. The drawing shows a football player in the act of making a touchdown. The ditty reads as follows:

"Frail weak Tommy couldn't play,
But to do so was his aim;
He drank milk and now he's strong,
And today he won the game."

Another ditty, above which is etched the "crooked man who walked a crooked mile" was submitted by Mrs. G. Poynor of Sikeston. It reads:

"There was a crooked man –
Who would have been quite straight,
If every day he'd found a glass
Of milk beside his plate."

A Sikeston business man submitted this ditty:

"There was a man in our town
and he was wondrous wise.
For the only milk he would drink
Was REISS Pasteurized."

Mrs. J. L. Osborn submitted this ditty:

"Oh boy, what a joy
To feel as fine as silk;
Please get wise, open your eyes,
Use nothing but REISS' Milk."

The round red Reiss Dairy milk bottles with poems continued from late 1938 into mid-1949 when the business moved to another new location and milk was packaged in cardboard cartons. The glass bottle phase of their business was over. Lonnie told me several times about them taking thousands of glass bottles to the landfill since there was no further need for them. The poems had appeared on quart, pint, and half pint bottles. The creamers were too small for a poem and the gallon jugs were maybe too big or too little in demand.

Fast forward to today where eBay and antique stores around Sikeston have made it possible for milk bottle collectors, milk bottle poem collectors, and Reiss relatives to continue feeding their addictions. Some guy (your granddad) even wrote a book about all this stuff and called it Reiss Dairy (of course). I have about 40 different bottles in my personal collection and have learned about 85 different bottle poems altogether. I even wrote my own Reiss Dairy poem to recognize this significant family history:

Reiss Dairy Epilogue

Reiss Dairy milk built strong bonds and strong bones.
John and Lonnie were good to family, friends, and crew,
And to Sikeston, their customers, and their homes.
May the Reiss and Standley legacies always remain true.

More pictures appear on the following pages. The first one is my great uncle John Reiss and his wife Mary Etta with their first daughter Jo Ellen. It was taken in 1913 in front of their dairy farm on the north edge of Sikeston, Missouri. They supplied milk to neighbors and other bottlers before opening their first dairy called Reiss Farm Dairy about 1935. Their first bottles were embossed with those words rather than the red paint they changed to about three years later. Those embossed bottles difficult to find on eBay.

John, Lillian and Mary Reiss about 1913

Below is John Reiss with his siblings and mother in 1925. He's in the upper right corner.

Back: William, Louie, Henry, John Reiss. Front: George, Anna Reiss, Margaret Reiss Dintelmann 1925

12

Above is the first Reiss Dairy building in a new life as a tax prep store. Below is the second Reiss Dairy building in a new life as an insurance office.

John and Mary Reiss' younger granddaughter is my second cousin Katy Standley. Her high school class in Sikeston, Missouri was having their 50th reunion on September 19, 2009. Katy obviously knew I had written the Reiss Dairy book three months earlier so she suggested I do a booksigning at the local Sikeston museum which is an old train station now called The Depot. I agreed and it was a lot of fun. I got to meet some of her classmates and several former Reiss Dairy employees from 50+ years ago.

Here's my cousin Katy in the middle. Below are several more photos from the booksigning.

14

Will, Kayla, Ava, and Blake, you need to know that your parents/aunt-uncle Heather and Adam drove 250 miles, 4 hours all the way from Springfield to Sikeston to surprise me at this booksigning. Not only was I surprised, but I was very appreciative. Here are the four of us in the Sikeston Cemetery at the graves of John and Mary Etta Reiss. We tried to have a late lunch at 3:00 at Lamberts in Sikeston which is famous for "throwed rolls" but even at mid-afternoon the wait was 1.5 hours. So caravanned back to Springfield and then Grand DD and I reached greater Dunlap at 10:30. It was a long but very unique day.

Love, Granddad

Rhode Island Reds by Franklin Reiss in 1932

Dear Will, Kayla, Ava, and Blake,   February 29, 2016

Happy Leap Day!!! This extra day happens once every four years so it's the first one for two of you to experience. It's like a free bonus for being great kids – an extra day of fun without increasing your age in years.

Here's a story about a radio presentation my uncle Frank Reiss made 74 years ago this coming Sunday on 3/5/1932 when he was a high school senior in Belleville, Illinois. He was talking about Rhode Island Red chickens he was raising on the Reiss family farm, probably as a 4H project. You may remember from my Granddad's Mondays story of 5/25/2015 that Frank and his younger brother Irwin (my dad) were charter members of the new 4H Chapter sponsored by the Broad Hollow Grange. Frank was president and always very comfortable talking in front of a group which served him well throughout his long career at the University of Illinois.

The **Rhode Island Red** is an American breed of chicken. It is a utility bird, raised for meat and eggs, and also as a show bird. It is a popular choice for backyard flocks because of its egg laying abilities and hardiness. The Rhode Island Red is the state bird of Rhode Island. It is one of only three state birds that is not a species native to the United States.

One of my dad's 4H projects was raising white Wyandotte chickens. The **Wyandotte** is a breed of chicken originating originating in the United States. The first examples of the breed appeared in the 1870s. Wyandottes are a docile, dual-purpose breed kept for their brown eggs and for meat. They appear in a wide variety of color patterns, and are popular show birds. Wyandotte hens are devoted mothers.

Sometimes Frank's Reds and Dad's Whites got together and made pink chickens like this or maybe some prankster just got carried away with food coloring. Perhaps you're familiar with a line of children's clothing called Pink Chicken, based in New York.

Will, Kayla, Ava, and Blake, let's get back to the heart of this story which is Uncle Frank's radio address. The two letters which follow are self-explanatory and very interesting. They are written by Katherine and Alwin Gasser who grew up about a mile south of the Reiss family farm in St. Clair County. Sometime in the 1920s they moved to a farm near Sikeston, Missouri where they continued as friends of John and Mary Etta Reiss who founded the Reiss Dairy. John was born on 11/4/1877 and Alwin on 8/7/1896 so they were a generation apart. Maybe the Gassers moved to Sikeston at the encouragement of the Reisses. They were farmers and raised grain to feed their chickens and beef/dairy cows. John Reiss was probably his customer. All four are buried in Sikeston.

Love, Granddad

Sikeston, Mo.
Mar. 6, 1932

Dear Friends,

Last nite we had the coldest nite this winter and also had snow yesterday all day. But none staid on the ground.

Yesterday (Sat) noon we tuned in on the farm hour and of all surprises, we heard Franklin Reiss of Belleville announced to speak on his project. Yes, we heard him and he was the only one I understood every word. His was a very good talk and I don't know what to say that is right. But I guess congratulations would be a good word. It really made me feel homesick for good old Floraville. Franklin must be quite a man by now. I guess he's going to college now.

We get to see Mr. & Mrs. John Reiss quite often. They are doing very well and are having quite an up to date dairy business.

We did very well with our farming last year. But the low prices of all farm produce is hard on all farmers.

We passed your house last summer, when we were at home, but you were all gone. It was the Sunday Smithton Homecoming was held. We are wanting to visit home again, this summer if possible. We have a flock of about 140 hens, mostly S.C. Rhode Island Reds and they are a paying flock both as egg and as poultry. Eggs are to date 8 cents in trade at the stores. We ship all our cream to Sugar Creek Creamery. It keeps us two pretty busy all the year around, but we are both well and like to work.

Gilbert is with his uncle on a farm at Gulin, Mo. now. He went to St. Louis about a year ago. He's 22 years now. Will close hoping to hear from you soon.

As always your friend,

Katherine Gasser

Sikeston, Mo.
March 6, 1932

Dear Friends,

We heard Franklin talk about his "Reds" Saturday. His voice came thru better than any of the young men who have spoken this winter. With better farmers and their increased yields, our chemists will be kept busy finding new uses and new outlets for farm products.

We seeded oats last Tuesday and Wednesday. We raised last year 58 acres corn, 20 acres wheat, 26 oats, 15 closer, 30 soybeans after small grains for hay and seed and 12 acres permanent pasture. We are still following the cropping ideas we started with except that we added the beans and increased corn. Soys have been raised as a cash crop. In future we shall increase clover and raise soybeans as a grain crop only to be fed to stock. All of the hay and most of the grain is fed on the farm as you can see when I say that we raise and feed out annually about 25 hogs and have on hand 18 head of dairy cattle.

Last year we added a new line. We fed one steer. Total cost of raising and feeding it $15. Returns $35.67, net profit $20.67. We expect to feed more.

Most farms here are straight grain or grain & cotton farms. S. E. Missouri has the soil, the climate and markets to have a prosperous agriculture. It has too much of a one crop system. A bad financing system and large land-holdings. We are about 98% tenant farmers. Most of these have stock and equipment mortgaged and in addition annually mortgage their crops in advance to finance the year's operation. A bad policy. Share cropping is a good way for a beginner to get a start at farming but as used here is an agricultural drawback. We need farmers here who are willing to stand on their own feet, and able to see beyond the end of their nose.

You have doubtless read a bit about Korean Lespedeza lately. I seeded some on my permanent grass pasture two years ago. It is wonderful. You cannot imagine how good it really is when used in this connection unless you have tried it. It produces fine grazing from July until October and grass will come up just as green as every next spring.

Hoping that we may hear from our old neighbors now and then, I remain.

Yours,

Alwin G. Gasser

Reiss Reflects on the Night Before He Left for College

Dear Will, Kayla, Ava, and Blake,   October 19, 2015

This is a story my dad wrote on March 26, 1987 for the "Sullivan Daily Times" in our Indiana hometown. All that follows is his except my final paragraph.

Even though it had been a warm sunny day, the delightful cool of an early September evening was settling in. It was about eight o'clock – we had just finished supper. Down on the farm, working hours went from daylight 'til dusk. As I had fed the chickens their evening scratch and gathered the eggs before finishing my chores by slopping the pigs, a strong feeling started to permeate the recesses of my mind. Was I finishing the last page of a stage of my life – because tomorrow I would be entering a new world?

It was this feeling that caused me to get up from the supper table and go for a walk in the light of a moon that was almost full. I walked into the orchard south of the house and climbed onto the roof of a brooder house where we raised baby chicks away from the contamination of the rest of the barn yard. From my vantage point, I saw the few lights of the village of Floraville, two miles to the west, the home of 106 Protestant people and the one-room school that I attended for eight years with the same teacher. The Evangelical Church spire was barely visible in the moon light. To the southwest, Paderborn with its 67 Catholics, their parochial school and their spired church with the cross on top and the country store also had memories for me – but one stood out.

I remembered it as vividly today as I did when it first happened when I was 8 years old. My two brothers, Frank and Bill, and I had gotten winter head and chest colds and we were feeling miserable. Pop decided we needed help. So he put on his overcoat and felt boots, lit the coal oil lantern and walked that mile and half each way across the fields to get us a dozen oranges and jar of Vicks Vapor Rub from that country store in Paderborn.

Tonight I was looking beyond Floraville and Paderborn into the indistinct world that lay beyond. There was a lot of uncertainty out there for me, but somehow I knew that starting tomorrow, I would take the first step to seek my destiny in a world I knew only vaguely through the books I had read.

Something caused me to turn around on my perch and look toward the house in which I was born 20 years ago. It was still the depths of the Great Depression, so I worked two years after high school and got a four-year scholarship to the University of Illinois before even considering going to college. In the summer kitchen, mom was doing dishes in the dry sink. We had no running water in the house. By the flickering coal oil lamp, Pop, with his reading glass was going over his favorite newspaper, the Chicago Tribune. (We didn't have any electricity either.)

I could stay here and farm. I'm sure Pop hoped that one of his three sons would follow his profession and till the land where he had spent 64 years of his life so far. As I sat on the brooder house roof that night, I was torn between two strong emotions. Stay here in relative security and work with my parents, who were extremely kind and good to me, or go out into that uncertain world which I saw so dimly beyond Paderborn and Floraville that moonlit night.

My parents were not domineering, so there was no reason for me to try to escape from something. No, I wasn't running away from something either. And the desire to be my own boss, which is so prevalent in the world today, was not a motivating force with me. I suppose the need for self-identity exists in all of us in varying degrees – but there was an unidentifiable something more.

In 1933 Frank and I, through the generosity of my brother Bill, took a bus to Chicago and saw the World's Fair and Lake Michigan and the Adler Planetarium. I knew if I was going to see the world and compete in that world, I would have to prepare for it. I would have to get an education to make my life more productive to build on the responsibility and the sense of values that I had learned at my mother's knee and from my father's helping hand and understanding counseling.

Tomorrow I would leave and Mom would cry for she knew – oh sure I would be back for Thanksgiving, Christmas, semester change and maybe summer vacations – but she knew that her youngest was leaving the nest to make a life of his own.

Later on my 21st birthday, she would write me a beautiful letter, which I still have, explaining that what I was doing was only natural – that is the way life is meant to be – and she would continue to wash my clothes and take care of me until I found a mate, a good girl, and then the life cycle would start over again. She and Pop would always love me as I would always love them – and oh, how right she was.

I heard a noise – I turned and saw my brother Frank – he said, "What are you doing Irv, taking a last long look?" This reflection would not be complete without one final observation. It was years later – four years in college, four and one half years in the U.S. Army, three years in Southern California and a few years in Sullivan, Ind., as chief of Meadowlark Farms with the responsibility for over 100,000 acres of land, that my father said to me, "Irwin, I always thought that you would be my farmer some day, but what you are doing is so much bigger and better than anything I could have offered you. You have my blessing." In a quivering barely audible voice, I said, "Thanks, Pop." This time I cried.

(EDITOR'S NOTE: Irv said that he and his two brothers now own the home farm where he was born, that it has been in the Reiss name since 1838, and that he has asked his children to keep it that way.)

Will, Kayla, Ava, and Blake, need I say more? All of Dad's generation have now passed to their greater rewards. What are we of the next three generations doing about preserving that legacy?

Love Granddad

1940 – 1949

1940 Population of St. Clair County is 166,899.

1940 States total 48, national population is 132.12 million.

1940 President is Franklin Roosevelt. Harry Truman is inaugurated in 1945.

1941 The Japanese attacked Pearl Harbor. The US declared war on Japan and Germany.

1944 D-Day where 155,000 troops from the US and 11 allied nations landed on the beaches of Normandy, France.

1944 The G.I. Bill of Rights is signed into law, providing benefits to veterans.

1945 The unconditional surrender of Germany ended World War II in Europe.

1945 The US drops atomic bombs on Hiroshima and Nagasaki. The unconditional surrender of Japan ended World War II in the Pacific.

1945 The United Nations is formed with 51 member countries.

1946 Bob Evans opened his first truck stop diner in Rio Grande, Ohio. There are now 600 restaurants in 19 states owned by the company. No franchises.

A New House on the Reiss Farm in 1940

Dear Will, Kayla, Ava, and Blake,   October 6, 2014

Here is a construction view of the west side of Grandma and Pop's new house in the middle of 1940. The builder is John Luetzelschwab who is walking the roof getting ready to lay two more rolls of tarpaper and then five bundles of shingles. Johnny is Grandma's oldest brother by 6.5 years and made his living as a carpenter and general contractor. He was charging my grandparents $0.50 per hour for his time. I don't know the other worker but it might be one of Grandma's other brothers – Herman, Jacob, or Frank. He even looks a little bit like my dad who had that summer off from college.

In the doorway is my Aunt Anita Reiss and her daughter June Ann who is age 3.5. They belong to Bill Reiss who is my dad's oldest brother.

A faint copy of the first floor blueprint appears on the next page. West is to the right and east to the left. Area is 896 square feet. The second floor has 3' knee walls so its central area is about 500 square feet. There is a full basement. Not shown is an enclosed porch along the east side which measures about 8 by 25 feet for another 200 square feet. It had windows on three sides and was a great place for fragrant geraniums which were always in bloom. The porch was often the lunch or dinner location for large family meals on holidays.

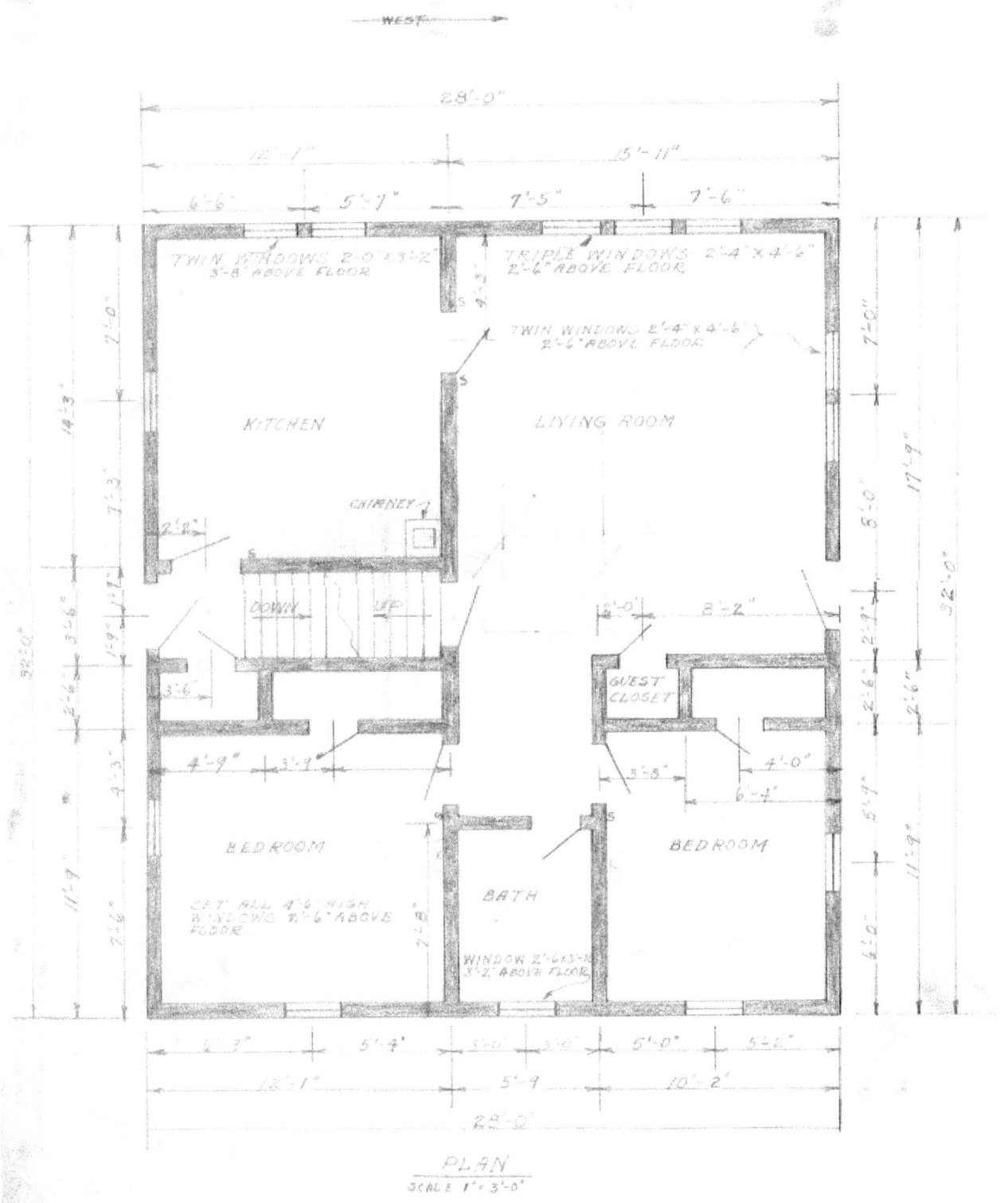

WEST →

PLAN
SCALE 1" = 3'-0"

GEO. W. REISS RESIDENCE

23

Here's a tally of eggs Johnny was buying from his sister during August and September. It was written on the back of his letterhead which you can see in reverse. Notice the egg prices are per dozen. Ask your moms what they pay now for eggs. I'm sure it's more than a penny apiece.

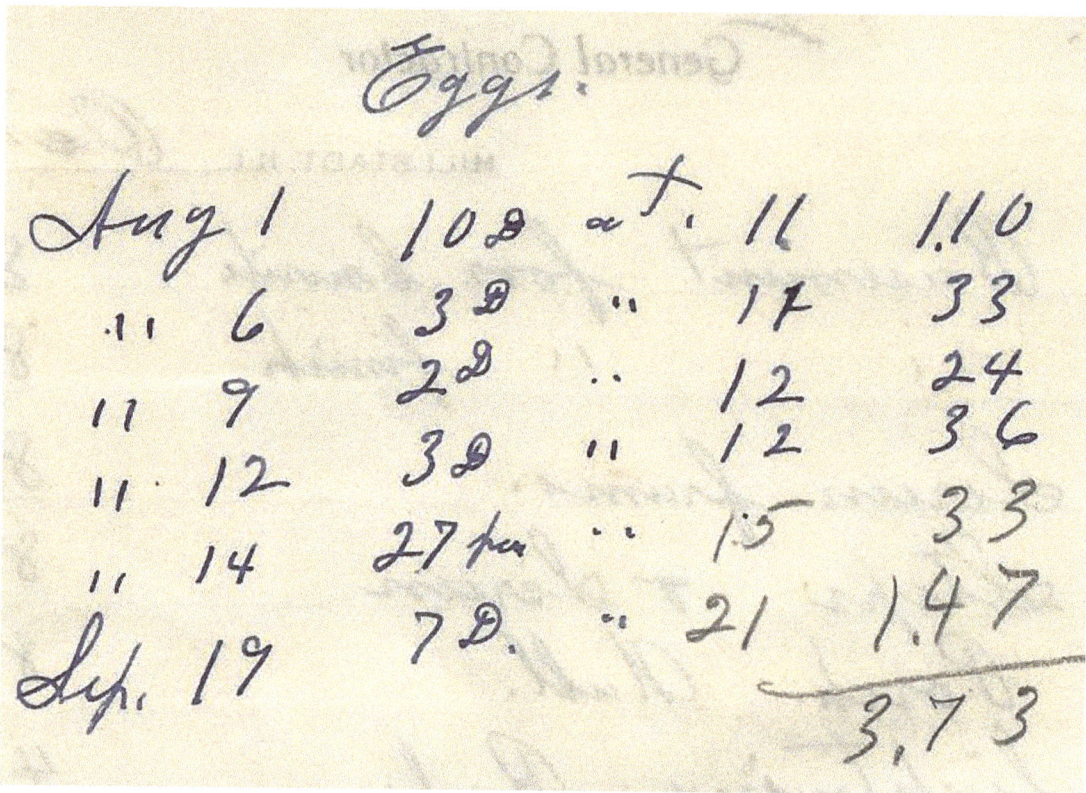

Will, Kayla, Ava, and Blake, the picture on the next page is my Grandmother Katie on her 53rd birthday March 25, 1943. She is standing outside the south porch door. That purse is probably a birthday gift. Notice that she is wearing an apron. That's not because she was cooking her own birthday dinner that Thursday. It's because she just liked to wear an apron, especially when going for walks with her grandchildren. Maybe it's a German or Swiss custom. That will be the subject of a future Granddad's Mondays story.

Love, Granddad

March 25, 1943

Dad's Letter from Fort Benning, Georgia in 1941

Dear Will, Kayla, Ava, and Blake,   July 28, 2014

Here's a four-page letter Lieutenant Irv Reiss wrote to his brother and sister-in-law, Frank and Gerry Reiss, 73 years ago tomorrow. He was in basic training in the US Army in Fort Benning, Georgia about two months after graduating from the University of Illinois. He had taken Advanced Reserve Officer Training Corps during his last two years of college which normally did not make a two- or three-year hitch with the Army mandatory. But World War II was just around the corner and Dad was obligated to serve.

The **Reserve Officers' Training Corps (ROTC)** is a college-based program for training commissioned officers of the US Armed Forces. ROTC officers serve in all branches of the US armed forces. Under ROTC, a student may receive a competitive, merit-based scholarship, covering all or part of college tuition, in return for an obligation of active military service after graduation. That funding is why Dad signed up for the two extra years of ROTC.

ROTC students attend college like other students, but also receive basic military training and officer training for their chosen branch of service through the ROTC unit at or nearby the college. The students participate in regular drills during the school year, and extended training activities during the summer.

The Army ROTC units are organized as brigades, battalions, and companies. Two years of ROTC was mandatory at my college, Rose Polytechnic Institute, later renamed Rose-Hulman Institute of Technology. Our student body totaled 1300 which was enough for a battalion but not a brigade. Maybe 10% of our student body took Advanced ROTC which involved the scholarship and service obligation.

ROTC History -- The concept of ROTC in the US began with the Morrill Act of 1862 which established the land-grant colleges. Part of the federal government's requirement for these schools was that they include military tactics as part of their curriculum, forming what became known as ROTC. Until the 1960s, many major universities required compulsory ROTC for all of their male students. However, because of the protests that culminated in the opposition to US involvement in the Vietnam War, compulsory ROTC was dropped in favor of voluntary programs.

Fort Benning History – During World War II Fort Benning had 197,159 acres with billeting space for 3,970 officers and 94,873 enlisted persons. Here's the main camp in 1941.

Dear Frank & Gerry,   7/29/1941

How's Mom & Pop? Uncle Irv is doing fine. Frank, thanks a lot for the pictures. They mean a lot to me. I'll get what I owe to you right soon now.

An attempt to tell everything that happens here would be futile. I think the expression "it can and does happen here" covers it very well. We set off 150 lbs. of dynamite in one charge the other day. You could have dropped our brooder house in the hole

We've got a little excitement today. Today we had bayonet drill. One hundred guys needed first aid. By 5 O'clock this evening 12 guys were sick. We lost two more on the way home. The ambulances picked up 10 more in the barracks by 6 o'clock. They left on stretchers feet first. Texas on my right didn't know where he was anymore. Miss. on my left couldn't stand up anymore. They called it heat prostration, but I know damn good and well it's food poisoning. 100 out of 200 reported for mess. We didn't have enough at our table to operate. It is now 8 o'clock, 35 are in the hospital and the barracks is full of sicks. I was OK up to an hour ago, now I don't know. Guys are being "knocked out" continuously. I'll finish this letter when I find out how long I'm going to last.

                                                            So long

Hello,   7/30/1941

I took the count of nine last night but I came out fighting. Company C was a sorry sight this morning. In spite of the ill effects of food poisoning and under a blistering sun, I went out and qualified for sharpshooter this morning on the Browning Automatic Rifle. I missed expert by one shot out of 110 shots. With the M-1 I put 11 shots in the bull and 4 hanging just out of the bull in 40 seconds at 200 yards. I've qualified on everything so far. We have 12 very rough GTs (graded tests) in our 12 weeks course. I've got two under my belt. 200 West Point grads blew in this week to take this course and learn a little military. Enough of that rot.

Somewhere in this letter there should be an $11.00 money order for you – $10.00 for an old debt and $1.00 for the Ag. Econ. picture. Also in the recesses of this envelope you should find a few samples of my photographic ability – or the lack of it. The comments on the rear should be self-explanatory. The pictures should ease the imagination somewhat.

Edit and I are still doing it up brown. I sent her a worry bird from Eastman, Georgia. You haven't eaten peaches until you have tasted the tree-ripened Georgias. Saw some immense tobacco warehouses near Savannah.

I got me a helluva cold during my rest cure at Warm Springs. They can give the damn place back to the Indians. I don't want it. I had a T-bone steak on a terrace overlooking a pine covered valley 1,000 feet below in Pine Mountain State Park last Sunday. This is the nuts – one weekend at the seashore and the next one in the mountains. Let's have a letter.

Love,
Irwin

The Edith that Dad mentions is his fiancée or maybe they were just engaged to be engaged. Her last name is Freedlund and her home town is Rockford, Illinois. Dad spent three days with Edith in Rockford in June 1941 before driving to Fort Benning. They had been an item on the U of I campus for some months or longer before Dad went on active duty. Edith sent him a picture of herself and a box of fudge for his birthday on 9/18/1941.

Here is a photo of Dad with Edith when she visited the Reiss Family Farm in the summer of 1941. I don't know if this is the first time she met Dad's parents, his brothers, and their wives, but it looked like everyone was having a good time. That looks like a pin on her dress from one of Dad's honorary agricultural fraternities.

Dad graduated from Basic Training at Fort Benning on 9/24/1941 and then drove his 1930 Model A Ford back to the Reiss farm in Illinois. He next appears at Camp Roberts, California on 10/13/1941 after driving 2200 miles in nearly four days from St. Louis. His carload stayed four nights in motels which he called "tourist cabins" in Lebanon, Missouri; Shamrock, Texas; Gallup, New Mexico; and Barstow, California. Camp Roberts is 12 miles north of Paso Robles and 15 miles from the Pacific Ocean.

Here's what a 1930 Model A Ford looks like. I remember riding in Dad's car about 1950 at the Reiss family farm. Some of the cushions and interior were a little beat up. I also remember the day he sold it for $25 to some young guy who came and towed it away.

Dad's letter of 10/15/1941 asks of Frank and Gerry: "Tell me – what do you do when your fiancée is 2500 miles away?"

Dad's letter of 12/7/1941, the day the Japanese attacked Pearl Harbor: "I'm up in the orderly room now. I'm acting company commander, I've just ordered every man restricted to the company area. I've posted guards armed with ball ammunition guarding every rifle rack and the storeroom. From now I'm carrying a loaded 45 automatic 24 hours a day. We've doubled the guard and given them careful instructions. The camp is full of Japanese. Our company has about 50 of them."

"All the coastal defenses have been ordered to 24-hour duty. All officers must appear in uniform. All orders and leaves have been canceled. I don't know what's going to happen, but regardless what does, I'll be doing my duty. And never forget that."

Dad's letter of 2/15/1942: "I am acquiring the scars of lost economic opportunity and I may acquire the scars of battle. But unless we have scars when the final peace arrives, we did nothing to bring it about. Destiny decreed my position – it is up to me to make the most of it."

Dad's letter of 3/8/1942: "Three weeks ago Edith asked to be released from our engagement. This week she wrote and said that she decided to marry another fellow. I can't understand why. I don't know any more than I've told you. I am still in love with her. It's needless for me to tell you how bad I feel." *Edith Marie Freedlund married Irvin Henry Landwehr on April 4, 1942 in her hometown of Rockford, Illinois.*

A week later Dad met Mary Leone Stephenson on **3/15/1942** which was her 21st birthday. Mom and Dad were married eight months later on 11/8/1942.

Will, Kayla, Ava, and Blake, isn't that a nice letter with an eventual very happy ending? Your great grandparents were married for almost 65 years. You can read all 1,000 of their World War II letters and those from close relatives in our book, From Burma With Love. My publisher, Author House, called on 6/10/2014 asking if I wanted to pay $700 for a company called Thruline Entertainment to rewrite our book as a movie script for consideration by Hollywood. Stand by!!!

Love, Granddad

The Japanese Attack Pearl Harbor

Dear Will, Kayla, Ava, and Blake,   December 7, 2015

This surprise attack happened at sunrise Sunday morning 74 years ago today on 12/7/1941 on the Hawaiian island of Oahu. Hawaii was a territory then and would not become our 50th state until 1959. My dad was already in the US Army stationed at Camp Roberts, California when this happened. Here is his letter of that date to his brother and sister-in-law in Urbana, Illinois.

Dear Frank & Gerry,   December 7, 1941

I enjoyed your letter, Frank. Congratulations on your work. I know you're doing a real job. Stay in there and pitch, my future looks black.

I'm up in the orderly room now. I'm acting company commander, I've just ordered every man restricted to the company area. I've posted guards armed with ball ammunition guarding every rifle rack and the storeroom. From now I'm carrying a loaded 45 automatic 24 hours a day. We've doubled the guard and given them careful instructions. The camp is full of Japanese. Our company has about 50 of them.

All the coastal defenses have been ordered to 24-hour duty. All officers must appear in uniform. All orders and leaves have been canceled. I don't know what's going to happen, but regardless what does, I'll be doing my duty. And never forget that. I think you and Gerry are the best brother and sister a guy could want. Take care of Junior and God bless you both.

                                                                Love,
                                                                Irwin

PS: I'm sending some pictures which I hope you'll enjoy. Camp Roberts is within range of artillery fire from the coast.

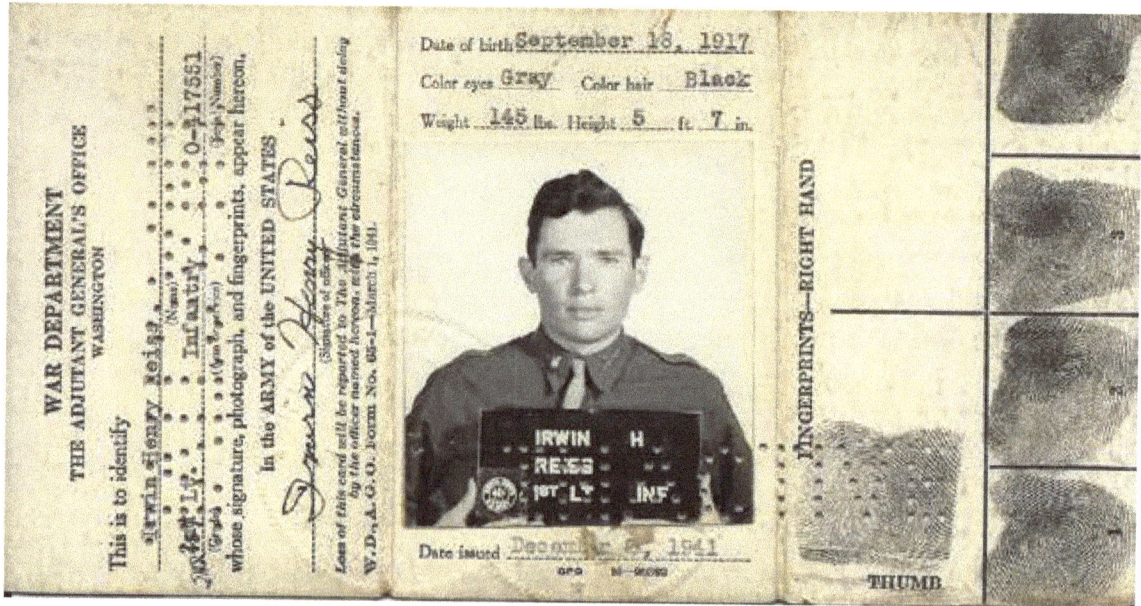

Notice the date below Dad's picture on his new ID card. It was issued the day after Pearl Harbor. Notice his photograph. I can see anger and determination.

Dad's Service Number was O-417551. Here's where that came from – By 1940, it was obvious to most in the U.S. military establishment that America would soon be involved in a major war. To that end, conscription had been introduced and the Army of the United States was founded to serve as a mixed volunteer and draft force raised to fight in the coming war.

Due to the vast numbers of personnel entering the Army ranks, a major expansion to the service number system was required. The original concept was to simply continue with the old service number system and begin with new numbers starting at 8,000,000. The Army, however, chose a more complicated design with new numbers beginning at 10,000,000. The eight and nine million series were reserved for special uses; the eight million service numbers would later be used strictly by female Army personnel while the nine million service numbers were never issued. Army officers continued to be assigned service numbers based on when they joined the officer corps with a service number range of 1 to 20,000. In 1936, the Army extended the service numbers to 499,999 and, in 1942, officer service numbers were extended again to 3,000,000. Officers of the Regular Army were assigned lower service numbers, with West Point graduates receiving the lowest of all in the 20,000 to 50,000 range.

By 1942, the Army had also discontinued the prefix "O" and established that all officer numbers would begin with a zero. For instance, an officer with the service number 2,345,678 would have the number written in military records as 02 345 678.

Grand DD and I were in Nagasaki, Japan 40 days ago on October 29. That's where the US dropped its second atomic bomb on August 9, 1945. We were part of a group of 16 current and former Peoria friends. Most were retired school teachers. Some of these couples had relocated to The Villages, Florida and we continue to see them every spring. Woody Siltman had organized our group cruise with Celebrity Lines which sailed from Yokohama, Japan on 10/25/2015 and arrived in Hong Kong on 11/7/2015.

Grand DD and I had known our travel details for over a year. We knew we would visit Nagasaki on 10/29/2015 which would include time at Ground Zero, 500 meters above which the atomic bomb had exploded and killed 70,000 Japanese. We had done our history homework. I was very curious what my personal reactions would be to visiting Ground Zero, an adjacent museum, various memorials, the harbor, and the rebuilt city. Here's some of that history from 1945.

In August 1945, during the final stage of the Second World War, the US dropped atomic bombs on the Japanese cities of Hiroshima and Nagasaki. The two bombings, which killed at least 129,000 people, remain the only use of nuclear weapons for warfare in history.

As the Second World War entered its sixth and final year, the Allies had begun to prepare for what was anticipated to be a very costly invasion of the Japanese mainland. This was preceded by an immensely destructive firebombing campaign that obliterated many Japanese cities. The war in Europe had concluded when Nazi Germany signed its instrument of surrender on May 8, 1945, but with Japanese refusal to accept the Allies' demands for unconditional

Surrender, the Pacific War dragged on. Together with the United Kingdom and China, the US called for the unconditional surrender of the Japanese armed forces in the Potsdam Declaration on July 26, 1945. This was buttressed with the threat of "prompt and utter destruction."

By August 1945, the Allied Manhattan Project had successfully detonated an atomic device in the New Mexico desert and subsequently produced atomic weapons based on two alternate designs. The 509th Composite Group of the US Army Air Forces was equipped with a Silverplate Boeing B-29 Superfortress airplane that could deliver them from Tinian in the Mariana Islands.

A uranium gun-type atomic bomb (Little Boy) was dropped on Hiroshima on August 6, 1945 followed by a plutonium implosion-type bomb (Fat Man) on the city of Nagasaki on August 9. Little Boy exploded 2,000 feet above Hiroshima in a blast equal to 15,000 tons of TNT, destroying five square miles of the city. Within the first two to four months of the bombings, the acute effects of the atomic bombings killed 90,000–166,000 people in Hiroshima and 39,000–80,000 in Nagasaki; roughly half of the deaths in each city occurred on the first day. During the following months, large numbers died from the effect of burns, radiation sickness, and other injuries, compounded by illness and malnutrition. In both cities, most of the dead were civilians, although Hiroshima had a sizable military garrison.

In between the bombings on August 8, 1945, the Soviet Union officially declared war on Japan, pouring more than 1 million Soviet soldiers into Japanese-occupied Manchuria in northeastern China to take on the 700,000-strong Japanese army. The dropping of the bomb on Hiroshima by the Americans did not have the effect intended, that of unconditional surrender by Japan. Half of the Japanese inner Cabinet, called the Supreme War Direction Council, refused to surrender unless guarantees about Japan's future were given by the Allies, especially regarding the position of the emperor/god, Hirohito. The only Japanese civilians who even knew what happened at Hiroshima were either dead or suffering terribly.

Japan had not been too worried about the Soviet Union who was busy with the Germans on the Eastern front. The Japanese army went so far as to believe that they would not have to engage a Soviet attack until spring 1946. But the Soviets surprised them with their invasion of Manchuria, an assault so strong that Emperor Hirohito began to plead with his War Council to reconsider surrender. The recalcitrant members began to waver. The Soviet Union also began to invade Japan, starting with their northern most island which was easy access from the Asia mainland. The Japanese became convinced it was just a matter of weeks before the Soviet Union would invade Tokyo, capture their emperor/god Hirohito, and execute him. ==That really got their attention.==

On August 15, just days after the bombing of Nagasaki and the Soviet Union's declaration of war, Japan announced its surrender to the Allies. On September 2, it signed the instrument of surrender, effectively ending World War II. Hirohito was no longer a god. The bombings' role in Japan's surrender and their ethical justification are still debated.

Nagasaki   **Hiroshima**

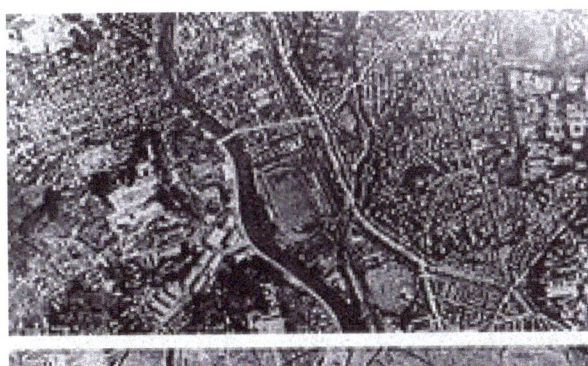

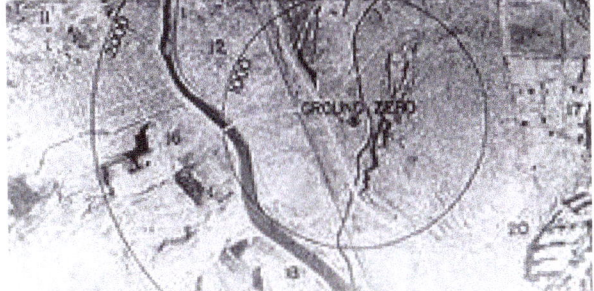

At left are pictures of Nagasaki before and after the bombing on 8/9/1945.

We learned on our visit to Nagasaki that the Japanese had invaded your mom/aunt Hany's country of Malaysia just hours before they bombed Pearl Harbor. Her country back then was called Malaya. That battle was between ground forces of the British Indian Army and the Empire of Japan. It was the first major battle of the Pacific War.

Here are pictures from the Nagasaki Atomic Bomb Museum adjacent to Ground Zero. At left is a replica of the 10-feet tall atomic bomb nicknamed Fat Man. At right is a clock damaged by the blast at 11:02 a.m.

33

This memorial marks Ground Zero or the Hypocenter as the Japanese call it. The plaque reads:

At 11:02 A.M., August 9, 1945 an atomic bomb exploded 500 meters above this spot. The black stone monolith marks the hypocenter. The fierce blast wind, heat rays reaching several thousand degrees and deadly radiation generated by the explosion crushed, burned, and killed everything in sight and reduced this entire area to a barren field of rubble. About one-third of Nagasaki City was destroyed and 150,000 people killed or injured and it was said at the time that this area would be devoid of vegetation for 75 years. Now, the hypocenter remains as an international peace park and a symbol of the aspiration for world harmony.

Here is the Peace Statue built by the people of Nagasaki in 1955 when the Peace Park was established. The bronze statue is 32 feet tall and weighs 30 tons. The right hand is raised upward to point to the threat of nuclear weapons while the horizontally extended left hand symbolizes peace. The gently closed eyes are said to offer a prayer for the repose of the bomb victims' souls. The face does not look Japanese because it is a "person who goes beyond human races."

Will, Kayla, Ava, and Blake, I mentioned at the start of this story that I was curious about what my reactions would be to visiting Ground Zero. Here's what's still stuck in my head from visiting Nagasaki, living 3.5 years in South Korea, visiting Japan half a dozen times, and working with their suppliers on Caterpillar business:

- The Japanese were brutal landlords in Korea, Okinawa, Burma, Manchuria, and other parts of China. To this day the South Koreans want nothing to do with them except access to their technology.

- My stock broker is Brett Douglas. His first wife, Iris Chang, wrote the 1997 international bestselling book, *The Rape of Nanking: The Forgotten Holocaust of World War II.* She learned so much dirt on the Japanese that she became greatly depressed and committed suicide on 11/9/2004 at the age of 36 leaving a husband and two-year old son. Brett has since married another Chinese lady.

- The War in the Pacific involved 4.5 years of my dad's life. I am so proud of his service and contributions in the US, Burma, and India. Also on the positive side, the war led to his marriage to Mary Stephenson, to 1,000 letters they exchanged in 1944/5 which are now in book form as *From Burma With Love*, and eventually to you four, his great grandchildren. That outcome is very good.

- I'm so glad my brother and I were able to take our dad to the 2004 dedication of the World War II Veterans Memorial in Washington, DC. Dad died in 2007.

- Thousands of Japanese citizens were victims of their belligerent military government. They did not deserve to be incinerated at Nagasaki.

- The world needs to get rid of ISIS.

Love, Granddad

Camp Roberts, California

Dear Will, Kayla, Ava, and Blake,   December 7, 2015

On September 18, 1941, my dad wrote to his brother Frank and sister-in-law Gerry from Fort Benning, Georgia. That was Dad's 24th birthday. He said he would complete Basic Training with the US Army in eight days and then drive home to the family farm in southern Illinois to rest and await orders.

His next letter dated October 15, 1941 is from Camp Roberts and reads – With my appetite for mountain driving thoroughly satiated and certain parts of my anatomy rather travel-worn, I arrived at Camp at 3:00 p.m. on Monday October 13. We traveled 2200 miles from St. Louis in 3 ¾ days. We spent four nights in tourist cabins (*motels*) – Lebanon, Missouri; Shamrock, Texas; Gallup, News Mexico; and Barstow, California. The Camp, if you ever have an occasion to consult a map, is 12 miles north of Paso Robles. The Pacific Ocean is 15 miles west. My request for a transfer to a non-combat unit was refused.

Dad was at Camp Roberts for three months in 1941, all of 1942, and about six months in segments of 1943. The best part of those training and teaching assignments was meeting an attractive redhead at the quartermaster's office on March 15, 1942. Her name was Mary Leone Stephenson and that day was her 21st birthday. They married eight months later on November 8, 1942. I know her better as Mom. The rest of their history during World War II is in our book, From Burma With Love, which contains 1,000 of their daily letters while separated by war for 15 months. Dad was in India and Burma. Mom and newborn me were in Atascadero, California.

My cousin Mark Stephenson who grew up in nearby Paso Robles recently forwarded a link to the following 11/15/1990 newspaper article about building Camp Roberts in 1940. It was a challenging history and thoroughly describes the difficulties of rushing that camp into existence, competing for living quarters amongst thousands of contractor workers, and just coping with the winds of war which were developing.

The bulldozer buried beneath Camp Roberts and other stories
Building of Camp Roberts recalled

Al Johnson, heavy equipment superintendent, kept the construction of Camp Roberts moving along during record rains in 1940-41.

CAMP ROBERTS — Fifty years ago next Monday, the peace and quiet north of San Miguel was shattered. The repercussions are still echoing today.

On Nov. 19, 1940, construction workers gathered on a ranch north of San Miguel to start grading building sites for Camp Roberts.

Large crews — working 10-hour days — completed the camp's West Garrison barracks in just 14 weeks.

Camp historian Al Davis also said the first troops to be trained at the new camp began arriving by train on March 15, 1941.

The entire camp — including the East Garrison area across the Salinas River — was completed by July 10, 1941.

The camp was built to house 30,000 soldiers but swelled to 46,000 during the height of training brought on by World War II. (*Here's the completed camp with the world's largest military parade grounds in the middle, equal to 14 football fields. That's the Salinas River with trees.*)

Before then, construction of Camp Roberts had brought an army of workers to the North County. At one time the civilian workers totaled almost 8,000.

One of them was Dorwin "Dutch" Avery, 76, of Templeton, who came down in late 1940 from Gilroy where he had worked on a ranch.

He said there were so many workers many of them couldn't find a place to live.

At first the nearest home he could find for his family was a motel in Soledad. Later he found an old four-room ranch house on Union Road four miles east of Paso Robles.

Avery's family had to share the house with another family. Avery, his wife, Ann, and their five children lived in two rooms. Their sixth child was born while they lived there.

The house had no inside bathroom, Avery said, or any water for that matter. He had to carry water home from town.

How could they live like that? "Hell, you couldn't find anything else," he said.

They lived like that for three years, he said, until they finally found a place to rent in Paso Robles. It wasn't any bigger but had water and an indoor toilet, he said, so his wife was tickled.

She wasn't pleased, though, when men kept walking up and knocking on their door for weeks after they moved in. Their home, it turned out, had been a house of prostitution, he said.

After the camp was built, Avery was hired there as a civil service employee in the roads, walks and grounds division. He worked there until he retired 30 years later.

Avery said he started out at the camp in December of 1940, about a month after construction began.

That was also about the time that the rains started. The winter of 1940-41 was one of the wettest on record.

Historian Davis said the rainfall that winter totaled 39.98 inches. The roads and ditches became rivers of mud, he said but the work never stopped.

Conditions were described in reports by Capt. J.T. Smoody, who oversaw the construction for the Army.

"Carpenters found it necessary to carry lumber to their worksite through knee-deep mud, and on occasion would be stuck so badly they would drop their load and would need assistance to be rescued from their predicament."

Davis reported that the wet weather delayed the construction of permanent roads. In many places, 4 to 6 feet of mud had to be removed and replaced with dry soil.

A legend grew up about a bulldozer that bogged down in the mud of what became the camp's huge parade field. The heavy machine was said to have buried itself so deeply that it was abandoned and covered over. Davis, after checking, found the legend was almost true.

He checked it out with Harley Davidson, a foreman for the camp's general contractor, Morrison-Knudsen. Davidson confirmed that a big piece of equipment did get mired in the mud, burying itself to top of its tracks, Davis said. But it wasn't abandoned, Davidson said. It was finally recovered by using 14 other pieces of heavy equipment.

Laborers earned $50 per week while bulldozer operators made $100. Foremen were paid $150.

That was for a 58-hour week, Davidson said, 10 hours a day, Monday through Friday, and eight hours on Saturdays. For those days, however, the pay was good and attracted thousands of workers. They had a big impact on San Miguel.

Real estate agent Bert Turnbow was quoted as saying highway lots that sold for $200 in August were bringing $100 per frontage foot in November.

The Elkhorn Bar in San Miguel, which had grossed about $300 per week, was bringing in $400 to $500 on weeknights by February 1941, and $700 to $800 per night on weekends. By July 10, 1941 the construction contract was officially completed. But there was still a lot of work to do.

That's what Iveus "Red" Evans found out 16 days later when he arrived from Texas. Evans, now 90, said he had planned to visit his brother and brother-in-law for just a week and then return to Texas. He still lives in Paso Robles.

Evans, a carpenter, was visiting his relatives on the job one day when the foreman walked up and told him he had been on the payroll since 8 that morning. Evans worked at Camp Roberts for the next 30 years.

He also helped build the USO building at 10th and Park streets in Paso Robles. It later became the city recreation building and is now being torn down. "I drove the first nail in the USO building," he said.

He held that job until his retirement in 1970 — except for about four months in 1942 and '43 when he was drafted into the Army.

He was 42, had a stiff leg and had only one eye. Evans thinks his being drafted had something to do with a conversation he had one night in a Paso Robles card room with a member of the local draft board. He doesn't talk about the details.

His wife, Irene, got the Camp Roberts post commander and post engineer to write letters saying they needed Evans back at the camp. The Army discharged him.

His wife also worked at Camp Roberts in the post laundry during the war. They raised all three of their children in Paso Robles.

Red Evans and Dutch Avery said there aren't many people left who worked with them at Camp Roberts in those early days. "They're dead," both said. But Camp Roberts is still alive, although it's been closed and revived a few times.

The war ended in August of 1945 and by July of 1946, Camp Roberts — which had trained 436,000 soldiers — was a ghost town, in caretaker status.

But it reopened on August of 1950 to train thousands of soldiers for the Korean War. By November 1953 the Korean War was over and Camp Roberts was again reduced to "ready" status.

But for an inactive post it remained very active, being used summers and weekends for National Guard and Army Reserve training.

Since 1971 the California National Guard has leased the camp from the Army, but it is also still used by regular Army troops from Fort Ord and it is the home of an Army satellite communications station.

Camp Roberts also still has an impact on the North County. It still provides many jobs, and residents often see truck convoys on the highways going to and from the camp.

Camp Roberts also stimulates the North County real estate market every few years because of recurring rumors that the camp will open again.

But since 1953 they've always been wrong.

Will, Kayla, Ava, and Blake, isn't that an interesting history. My dad arrived shortly after Camp Roberts opened in mid-1941. Many of the finishing touches continued after he reported for duty. Before my folks were married, Mom lived with her parents, Andrew and Daisy Stephenson, 25 miles south in Atascadero. The area housing demand was so strong that they converted their detached garage into a small cottage which they rented to Army officers who arrived and departed every two or three months.

You know the Japanese attacked Pearl Harbor 74 years ago today on December 7, 1941. Can you imagine what was going through my dad's head – here he was 2,200 miles from his parents, his brothers, and his (then) fiancé Edith Freedlund. His intended career in agriculture was now on hold for several more years. He was in a combat unit. His future was extremely uncertain. What's next? Would he be wounded? Would he even survive? It's very appropriate that NBC news commentator, Tom Brokaw, calls this "The Greatest Generation!!!"

Love, Granddad

War Bond

Dear Will, Kayla, Ava, and Blake,   May 4, 2015

Upon graduation from the University of Illinois on June 11, 1941, my dad entered service with the US Army as a Second Lieutenant. He had taken Advanced ROTC which paid part of his college expenses so he was thereby obligated to serve for four years. Six months later the Japanese attacked the US Fleet in Pearl Harbor, Hawaii on December 7, 1941. The US formally declared war on Japan the next day on December 8 and then on Germany on December 11.

Here's the bond my dad bought for his dad (whose name should be Reiss instead of Russ) in October 1942. These bonds were a major revenue source the US Government used to finance the war effort. Dad and Mom were married the next month on November 8, 1942. Their lives were getting extremely complex for all kinds of financial, rationing, separation, military, and world political reasons. I cannot comprehend. That's why NBC newsman, Tom Brokaw, calls this the Greatest Generation!!!

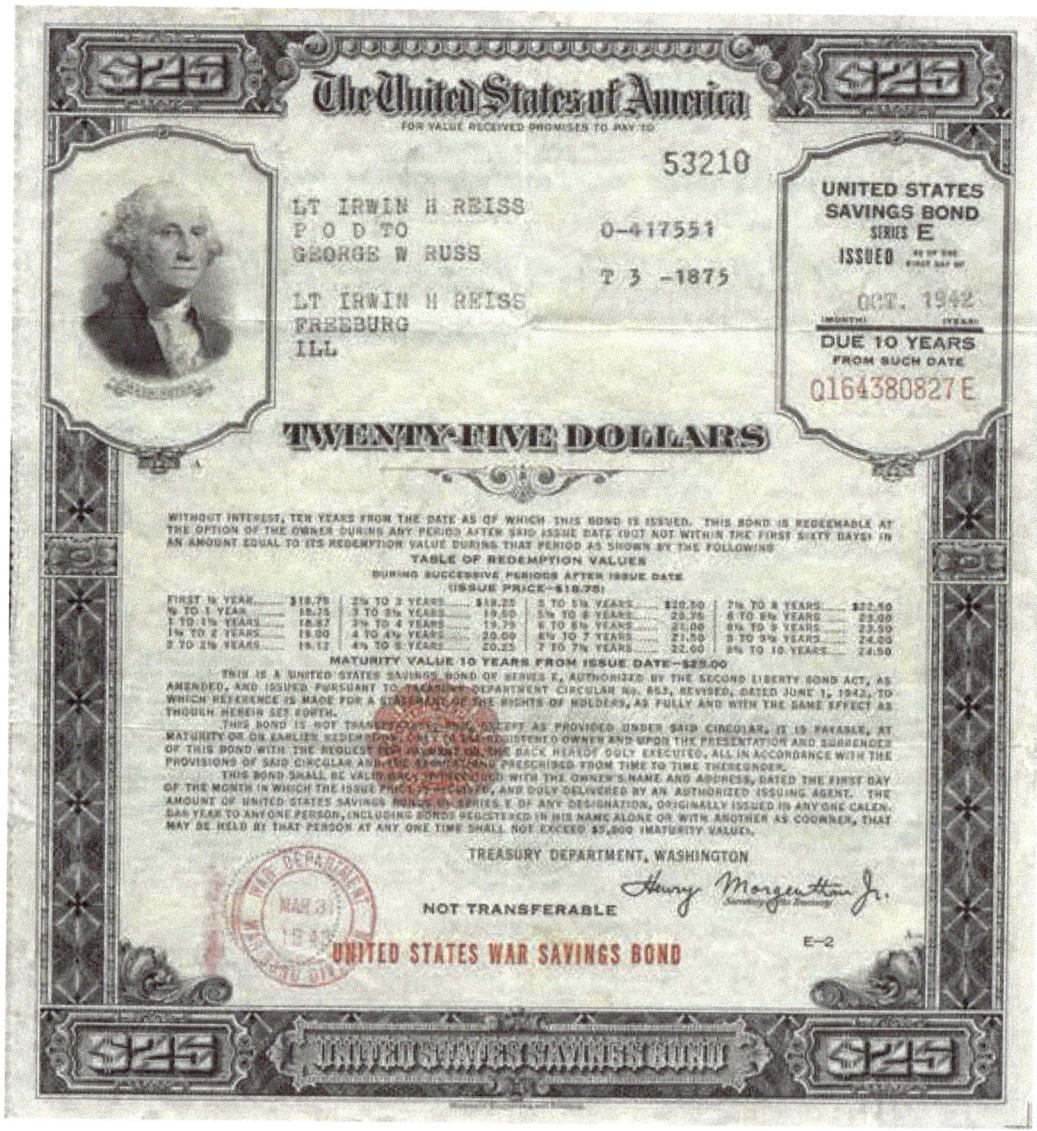

Here are parts of a letter Mom wrote to Dad six days after I was born on 6/12/1944. Some of it involves war bonds. She was still in the hospital since the normal stay back then was ten days.

June 18, 1944
Letter #17

My precious daddy,

Today is our 6th day in the hospital and we are on the last lap. So far I haven't seen Stevie yet today, but they will bring him in at 10 this morning – it is now 9.

Mom said the write-up about the baby in the "News" was a scream. They called it a "Patriotic baby" and a "War Bond Baby" because it was born the day the 5th War Loan Drive started. I'll see if I can send you a copy. So far it hasn't appeared in the "Baby Talk" column in the San Luis paper, but they usually write it up real dippy too.

The article in the June 16 "Atascadero News" reads: REISS SON BORN – Lieut. and Mrs. Irwin Reiss (Mary Stephenson) are the proud parents of a nine pound son, Stephen William, born at the Mountain View Hospital in San Luis Obispo on Monday June 12, Flag Day and the opening day of the Fifth War Loan Drive. It was also Civilian D Day.

Last nite I gave the hospital a check for $75.54 in partial payment of my bill. Now our checking account balance is $875, but I have to add your $240 and my $40 so that makes it $1,155. I think that after I pay the doctor's bill, I'll buy another $500 bond for $375.

Lots of kisses from me, dear, and lots of juicy, wet ones from Stevie.

Always your two babies,

Your Mary and your Stevie

Fireside Chat 30: Opening Fifth War Loan Drive (June 12, 1944) by President Franklin Delano Roosevelt

Less than a week after D-Day, Roosevelt calls on Americans to do their duty to support the war by buying Treasury bonds as part of the fifth war loan drive. Here are excerpts from his radio address to the people.

Ladies and Gentlemen:

All our fighting men overseas today have their appointed stations on the far-flung battlefronts of the world. We at home have ours too. We need, (and) we are proud of, our fighting men – most decidedly. But, during the anxious times ahead, let us not forget that they need us too.

It goes almost without saying that we must continue to forge the weapons of victory – the hundreds of thousands of items, large and small, essential to the waging of the war. This has been the major task from the very start, and it is still a major task. This is the very worst time for any war worker to think of leaving his machine or to look for a peacetime job.

And it goes almost without saying, too, that we must continue to provide our Government with the funds necessary for waging war not only by the payment of taxes – which, after all, is an obligation of American citizenship – but also by the purchase of War Bonds – an act of free choice which every citizen has to make for himself under the guidance of his own conscience. Whatever else any of us may be doing, the purchase of War Bonds and stamps is something all of us can do and should do to help win the war.

Tonight, therefore on the opening of this Fifth War Loan Drive, it is appropriate for us to take a broad look at this panorama of world war, for the success or the failure of the drive is going to have so much to do with the speed with which we can accomplish victory and the peace.

For all of the things which we use in this war, everything we send to our fighting Allies, costs money – a lot of money. One sure way every man, woman and child can keep faith with those who have given, and are giving, their lives, is to provide the money which is needed to win the final victory. I urge all Americans to buy War Bonds without stint. Swell the mighty chorus to bring us nearer to victory!

Fifth War Loan – June 12, 1944 marked the beginning of the most ambitious war financing campaign. The $16 billion goal of the Fifth War Loan was the largest of the eight campaigns, but by its conclusion on July 8, 1944, $20.6 billion had been sold. It came at a critical time, as the tempo of war had increased dramatically. Production rates were hitting new peaks, while availability of goods was low and consumer earning rates were high. Will, Kayla, Ava, and Blake, I still have this war bond that Dad bought almost 73 years ago. Face value was $25 but the current redemption value is $97.45. The yield rate from issue was 4.16% but further growth stopped after 40 years in 1982. There's a bond like this on eBay right now for $98. But ours is a significant family memory so I think we'll keep it for you four grandchildren and for your future grandchildren.

Love, Granddad

Dog Tags

Dear Will, Kayla, Ava, and Blake,   November 5, 2012

This is a very special subject which fits nicely with my other Granddad's Mondays of today which is the 11/8/1942 wedding of your great grandparents, Irwin and Mary Reiss. This Granddad's Mondays is about dog tags.

Dog tags were probably first developed to fit on a dog's collar so that if the dog ran away, the people who found it could then contact the owner and see that the dog was returned. The dog tag contained basic information. Here's what I found on Google about military dog tags for soldiers.

A **dog tag** is the informal name for the identification tags worn by military personnel, named such as it bears resemblance to actual dog tags. The tag is primarily used for the identification of dead and wounded and essential basic medical information for the treatment of the latter, such as blood type, history of inoculations, and religious preference. Dog tags are usually fabricated from a corrosion-resistant metal or alloy such as aluminum, monel, or stainless steel. In the US military, two identical tags are issued. One is worn on a long chain around the neck; the second on a much smaller chain attached to the first chain. In the event the wearer is killed, the second tag is collected, and the first remains with the body.

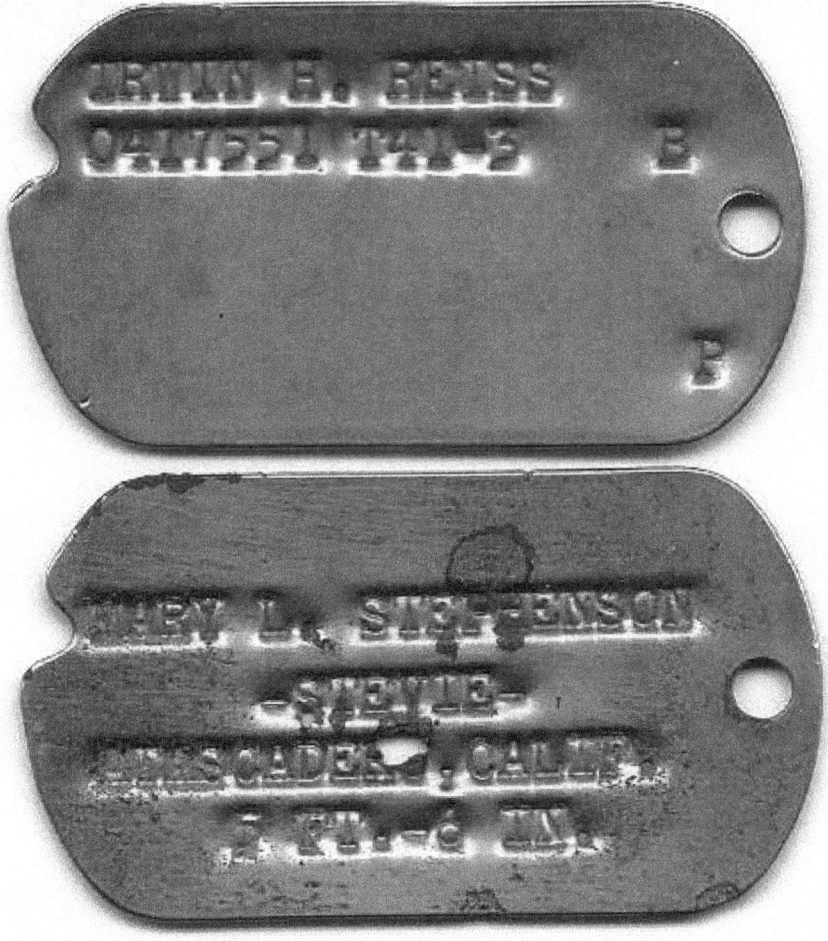

The first tag at left belonged to your great grandfather, Irwin Henry Reiss, whose serial number was 0417551. That suffix of T41-3 may refer to March 1941 when Dad was activated from the ROTC program at the University of Illinois into the US Army.

The second tag belonged to your great grandmother Mary Leone Stephenson before she married Dad on 11/8/1942. Her tag mentions her maiden name, her nickname of "Stevie," her home of "Atascadero, Calif.," and her height of "5 ft. 6 in." Mom was a civilian employee in the Quartermaster's Office at Army's Camp Roberts 27 miles north of Atascadero when she met Dad on her 21ˢᵗ birthday on March 15, 1942. She probably had one of her military friends at the camp make this bootleg dog tag for her. I had not realized that Mom went by "Stevie" as a nickname. She might as well have though because both of her brothers did as well as several nephews in the next generation.

Here's the incredible part – Mom actually lost this tag in the front left hillside of her home in Atascadero some time between when it was made in late 1941 and mid-1946 when she and Dad moved to Vista in San Diego County, California. Her tag laid on that hillside for at least 65 years under a shallow layer of dirt until a year ago when it was found by Greg Ravatt who along with his wife Tina Mayer had bought that home about 2002. They were doing some landscape work last year, found Mom's dog tag, and saved it.

My brother Ken and I were in Atascadero two months ago on September 15 for a double family memorial service for Mom's younger brother Andy and his wife Mary Alice who both died within the last nine months. After the service Ken and I visited Mom's old house without an appointment to see if Greg or Tina were home such that we could tour the inside and take pictures. Greg and his daughter were home so we got a great guys' kinda tour where everyone ignored unmade beds, etc. Greg and Tina are both architects and had done extensive research on this home and how it was divided into apartments during World War II and later. He showed us the former maid's quarters and double stairway to the second floor. Greg's daughter called her mom just to mention what was going on at which point her mom mentioned the old dog tag and that she should give it to us. We eagerly and very appreciatively accepted the gift so now that tag is back in our family possession some 70 years after it was made.

So, Will, Kayla, Ava, and Blake, isn't that an interesting story about your great grandparents' dog tags. ==And the best part is that both tags are now on the same metal ring for the first time ever.== The lost has been found and reunited with its partner!!!

Love, Granddad

Irv and Mary Reiss Wedding (1942)

Dear Will, Kayla, Ava, and Blake,   November 5, 2012

Your great grandparents, Irv and Mary Reiss, were married 70 years ago this coming Thursday on 11/8/1942. They had met on 3/15/1942 which was Mom's 21st birthday. Dad was in the US Army stationed at Camp Roberts, California and Mom was working there in the Quartermaster's office. So they had a quick romance and were married less than eight months after they met. It must have been love at first sight. Here is the receipt for the $2.00 Marriage Application fee in the San Luis Obispo County, California.

Here are newspaper articles about the Saturday night rehearsal dinner, the Sunday wedding, the wedding invitation, and the wedding announcement. Because of the expense, gasoline rationing, and wartime travel restrictions, none of Dad's parents or brothers and their wives were able to attend the wedding. His best man was Walter Keith who Dad knew from their classes together at the University of Illinois. Dad had been Walt's best man when he and Marge were married several months before. After the war the Keiths settled in Urbana, Illinois where Walt was a professor of landscape architecture at the University of Illinois. So the Reisses and Keiths stayed lifelong friends.

Stephensons Host at Pre-Wedding Dinner Saturday

Mr. and Mrs. A. T. Stephenson were hosts at a very pleasant dinner given at their home on Rosario Avenue Saturday evening, preceding the wedding of their daughter, Mary, and Lt. Reiss on the following day.

Covers were laid for Lt. and Mrs. Walter Keith, Lt. and Mrs. Martin Gundlock, Lt. and Mrs. Francis Nagle, the Misses Eleanor Cornelius, Lucille Ray and Thais Shaves, Rev. Anton Hanson, Rev. and Mrs. Lowell A. Young, Mr. and Mrs. William Watson, Andrew Stephenson, Jr., Mrs. Harry S. Gray, Mrs. E. D. Jarvis, Mrs. Thomas Garrity, Patricia Eberlein, Miss Mary Stephenson, Lt. Irwin Reiss and the host and hostess. A pleasant social evening followed the dinner.

CUSTOMER'S RECEIPT   253-34
GWEN MARSHALL
COUNTY CLERK
San Luis Obispo, California, Oct 21 1942
M Irwin H Reiss

QUAN.		AMOUNT
	Complaint No.	
	Petition No.	
	Demurrer No.	
	Answer No.	
	Execution No.	
	Certificate to Copy No.	
	Copartnership	
	Marriage Application	2 00
	Copy, Preparing	
	Copy, Comparing	
	Copy, Exemplified No.	
	Acknowledgment or Affidavit	
	Incorporation No.	
	Qualifying Notary	
	Registering	
	Searching Record	

A. Carlisle & Co., San Francisco

Mr. and Mrs. Andrew Tynes Stephenson
request the honour of your presence
at the marriage of their daughter
Mary Leone
To
Mr. Irwin Henry Reiss
First Lieutenant, Army of the United States
On Sunday, the eighth of November
At four o'clock
Community Church
Atascadero, California

Stephenson – Reiss Nuptials performed at Atascadero

At one of the loveliest weddings of the fall season, Miss Mary Leone Stephenson, daughter of Mr. and Mrs. Andrew T. Stephenson of Atascadero, made her nuptial vows with 1st Lt. Irwin Henry Reiss, son of Mr. and Mrs. George Reiss of Freeburg, Ill., at the Community Church of Atascadero last Sunday at 4:00 p.m.

The double ring ceremony was performed by Rev. Hanson of Glendale, assisted by Rev. Lowell Young.

Miss Stephenson was a picture bride in ivory satin with a full length train bordered in Venetian lace. Her gown was fashioned with a fitted bodice featuring a square net yoke, edged with an inset of Venetian lace. A filmy veil falling the full length of the train was caught with a coronet of seed pearls. She carried a bouquet of white roses with a shower of white sweet peas. Her father gave her in marriage.

Miss Eleanor Cornelius, with whom she has been a classmate since they were in the first grade of school together, was maid of honor. She wore a pale blue georgette with a fitted waist band, into which the top bodice was gathered. The skirt was full and on her head was a matching net coronet with a shoulder veil. Her bouquet was of Talisman roses.

The bridesmaids were the Misses Lucile Ray of Berkeley and Thais Shaves of San Jose, both college classmates of the bride. Miss Ray was in pale aquamarine and Miss Shaves in pale pink, both being gowned in identical design to that of the maid of honor. They each carried a bouquet of white and pink-tinted bridesmaid roses.

First Lt. Walter Keith of Camp Roberts served the groom as best man, and the ushers were Lt. Gundlock and Lt. Francis Nagle, both of Camp Roberts.

Preceding the ceremony, Miss Dorothy Maltby of Paso Robles, a friend of the bride sang "O Promise Me" and "Because."

Mrs. Walter Keith presided at the organ, playing Lohengrin's Wedding March as the bride came down a white carpeted aisle, between six tall white cathedral candles to the altar which was surrounded with four candelabra of seven tapers each. The pew markers were of white mums and an arrangement of fern and mums formed a background in the chancel. Floral arrangements were by Mrs. Harry Gray, Mrs. Edwin Jarvis, and Mrs. Thomas Garrity.

Approximately 150 attended the wedding, after which a reception was held in the social hall of the church, which was beautifully decorated with white mums.

The bride's mother wore a gown fashioned with a white lace bodice and sheer black velvet skirt, with a black hat and accessories. Her corsage was of gardenias.

The parents of the bridegroom were unable to be present.

A four-tiered wedding cake topped with a miniature officer and bride was cut by the bride. Tiny fancy cakes were presented to the guests, with Mrs. William Watson of Los Angeles in charge. Presiding at the punch table were Mrs. Martha Wilsey of Halcyon and Miss Jean Russell of Atascadero.

Following the reception, the bridal party, and the family and close friends of the bride and bridegroom were entertained at the home of the bride's parents where the bride's bouquet was caught by Miss Shaves.

The young couple left immediately for a short honeymoon in southern California, and upon their return will make their home at Atascadero while Lt. Reiss is stationed at Camp Roberts.

Mrs. Reiss chose for her going-away outfit, a blue wool jersey with a silver fox chubby, and she wore brown accessories.

The bride attended schools in Atascadero and two years at San Jose State College. She was employed as a secretary in the quartermaster's office at Camp Roberts prior to her marriage.

The bridegroom is a graduate of the University of Illinois where he received a B.S. degree. He is affiliated with the following honorary societies: Gamma Sigma Delta, Alpha Zeta, Phalanx, Alpha Tau Sigma, and Sigma Xi international scientific honor society.

He was ordered to active duty at Fort Benning, Ga. in June of 1941 and has been stationed at Camp Roberts since October.

Out-of-town guests at the wedding included Andrew Stephenson, Jr., brother of the bride, who is attending Bellerman College at San Jose. Her other brother Lt. Elliott Stephenson, who is stationed at Camp Davis in North Carolina, was unable to be present.

Also attending were Mr. and Mrs. William Watson of Los Angeles, and Mrs. A. T. Breckell, a cousin of the bride, also of Los Angeles.

The bride was extensively entertained prior to her marriage, a miscellaneous shower being given by the maid of honor, Miss Cornelius; a dinner party by Capt. and Mrs. Theodore Tellefsen, Capt. and Mrs. Robert Corfman, and Lt. and Mrs. William Wilson, and a breakfast by Mrs. Holschue.

Mary Stephenson becomes bride of Lt. Irwin Reiss
Candlelight Ceremony at Community Church Sunday afternoon

A beautiful and impressive double ring ceremony united Miss Mary Leone Stephenson and Lt. Irwin Henry Reiss in marriage at the Community Church Sunday afternoon, Nov. 8, in the presence of a large assembly of friends and relatives from various parts of the state.

The church auditorium presented a beautiful, green woodsy setting for the ceremony, with giant ferns arranged by Mesdames Harry Gray, Thomas Garrity, and E. D. Jarvis, covering the walls from floor to ceiling and banking the altar, while the windows were covered with lacy, green curtains of ferns and greenery. The ferns at the front were dotted with white flowers from the Perrine greenhouses, and flanked with tall candelabra, holding seven white tapers each. Other white candles in silver floor holders, burned on either side of the center aisle. These, with the wall sconces and the floor lighting of the ferns at the altar, provided the lighting for the candlelight ceremony.

Mrs. Keith Pianist

Mrs. Walter Keith took her place at the grand piano to accompany Miss Dorothy Maltby of Paso Robles in singing "Oh Promise Me" and "Because" and then played the Lohengrin wedding march, as the bridal procession started down the long aisle.

Rev. Anton Hanson of Glendale took his place at the altar, accompanied by the groom and his best man, Lt. Walter Keith, with the ushers, Lt. Frances Nagle and Lt. Martin Gundlock. The bride's three maids were Eleanor Cornelius, made of honor in ice blue chiffon, Lucille Ray in turquoise blue chiffon, and Thais Shaves in ashes or roses chiffon, all carrying roses.

The bride entering on the arm of her father, A. T. Stephenson, was radiant in ivory satin and Venetian lace with train and long veil, carrying white roses and sweet peas as a shower bouquet.

Reception Held

At the close of the beautiful service, with its clearly voiced responses, a reception was held for the bridal party in the social hall adjoining the auditorium, where refreshments were served from the beautifully appointed buffet table centered with the three-tiered bride's cake, cut by the bride with the sword loaned by Capt. T. Tellefsen.

Those serving at the tables were Mrs. William Watson, Mrs. Albert Breckell from Los Angeles, and Mrs. Martha Wilsey and Miss Jean Russell of Atascadero.

Prominent among the out-of-town guests at the wedding were Mrs. G. W. Jorres of Evansville, Ill., Miss Lucille Ray of Berkeley, Miss Thais Shaves of San Jose, Mr. and Mrs. William Galtan, Mr. and Mrs. Terry Davis, Mr. and Mrs. Truman Harris, Mr. and Mrs. Herbert Reinert, and Miss Dorothy Maltby, all of Paso Robles; Mr. and Mrs. William Watson and Mrs. Albert Breckell of Los Angeles and Andrew Stephenson from San Jose.

Lt. and Mrs. Reiss left shortly after the reception on their wedding trip in southern part of the state and old Mexico. The bride was wearing a traveling suit of powder blue wool jersey with fur chubby and brown accessories.

Mr. and Mrs. Andrew Tynes Stephenson
announce the marriage of their daughter
Mary Leone
To
Mr. Irwin Henry Reiss
First Lieutenant, Army of the United States
On Sunday, the eighth of November
One thousand, nine hundred forty-two
Atascadero, California

November 22, 1942

Dearest Mother & Dad,

Things have finally slowed down to where I can get a few things done. I have been out in the field since last Monday. 7½ months behind a desk and then the field is pretty hard. I have been in the field from 630 in the morning until 800 at night. The first day out I walked 12 miles. Boy I thought I'd fold up. This week we are on task force and confined to the post, consequently I am back in my room in the barracks.

Mary and I are still living with her folks. We have two rooms. Mary came out to see me yesterday. She is coming out for Thanksgiving dinner.

Mother & Dad, the wedding gift was very nice. The gold piece created a sensation.

I've been getting up at 4:30 in the morning in order to get to work on time. Tell Frank & Gerry we'll write as soon as I get time.

Our wedding gifts total 109 now. We got a solid crown silver tray from Capt. Kimball. We even got presents from General & Mrs. Ryan in Cleveland, Ohio. Some came from Canada, others from New York City.

Mrs. Robert Franke came to Camp Roberts Sat. I called the Guest House but she wasn't there. The weather is nice and warm. Stay well and write soon.

Love,

Irwin & Mary

This $20 gold coin dated 1873 was the wedding gift from Irv's parents, George and Katie Reiss, to Irv and Mary. That is the year Irv's father was born on the family farm in St. Clair County, Illinois in a log cabin built by his grandfather Adam Reiss in 1834.

Will, Kayla, Ava, and Blake, isn't that a terrific story with lots of details about how your great grandparents, Irv and Mary Reiss, were married just 7 months and 24 days after they met. It was a great match because they were married for almost 65 years.

Love, Granddad

Cedar Row Farm Gazette

Dear Will, Kayla, Ava, and Blake,   October 21, 2013

Here's a picture of the two rows of cedar trees on our family farm, one in the foreground next to the road and one in the distance beyond the pond. That kid in the center left is me at age 13 in 1957. My grandfather George Reiss planted those two rows of trees about 1920 and then he named his farm "Cedar Row Farm." I remember my dad helping me address letters that I would write to my grandparents. He always made sure the second line of the mailing address said "Cedar Row Farm" because he and his parents were very proud of that name.

I visited our farm yesterday and took lots of pictures for my next book. I also interviewed my cousins Lavern and Lucille Lang to get lots of background information since they farmed our farm from 1954 for 45 years. I also interviewed Marcella Klein who is age 93.5 and still lives alone on the next farm west since 1940 after being born on the next farm south on 2/20/1920. She is very very sharp with a great memory, fast talker, and definitely does not act her age.

I walked the nearest row of cedar trees. There are 40 of them all about 18 inches in diameter. Fortunately they have all grown into the metal pasture fence that exists along that road. That makes them totally worthless for timber value since their trunks contain so much metal.

Here's a letter from my grandparents, George and Katie Reiss, that was written 71 years ago this past Friday to my parents who were married three weeks later in California.

Cedar Row Farm
R. R. No. 1
Freeburg, Ill.
October 18, 1942

Dearest Irwin and Mary,

This is Sunday evening about four hours since you called us. Your call surely perfected the day. I was so happy to hear both your voices. Dad asked me tonight; how did Irv's and Mary's voice sound? I told him it sounded as tho they were as happy as we were. I could hear you better than ever before in spite of all the noise and laughter which was going on in the dining room where the crowd was eating supper as it was around 5:30. About half of the crowd had left before. Dad kept telling them be quiet. Mom's talking to Irwin. Anita was just at the door and wanted to have a chance to talk to you both way out in California. She too thought Mary has a very sweet voice.

Irwin, Dad asked me what such a call costs and how we could get you if we ever wanted to call you. Did you call from Mary's home?

We were so happy to have Franklin with us yesterday and today. Time was too short to take baby George on such a rush trip, so Gerry stayed home with him. He has been getting his shots against those different diseases and some of them gave him a high fever. Don't you think he looks cute on the picture where Dad and I are holding him.

Here is who was all here. Mr. & Mrs. Ferd Reiss, Mrs. & Mrs. Kenneth Bivert, Mr. & Mrs. Earl Reiss, Mr. & Mrs. Will Reiss, Mr. & Mrs. Henry Reiss, Jeanette Reiss, Mr. & Mrs. Robert McCall & daughter Jane, Mr. & Mrs. Will Feder and Doris, Aunt Katie, Pearl and Melvin Sukard, Mr. & Mrs. George Dintelmann & Dale. Mr. & Mrs. Edwin Dintelmann and Uncle George Dintelmann, Bill & Anita and June Ann, Uncle Henry Lang and sons, and Uncle Herman & Frank, and Franklin, Dad and myself. Everybody was so happy. There was a constant chatter and laughter. Irwin, if you get a furlough, would you come by train? I think it would be the easiest and cheapest. So good luck to you, children.

I hope you can read the enclosed "Cedar Row Gazette." Maggie started it, so if you have time, then write to her once. 2720 Benbow in Alton, Ill.

Cedar Row Gazette, October 18, 1942

Dear Irv: Another one of these Reiss gatherings where good food and conversation predominate. Congratulations to you and Mary! Hope to see you in November.

The Dintelmanns – Marge, Dale, George

From Uncle Will – Hello Irwin. Had a fine family gathering here today. Have been working very hard this summer so much so that we did not even take a vacation. Looking forward to seeing you back here with us all again.

Love and good wishes from Will & Mabel

Dear Irwin: Altho the weather has not outdone itself to be pleasant, everybody here seems to have been in a very pleasant mood. Everybody is talking about gas rationing. I really think it's just a means of conservation if not a waste of time. I understand you like your location a lot better – could it be the new acquaintances. I wish you all the luck and happiness you deserve.

Sincerely yours, Beulah & Edwin

Dear Irwin, You'll probably read a lot more interesting than this but anyway I hope you enjoy it all. Frank was down and brought pictures of George. Oh boy, what a boy. Bill went to work at 3 o'clock so you won't see him in the chain of letters. I'm going home later with Earl and Helen Reiss. That's all, I'm tired so how about you writing some time.

Love, Anita & June (signed by both)

Dear Irwin, This really has been a delightful day and we are much indebted to your mother and Anita for planning it. The day has been made perfect by your call a few minutes ago. Your mother's eyes were shining when she came away from the phone. We do hope you get to bring your bride home before long and that we can manage to see you. Best wishes and much luck.

Syvilla

Dear Irwin, Earl Reiss & June Ann are playing hide away with an acorn & June Ann seems to be having a great deal of fun doing it. Was surprised to hear you getting married, but I wish you both luck & success in the future years. Will close & hoping to see you when you are home.

Doris Feder

Dear Irwin, I was about to start this as you called from California just now. I took June Ann walking in the woods and we came upon the remains of a snake. June Ann said, "Let's go back the other way. I don't want to run into any more snakes." So we did. By the time we got back, Bill had left for work and Anita and June Ann are going back with Helen and Earl.

Franklin came down on the train for the weekend but Gerry and Georgie stayed home. He went back to St. Louis with Uncle Henry to catch the train back.

It's been so dry here that the little splatter that started isn't doing much good. June Ann came to me after she talked to you and said, "Now I can tell my teacher that I talked 2,000 miles away." We're ready to leave so –

Jane McCall

Will, Kayla, Ava, and Blake, this letter with enclosed Cedar Row Gazette was published in my last book, <u>From Burma With Love</u> which you probably haven't read yet. The italics below was a transition paragraph in that book which provided background information. It's here again for the same purpose. Have a great week.

Love, Granddad

Irv's parents, George and Katie Reiss, are the third generation owners of the 360-acre Reiss Family Farm. It is located about twenty miles southeast of St. Louis or twelve miles south of Belleville, Illinois which is the county seat of St. Clair County. The farm has two 100-yard long rows of cedar trees next to the west lane and the northwest line, hence the "Cedar Row Farm" name in the return address and "newspaper" title. The farm was established by George's grandfather Adam Reiss with his first purchase of 40 acres in 1834 at $1.25 per acre. Significant farmstead buildings in 1942 are a log cabin built in 1834, a log granary built in 1834, a three bedroom home built in 1889, a large two-story barn built about 1920, and a three bedroom home built in 1940. George and Katie's three sons were all born upstairs in the 1889 house – William on 5/6/1912, Franklin on 10/31/1915, and Irwin on 9/18/1917. The family raised chickens, hogs, and various crops. All farming was done by horses. They never owned a tractor. The farm was a popular place for frequent family gatherings because there was lots of space, a pond for fishing, a big orchard, and woods for hiking.

Learning Chinese at Yale University

Dear Will, Kayla, Ava, and Blake,   March 7, 2016

During World War II, a total of 418 men (176 officers and 242 enlisted men) received instruction at Yale University in New Haven, Connecticut in the Chinese language to equip them to train Chinese troops in all phases of modern warfare. My dad was one of the officers who was trained at Yale from 7/15/1943 to 11/30/1943 or 4.5 months. That class of men appears below. One of the major qualifications the Army used in selecting these men was their existing ability to speak more than one language. For my dad, it was English and German.

You can see ranks in front of each name. Most were first or second lieutenants and two were captains. Serial numbers appear after each name. The INF means "Infantry", FA means "Field Artillery" and CAC means "Coast Artillery Corps." These men and their wives did everything together for those 4.5 months. They ate at a lot of Chinese restaurants and socialized together. They rented separate houses in New Haven but otherwise everything else was as a group. They got to be good friends.

CAPT WILLIAM W. HENTHORNE	0447708	INF
CAPT YUANE SHELTON	0352563	CAC
1ST LT LUDWIG P. GILLIS	01300474	INF
1ST LT JOSEPH J. LEBEDA	0391247	INF
1ST LT DAVID B LOVEJOY	01290777	INF
1ST LT IRWIN H REISS	0417551	INF
1ST LT DAVID W STEWART	01170571	FA
1ST LT TURNER WHITE III	0497311	FA
2ND LT ROBERT J CHAN	01321994	INF
2ND LT ROWLAND ROBERTS	01172246	FA

The last group of trainees left Yale on 11/30/1945. In 1947 the Yale Chinese Language School was renamed the Institute of Far Eastern Languages (IFEL). From 1951 through early 1965, during the presidencies of Truman, Eisenhower, Kennedy and Johnson, the US Air Force contracted with Yale University for training in selected Asian languages for Cold War intelligence operations performed by the US Air Force Security Service under National Security Agency direction. In the 14 year period, over 3,000 airmen completed intensive language courses, primarily in Chinese and Korean, at IFEL.

The Chinese language is very difficult for Western people to learn and understand because it uses sounds that we don't use and because there is no Latin alphabet. These red letters are my name with the first two characters being just initials. How in the world could you sound out something like that?

Each man in Dad's group got 14 days leave when classes concluded at the end of November. Mom and Dad drove to Niagara Falls and eventually all the way back to California so Mom could live with her parents in Atascadero. At this point she was three months pregnant with their first child (AKA me). A few days later Dad, Mom, and her younger brother Andy drove to San Francisco so Dad could take an eastbound train to Camp Reynolds, Pennsylvania for more training. Mom and Andy drove back to Atascadero. One of Dad's train stops was in North Platte, Nebraska where local citizens fed all soldiers on the train a nice Christmas Day meal. He arrived in Chicago on December 26 and two days later reported to Camp Reynolds near Greenville, Pennsylvania. His group of ten Chinese linguists sailed from New York on 2/19/1944 aboard the Aircraft Carrier USS Wake Island. They stopped in Brazil and South Africa before docking at Karachi, India (now Pakistan) on 3/29/1944.

On 4/16/1944 they received orders were travel by train to Ramgarh Training Center in northeast India. Here's some history on that center and why Chinese linguists were needed to help with training refugee Chinese soldiers.

The camp that would later become the Ramgarh Training Center in Bihar, India was originally a prisoner of war camp for Germans and Italians captured by British and Commonwealth troops in North Africa. In early 1942, as Burma became overrun by the Japanese, 9,000 men of the Chinese 5th Army fled into India alongside of their British allies. Ramgarh was selected in June 1942 as the new base for these Chinese troops, who were now collectively named "X Force". Although the Chinese had by this time almost five years of fighting experience under their belt, the Japanese having escalated the Sino-Japanese conflict into a full scale war in July 1937, most Chinese troops were conscripts who received little or no training. Thus, Ramgarh was immediately defined as a training camp for these survivors of Chinese 5th Army. By the end of June 1942, the first of the US Army instructors arrived; the first of the Chinese arrived in the following month by rail. In addition to instructors, the United States would also provide radios, rifles, artillery pieces, tanks, and trucks. Meanwhile, the British provided the large amount of food that this training center would require, and the funding to pay the wages of the Chinese soldiers. The first of the trained units returned to the front lines in April 1943, followed by units in September 1943 who they would play a part in the opening of the Ledo Road supply route. As space at the training center was freed up, units of Chinese 30th Division began to be brought in in July 1943. By the end of 1943, the center would turn out 5,368 officers and 48,125 men. Ramgarh would leave the legacy as the first US-manned military training center outside of the United States, and would remain the only one until another training center was established in Kunming, Yunnan Province in southern China later in the war.

Dad's group was disbursed within Ramgarh. Within a month several of his group asked for transfers for various personal reasons. One was William Henthorne who was transferred to a combat unit in Burma (now Myanmar) on 5/24/1944. He is the artist who drew Dad's Yale graduation cartoon. Here are various comments from Dad's daily letters to Mom about staying connected with his group.

6/25/1944 – I am going to Calcutta for a few days soon. The fellows, with the exception of Henthorne who left our group a long time ago, are back here again. White is out of the hospital again. *Dad didn't know it then but William Henthorne was killed in action ten days earlier in Myitkyina, Burma on 6/15/1944 at the age of 23.*

6/26/1944 – This morning I spent about an hour in the Chinese wards at the hospital trying out what Yale had endeavored to teach me. I created quite a fervor and was immediately surrounded by an eager group. . . . . It is very difficult for the western man to understand the Oriental mind. I find that the outside reading that I did at Yale helps me very much in overcoming obvious first impressions.

7/5/1944 – You asked about Bill and Turner. Bill was separated from our group permanently, but Turner was only gone a few days. Some of the fellows have volunteered for various duties that don't come under the scope of what we were trained for; so our group may be split up still further. Our original project is not materializing very fast.

7/6/1944 – While doing business at headquarters downtown, I met two of the Chinese boys from some of the previous classes. From them I learned that Chan and Lovejoy went through here a few days ago. That means that they are no longer with our group. That leaves six of us now.

7/14/1944 – From your PS, I take it that my spelling is still atrocious. Blame that on the Yale Romanization system. I write words as they sound. Anyway, I will acknowledge my errors. Trousers instead of trowsers, laundry instead of lawndry, and so on.

7/17/1944 – Although we are teaching at Ramgarh, that is more or less marking time for officers of our training. Lovejoy and Chan got tired of it and volunteered for line duty. They are in combat in Asssam. I don't think that they should have volunteered since they are trained for something else.

7/18/1944 – I had a letter from Joe today. He tells me that he is getting very bad headaches from the heat. He says that only he, Lou, and Shafto are together yet. Turner and Stewart however are still in the camp.

7/25/1944 – Had a short note from Joe and Lou today. They both say to say hello to you and send their congratulations on the 9 ¼ pounder who has been crowned champ of the four. Neither one of the two appears very content with their present work. I think it will change very soon because one of these days we will get to our permanent stations.

7/26/1944 – I saw Roberts today as he was passing through. About all that you can say for our group is that we are all still in the China-Burma-India Theater. We are now scattered thousands of miles apart and never will get back together again. He had a letter from Chan who has been in action for some time now. I haven't heard anything from Bill in a month. Gillis is off to somewhere, a desk job I think. Joe and I, while not together, are both on temporary duty. Roberts just spent a week in the hospital.

8/7/1944 – I'll be glad to see Joe again. He is the only one left where I am going. One of the first things that we will do is compare pictures of our sons.

8/11/1944 from Mom – I did have a nice long letter from Marge Lebeda. She said Joe said, Bill H. went into combat too. Joe Jr. is 6 months old now and has several teeth.

8/11/1944 – You can now call me Lt. Irwin H. "Casual Officer" Reiss. I have a new job but it's temporary. As soon as I have two years in unassigned, I'll ask to go on an inactive status. Anyway, I am very busy. I got dumped in the middle of a job that I don't know a damn thing about – yet.

8/14/1944 – Stewart and I had dinner together at his mess hall last night. He had an issue of "Yank" magazine which had a write-up on the "GI Bill of Rights." The back to school movement looks very inviting.

8/15/1944 – Well, I am all packed up again and am making farewells around here. I had dinner with Turner at his mess hall last night. After dinner we sat around and talked for a couple of hours. He is going back to school too after the war.

8/18/1944 – I went to see White in the hospital last night. This time he has malaria.

8/30/1944 – I suppose it is permissible now to tell you that Bill Henthorne was killed in action a couple of months ago. He was reported missing to Betty about a month ago. I don't know whether she knows definitely or not. Anyway, don't tell her.

Will, Kayla, Ava, and Blake, that's quite a history, isn't it. Dad's new job was as a labor officer along the Ledo Road in northern Burma where he hired up to 2,000 local villagers per day to work on that road. Those daily letters make up the rest of our book, <u>From Burma With Love</u>. That job lasted about six months before Dad returned to the US to rejoin his family which now included a son. He and I met for the first time on Easter Sunday 1945 when I was nine months old. You can see why news commentator Tom Brokaw calls these World War II veterans and the home force that supported them, **"The Greatest Generation."** We need to continue to pray for peace. Below is what I found on Bill Henthorne.

Love, Granddad

Capt. William W. Henthorne

Birth: Sep. 13, 1920
Death: Jun. 15, 1944, Myanmar (Burma)

MARQUETTE, Iowa. - Funeral services for Capt. William W. Henthorne, son of Mr. and Mrs. A. W. Henthorne of Marquette, who was killed in action at Myitkyina, Burma, June 15, 1944, will be held at 2 p.m. Tuesday at the Pilkington Funeral home in McGregor. The Masonic lodge of McGregor and Marquette of which Capt. Henthorne was a member, will conduct rites, assisting the Rev. E. G. Steinman, pastor of the Methodist church. Burial with military honors will be in Pleasant Grove cemetery at McGregor, the Marquette Legion conducting. Henthorne was born Sept. 13, 1920. He was graduated from the University of Iowa in May, 1942, and the following month reported as second lieutenant at Fort Benning, Ga. After a year there, serving part time as an instructor and being promoted to the rank of a captain, he was sent to Yale university to take a four month course in the Chinese language. He married Betty Bickel of McGregor Dec. 5, 1943, and the following February went overseas to India where he was stationed until June, when he was sent to Burma. (The LaCrosse Tribune, LaCrosse, WI, Sunday, Dec. 19, 1948, p. 20, Col. 1)

Burial:
Pleasant Grove Cemetery
McGregor
Clayton County
Iowa, USA

Fruitcake for Christmas

Dear Will, Kayla, Ava, and Blake,   December 23, 2013

This letter was written 69 years ago today by your great grandfather Irwin Reiss while he was serving in the US Army in India and Burma during World War II. It was probably his first Christmas without any immediate family nearby. He was writing to his wife who is your great grandmother Mary and to his six-month old son who you now know as Granddad. We two were living with Mom's parents in Atascadero, California. Dad was a patient in the 20th General Hospital in Assam, India where he had been admitted for severe headaches. He was not allowed to mention the hospital name due to censorship reasons. This letter is one of nearly 1,000 in a book published by Author House called From Burma With Love. Here's the letter.

> Somewhere along the Ledo Road
> Assam, India
> December 23, 1944

My precious Mommie and Stevie,

How are my darling baby girl and boy today? I am still in bed 19. And as far as I know no nearer to getting out. The Colonel got me in and it looks muchly as if he were going to have to get me out too. I didn't have any mail today and so far I haven't received any package from Mother or Frank, both of whom have sent some.

Everybody in the ward has been passing around nuts and candy, so tonite I unwrapped the fruitcake and I'll pass it around later. You can tell Mom it is still in very good condition and I'm sure it will taste good.

I again read practically all day. I am beginning to tire from so much reading. At present I am reading Oct. "Readers Digest," Nov. 26 "Time," Grapes of Wrath, and a biography of Andrew Jackson. And tonite I am going to start on a western story for still more diversion. If I am to finish all these, I'll be here quite a while yet.

I read some comments on the cigarette shortage. It is a blessing in disguise, believe me. Out of the group of five officers who lived together at my former station – not one of us smoked.

I washed my hair yesterday, so today they are all over the place. I must get a haircut soon. My hair is still wavy. Stephen certainly should have wavy hair. What color is it now?

How does your new prescription suit your eyes? Did you have to get stronger lenses or just what was wrong?

Irwin Jr. came in for his share of admiration today. I have him sitting so that I can see him even when I'm under my mosquito bar. And of course I always have my pictures of you with me. I think my little family is the most wonderful in the world. I love you and our Stevie with all my heart.

> Yours own Daddy, Irvie Always

The article below on the same subject was written from memory by Irv Reiss for his local newspaper in Sullivan, Indiana 48 years after he wrote the letter above to his wife and infant son. It is one of 150 articles he wrote for the "Sullivan Daily Times" between 1984 and 2004. Those articles plus dozens of professional papers and speeches all appear in another book published by Author House called Family, Farming and Freedom.

12/11/1992 Americans Pooled Goodies for Christmas in Mogaung

Christmas is an annual event that I have eagerly looked forward to for over three score years and 10. Call me a child if you will, but my interest and excitement in the December 25 celebration has not diminished – but the factors that stimulate that interest and excitement are different than they were when I first learned about Christmas.

Let me be candid with you, I think celebrating Christmas brings families closer together – every Christmas Eve down on the farm we (our family) went to church where the Sunday School children put on a beautiful program. In the early years the huge Christmas tree had real candles that had to be lighted and extinguished when they burned short. The danger of fire always added to the excitement of taking part in the program and waiting for the bag of goodies – apples, oranges, candy, and peanuts that we got when the service was over. After we got home – by walking the 2 miles, riding in the horse-drawn surrey or the model T Ford – we could eat from a bowl of candy and cookies that each one of us – Mom and Pop included – had under the tree. We sat around the stove that added heat to the warmth that existed among our family members. And by the way, Mom had made all the cookies and candy in her kitchen.

Christmas Eve 1944 I wasn't in that family circle – I was in Mogaung, Burma on the other side of the world, over 10,000 miles from home thinking among other things about my son, whom I had never seen, hopefully celebrating Christmas in some way with his mother. Where, you ask, is Mogaung, Burma? It is on the road to Mandalay in the northern part of the country of Burma in the Far East. How did we celebrate Christmas. There were just four of us working in that vermin-infested jungle. We pooled whatever goodies we had from home. I had about half a fruitcake that Mary's mother had sent me weeks before. But even under these extreme circumstances we felt a closeness among four people who had nothing in common except that we were soldiers in the U.S. Army doing what we had been ordered to do.

Traditionally, we have always used Christmastime as a period for fellowship and kinship and a renewing of the ties that bind our hearts in Christian love. We send more than 100 Christmas cards every year, most with personal messages to friends and relatives with many of whom this is our only yearly contact. And what a delight it is to hear from them in return.

I am a great believer in the family as a basis of our society. I hope and pray that the spirit of Christmas – symbolically, Santa Claus, if you will – will continue to prevail in the hearts and minds of children, parents and grandparents and act as a catalyst to bring and keep families together. Merry Christmas.

Will, Kayla, Ava, and Blake, it looks like Grandpa Irv forgot which country he was in when he wrote that newspaper article 48 years after that Christmas of 1944. Not a big problem because his message still comes through loud and clear. Now for the rest of the story – here is the recipe for that Christmas fruitcake. My grandma Stephenson used it from before 1930 onward so it has stood the test of time. Now I think you three and I, with a little help from the three moms in our family, should make one of these fruitcakes in the next two days before Christmas. Whaduyathink?

Love, Granddad

1 lb of white raisins
½ lb of preserved citron
1 lb of preserved pineapple
1 lb of glazed cherries
¼ lb of minced preserved orange and lemon peel
1 lb of nut meats
3 cups sifted flour
1 cup shortening
1 cup sugar
5 eggs
¼ teaspoon of salt
2 teaspoons of baking powder
¼ cup of pineapple or orange juice
1/1/2 teaspoons of vanilla

Cut up fruits and nuts coarsely and mix thoroughly with one cup of flour. Work shortening with a spoon until fluffy and creamy. Gradually add sugar while continuing to work with spoon until light. Add eggs, one at a time, beating after each. Sift remaining two cups of flour with salt, baking powder, and add alternately to mixture in thirds with fruit juice and vanilla. Fold in the floured fruits and nuts. Pour into two loaf pans about 9" by 5" by 3" which have been greased and lined with waxed paper. Bake at 300 degrees for 2 ¼ to 2 ½ hours until done.

B. J. Elder

Dear Will, Kayla, Ava, and Blake,   January 4, 2016

Here are parts of two letters my dad wrote in July 1944 from India when he met this young girl and her father during World War II. Dad was serving in the US Army helping build a road from Ledo in eastern India, through northern Burma, and into central China. The first stretch was called the Ledo Road which was part of the overall Burma Road. The roads would bring goods and military supplies from eastern India into central China since all Chinese seaports were being blockaded by the Japanese. You can Google both road names. The letters he is answering came from Mom who was in the hospital in San Luis Obispo, CA following my birth on June 12.

India
July 15, 1944 at 2100

My own darling babies,

How are you two? Three letters from you today, Sweet, and they were very lovely. They were written on your 6, 7, 8th days in the hospital. Darling, I am so very happy about our baby and I know that you are a wonderful mother to him. He is our very own, dearest, and I'm so very proud of him and you.

Today I am to meet some people who have just been evacuated from China. He is a former professor of Yale University in China. I am looking forward to an interesting discussion.

Well, I have rambled on here about my little experiences, but the big thing in my life is on the home front – you and Stevie. I have read and reread your glowing accounts of our baby and I know that you are as happy about him as I am.

Your own devoted Daddy,
Irvie

The **Yale-China Association**, *founded in 1901, is a private, nonprofit organization with more than a century of experience contributing to the development of education in and about China and to the furtherance of understanding and knowledge between Chinese and American peoples.*

The Yale-China Association was first incorporated as the Yale Foreign Missionary Society, and was known informally as Yale-in-China as early as 1913. It was nondenominational from its beginnings and by the 1920s had ceased to be an overtly missionary enterprise. It was re-incorporated in 1934 as a secular organization, the Yale-in-China Association. The city of Changsha in Hunan Province was chosen as the base of operations in China.

The war years (1937-45) placed enormous strains on the Yale-in-China institutions, especially the Hsiang-Ya Hospital, which cared for the seemingly limitless war casualties and refugees. Yale-in-China's wartime experiences were difficult, and many of the Changsha facilities were damaged by invading Japanese troops. Nevertheless, these challenges served to inspire renewed commitment on the part of both American and Chinese faculty and administrators. The Yale-in-

China staff who returned to Changsha in September 1945 were determined to rebuild the campus and resume their pre-war operations.

India
July 16, 1944

My darling Mary and Stevie,

Darling, he is beautiful! And he is much bigger than I thought he would be. The pictures are very lovely, darling. He is a perfect baby and he looks so healthy and strong. I'm so proud of you, darling. I showed Dr. Rugh Stevie's picture and he thought him a very handsome boy. I had five letters from you today, Sweet. I have all but three up to and including July 1.

I mentioned Dr. Rugh earlier in my letter. He and his daughter came out to see me this afternoon and we had a very pleasant talk. He is the new man from Yale-in-China that I told you about. He has been in China the past eight years and his very charming seven year old daughter speaks Chinese very fluently. He is from Los Gatos, Cal. and will either call you or drop you a card telling you that he has seen me. He knows Prof. Kennedy and Dr. Fenn for the addresses of some people to contact in the field of Agricultural Economics over here.

I love you and Stevie tremendously much and I think that we have a wonderful son, baby.

Your very own devoted Daddy,
Your Irvie

I Googled "Rugh Yale China" and got several hits including the italics above about the Yale-China Association. I also found this entry of Dr. Rugh's young daughter that Dad met in 1944.

BJ Rugh Elder – BJ began her childhood in Changsha, where her father ran Yale-in-China educational and medical program established by Yale University. As the Japanese invaded, Yale-in-China and the Rugh family had to move to Yuanling, deep in the Hunan Province. But even there, air raids became a routine part of daily life. BJ's memoir of her childhood years, The Oriole's Song, was recently published by Eastbridge in 2003.

So then I Googled "BJ Rugh Elder" and got more hits including her phone number and address in Philadelphia and a summary of her book on the next page. I called her and introduced myself which led to the letters which follow. I sent her my autographed book titled From Burma With Love and she sent me hers.

Will, Kayla, Ava, and Blake, in Googling "B. J. Elder" today for his story, all I found was a former NBA basketball player. So I re-Googled her including her maiden name. One of the hits under her fuller name is my book since she is mentioned in it!!! How cool is that?

Love, Granddad

THE ORIOLE'S SONG by BJ Elder
An American Girlhood in Wartime China

BJ Elder, born Betty Jean Rugh *in 1933 in Hunan Province, spent most of her first sixteen years in China. Now retired, she lives with her husband in Philadelphia, where she raised two daughters, earned a graduate degree, and worked as a Nurse Practitioner.*

The Oriole's Song is a love story – love of family, of entwined cultures, of life itself – during and after the turmoil of war. This beautiful recollection of an American girlhood in China during World War II and of an adult homecoming decades later ... is a continual delight with large insights and small moments made exquisite by delicate prose.

On May 17, 1951, Dwight Rugh – a Yale-in-China representative for twenty years and one of the last Americans remaining in China after the Communist Revolution – was taken from his home in Changsha to a mass rally where he was denounced as an imperialist spy. Twenty-three years later, his daughter was one of the first Americans to enter China after it reopened to the West. Despite the fact that the Cultural Revolution was in full sway, she visited the site of her father's "trial" and met with some of his friends and colleagues who had been compelled to participate in the proceedings.

In this evocative and beautifully written memoir, BJ Elder tells the remarkable story of her family and what it was like for her, an only child, to grow up in China during the Second World War. Born in Hunan, hers was a childhood spent in two languages and "between two names." In a remote river town, she shares the terrors and enthusiasms of her Chinese friends, hides from Japanese bombs, struggles over Chinese calligraphy, and spends enchanted summers in a hidden valley. Yet she thinks of America as "home." When the family goes home to the United States, however, she finds herself drawn back to the country of her birth.

Betty R. Elder
162 Kendal Drive
Kennett Square, Pennsylvania 19348
610 388 2179
belder7496@aol.com
Husband is David L. Elder

700 Savanna Court
Dunlap, Illinois 61525
December 24, 2011

Mrs. Betty Jean Rugh Elder
162 Kendal Drive
Kennett Square, Pennsylvania 19348

Dear B. J.,

Thanks again for sending a copy of your book, The Oriole's Song, about your upbringing in China and parts of Asia. Well, my book of fifteen months of my parent's daily letters during

World War II is now finished and a copy is enclosed for you. It's called <u>From Burma With Love</u>. Read Dad's letter of July 16, 1944 on pages 303/4/5.

These books arrived from the publisher this week so my gift to you will not arrive in time for Christmas. So let's call it a Happy New Year gift. I wish you and your family all the best for the coming year.

Yours truly,
Stephen W. Reiss

162 Kendal Drive
Kennett Square
,Pennsylvania 19348
January 16, 201

Stephen W. Reiss
700 Savanna Court
Dunlap,
Illinois 61525

Dear Steve,

Your book was waiting for us when we returned from visiting our daughters in California last week. Thanks so much. What a marvelous achievement! I have only had a chance to look it over so far, but what I've read is fascinating and makes your parents very real. Congratulations.

I read the reference to my father and me with interest. You were very generous to use so much space on us and on Yale in China. (now officially called "Yale-China")

It's of special interest to me that many of your father's letters were written from Burma. My husband, Dave, previously in charge of Asia Programs for the American Friends Service Committee, now, after retirement, is working as a consultant to a local Foundation interested in supporting food security programs in Burma/Myanmar. He visits the work in Burma twice a year and will leave in a few weeks on his next trip.

We are particularly pleased with the recent movement towards greater democracy in Burma. It makes me thankful once again to be living "in interesting times".

May the new year be good to you. I look forward to further contact and discussions with you.

B.J. Elder

CBI Boots for Stevie

Dear Will, Kayla, Ava, Blake,   February 24, 2014

Sixty-nine years ago yesterday my dad sent the following letter to my mom and me in Atascadero, California. He had been serving with the US Army for 14 months in India and Burma. Dad was slowly making his way home from Burma to the United States. He had taken several military flights from Ledo in Assam Province in eastern India to layover in northwestern India for about a month to improve his health while additional ongoing flights became available for returning servicemen. That base bordered the Thar Desert and was much more comfortable that the heat, humidity, and rains in Burma.

                                                                                 India
                                                                                 February 23, 1945

Mary & Stevie, my darlings,

How are you today? It is now a confirmed fact that we will not leave this month anymore. I would have gone out last night probably if Lily Pons and Andre Kostelanetz had not taken the plane. Five people rode in a plane that could carry at least fifty.

Darling, I spent some more money today. I bought a very lovely hand engraved solid brass flower bowl. It is about ten inches in diameter and will make a lovely centerpiece filled with flowers as only you, my darling, can arrange them – it's for our home, dear. If I can get somebody's package privilege for February, I'll mail it. The gift that I had made for Stevie is finished too now, however, I will bring it home.

Take care of yourself and our baby, darling. I love you with all my heart.
                Your affectionate Daddy,
                Irvie forever

Here is the gift Dad had made for me. It's a small pair of combat boots with the China-Burma-India patch on the side. Maybe you've seen them on display in my den. Here's an interesting story of how that CBI patch was developed.

Assam is a state in northeastern India. Lt. General Raymond A. Wheeler was born in Peoria, Illinois in 1885 and graduated from the US Military Academy at West Point. In autumn 1943, he was appointed to

70

the South East Asia Command of the South East Asian Theater of World War II on the staff of Admiral Lord Louis Mountbatten. He would be involved in building the Ledo Road to bring supplies into central China. Lt. Reiss would also be involved in that Ledo Road project and soon traveled by aircraft carrier through the south Atlantic and around Africa to India in early 1944.

China Burma India Theater (CBI) was the name used by the US Army for its forces operating in conjunction with Allied (British and others) air and land forces in China, Burma, and India during the war. The famous CBI patch has an interesting development history according to Brig. Gen. Frank Dorn.

"After the Allied collapse in Burma and General Stilwell's march over the mountains to Assam, the American effort in the CBI Theater was concentrated in India, particularly at the port of Karachi. In July and August, 1942, General Joseph W. Stilwell, the Theater Commanding General, left his Chungking, China headquarters for an extensive inspection tour of India. As his aide-de-camp, at that time, I accompanied him."

"While in Karachi, the local U. S. Commander informed Stilwell that relations between British and American troops were not good - all because their tropical uniforms were almost identical. When the military police of either army received a call to put down a brawl (a many times nightly performance), they arrived swinging night sticks indiscriminately. British soldiers objected to American MPs breaking their heads; and American GI's objected just as strenuously to lumps and bruises applied by British clubs. Normal differences of opinion and fights in bars and night spots had accelerated at a rapid and disturbing rate."

"Stilwell decided that his men should be designated by some easily recognized emblem in order to reserve their heads for American MPs only. The local British commander concurred that this could be the solution to the restoration of British-American relations."

"That evening when we returned to New Delhi, Stilwell told me to dream up a solution fast; perhaps some form of shoulder patch that would be distinctive and could be turned out in large quantities. After much scribbling, I came up with a simplified U. S. shield on whose blue field the Kuomintang Sun of China and the Star of India were imposed. Since the emblem of Burma was a peacock and we had just lost the whole country anyway, I did not even try to include it."

"I arranged with an Indian tailor shop to make up a few samples of my proposed patches and wore one on my own left shoulder that night at dinner with Stilwell and half a dozen of the New Delhi headquarters staff and command. The old man spotted my creation at once with a characteristic "What-the-hell-is-that-you've-got-on-your-sleeve, Dorn?"

"I replied that it was the brand new shoulder patch of the CBI Theater and gave him one of the samples which he asked me to pin on at once. He then turned to General "Spec" Wheeler and directed that an initial supply of thousands be made and distributed immediately to all U. S. troops in India and China. Thus the now famous emblem was born out of the necessity to preserve good relations - and heads - in India."

Will, Kayla, Ava, and Blake, that's quite a gift and quite a story, don't you think. Now, nearly 70 years after my dad had these boots made, I can fully appreciate his thoughtfulness with such a unique gift that reflects his 51 months of military service, his participation with the famous CBI campaign, and his expectations for his new young family. I've inherited about a dozen CBI patches from my dad plus that many more of the Ledo Road patch below.

Love, Granddad

There was also a patch developed for the Ledo Road soldiers. Here is that story of the **Ledo Road Shoulder Sleeve Insignia.**

The Ledo Road was well on its way to completion and would need a symbol. In April of 1944 a competition to design a Ledo Road shoulder patch was announced by General Pick.

PICK SEEKING INSIGNIA FOR LEDO ROADSTERS

LEDO ROAD—Along the Ledo Road this week, Brig. Gen. Lewis A. Pick has approved a sketching contest to discover a design for a Ledo Road insignia.

The contest is open to all who have taken part in the building of this project. The reward will be a two-weeks furlough.

T/4 Robert Smith, a cartographic illustrator assigned to the 20th General Hospital, had samples made for his design entry.

His design shows the road curving through the mountains, across the green hills of Burma, and disappearing into the Chinese sun. Three red, white and blue stripes are at the top. Three white stars in the larger red stripe represent the countries involved of China, Burma, and India. The border is green. Smith's design won the competition.

Although approved locally for uniform wear, the insignia was never officially approved by the U.S. Army. Having been created over two years after construction of the road began, most who were qualified to wear it, never did, at least not until they were sent home.

I'm Coming Home

Dear Will, Kayla, Ava, and Blake,   January 26, 2015

This story was a significant news item 70 years ago this coming week. That news appears in the title above and in the next two letters which were sent by your great grandfather Irwin Reiss, saying that the US Army was sending him home to his family in California after 4.25 years of service during the Second World War. The first letter went to his wife and son (aka me) and the second letter went to his brother and sister-in-law in Urbana, Illinois as an enlarged microfilm copy.

Along the Ledo Road
January 29, 1945

My sweet wife and baby,

How are you today, sweet? And how is our darling boy? My mail today consisted of one envelope containing my Jan. 8 *Time* magazine.

The significant news today is that the medical board has decided to send me to the U.S.A. I don't think the full realization has hit me yet. I looked at a picture of you and Stevie – and it is now probable that within a couple of months I'll have you in my arms. You can tell Stevie his Daddy is coming home.

I spent part of today gathering material for my lecture tomorrow. I have another one on Thursday. I'm all worn out again today from the exercises this afternoon. I played badminton, softball, and basketball.

Was Stevie good today? And did he kiss Mamma last night? Take good care of him and yourself, dear. I love you so very dearly. All my love and kisses.

Always your devoted,

Irvie

Here's a V-Mail that Lt. Irwin H. Reiss sent 70 years ago this Friday saying that he was on his way home from India. **V-mail**, short for **Victory Mail**, is a hybrid mail process used during the Second World War in the US as the primary and secure method to correspond with soldiers stationed abroad. To reduce the logistics of transferring an original letter across the military postal system, a V-mail letter would be censored, copied to film, and printed back to paper upon arrival at its destination.

This V-Mail measures 4.25 by 5.25 inches and is folded in half to fit into an envelope that measures 3.75 by 4.75 inches. The envelope has a window so the Urbana address of Frank and Gerry Reiss in Urbana is visible.

73

These two letters are the best news of about 1,000 that my folks exchanged daily during the fifteen months they were separated. Dad was in India and Burma and Mom (with newborn me) was in California. Those letters included about 50 from Irv's parents and relatives. I transcribed all those letters and published them in a book titled, <u>From Burma With Love</u>.

Will, Kayla, Ava, and Blake, something really incredible happened as I typed all those letters as 2.27 million keystrokes or 426,092 words on 664 pages. I, as an adult, got to meet my parents when they were in their mid-twenties, something which is otherwise impossible. There are 70 years between the original writing and the transcription but it was all instantaneous conversation because I already knew the players and the situation. I am thoroughly proud of Mom and Dad and totally blown away by what they had to live through. You'll have those same thoughts and conclusions when you read our book.

Love, Granddad

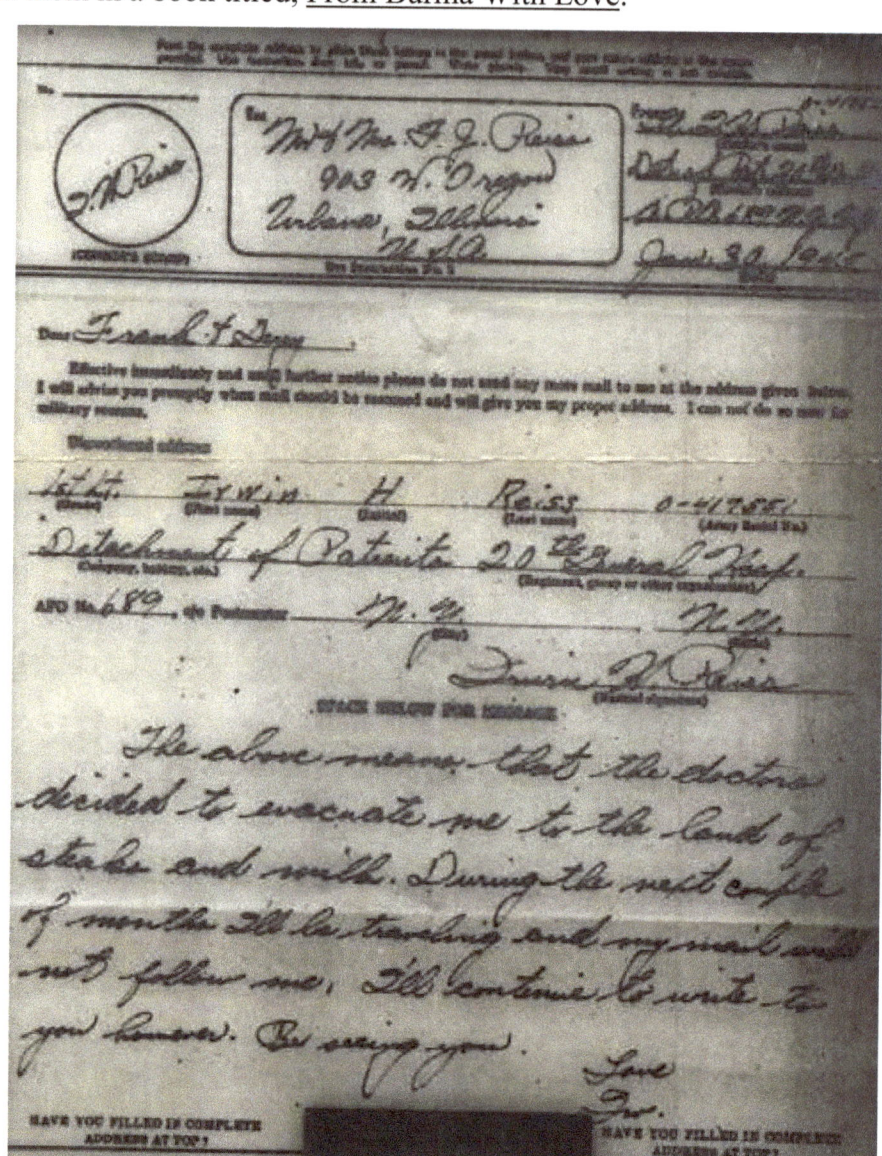

Irv Reiss World War II Medals and 2004 Memorial Day

Dear Will, Kayla, and Ava,   May 28, 2012

Today is Memorial Day. It's when we honor American men and women who served in all branches of the US military, especially those who died defending our country during times of war.

Memorial Day is a federal holiday observed annually on the last Monday of May. Formerly known as **Decoration Day**, it originated after the Civil War to commemorate fallen Union soldiers. By the 20th century, Memorial Day had been extended to honor all Americans who have died in all wars.

By the early 1900s, Memorial Day was an occasion for more general expressions of memory, as people visited the graves of their deceased relatives, whether they had served in the military or not. It also became a long weekend increasingly devoted to shopping, family gatherings, fireworks, trips to the beach, and national media events such as the Indianapolis 500 auto race, held since 1911 on the Sunday of Memorial Day weekend.

The preferred name for the holiday gradually changed from "Decoration Day" to "Memorial Day," which was first used in 1882. It did not become more common until after World War II, and was not declared the official name by Federal law until 1967. On June 28, 1968, Congress passed the Uniform Holidays Bill, which moved four holidays, including Memorial Day, from their traditional dates to a specified Monday in order to create convenient three-day weekends. The change moved Memorial Day from its traditional May 30 date to the last Monday in May.

My dad, your great grandfather Irv Reiss, served in the US Army from June 27, 1941 to September 17, 1945 (a day before his 28th birthday) for a total of about four years and three months. He had taken Advanced Army Reserve Officer Training Corps (ROTC) at the University of Illinois which led automatically to the officer position of Second Lieutenant in the US Army upon graduation. Later on he was promoted to First Lieutenant. He was trained at Fort Benning in Georgia, Camp Roberts in California where he met his future wife, Fort Washington in Maryland, Yale University in Connecticut, and Camp Reynolds in Pennsylvania before sailing on the aircraft carrier Wake Island from New York to Karachi, India in early 1944. He was stationed at Ramgahr Training Center in India and at several points along the Ledo Road in Burma (now Myanmar) where he was a labor officer hiring up to 2,000 local coolies to work on that road which led from Ledo, India to Myitkyina, Burma on the Ayeyarwady River.

Your great grandfather was awarded five medals for his service during World War II. From left to right on the next page are The American Defense Service Medal, The American Campaign Medal, The Asiatic-Pacific Campaign Medal, The World War II Victory Medal, and the Lapel Button for Honorable Service. I have replacement medals of all these that your great grandfather was awarded and will be very happy to show them to you some day.

The **American Defense Service Medal** is a decoration of the US military, recognizing the service before America's entry into the Second World War but during the initial years of the European conflict. The medal is authorized to military members who performed active duty between September 8, 1939 and December 7, 1941. Members of the US Army received this medal for any length of service during the eligibility period, provided that they were on orders to active duty for a period of twelve months or longer.

The **American Campaign Medal** is a decoration of the US armed forces which was created on November 6, 1942 by an executive order issued by President Franklin D. Roosevelt. Originally issued as the "American Theater Ribbon," the decoration was intended to recognize those service members who had performed duty in the American Theater of Operations during World War II.

The **Asiatic-Pacific Campaign Medal** is a service decoration of the Second World War which was awarded to any member of the US military who served in the Pacific Theater from 1941 to 1945 and was created on November 6, 1942 by an executive order issued by President Franklin D. Roosevelt.

The **World War II Victory Medal** is a decoration of the US military which was created by an act of Congress in July 1945. The decoration commemorates military service during World War II and is awarded to any member of the United States military, including members of the armed forces of the Government of the Philippine Islands, who served on active duty, or as a reservist, between December 7, 1941 and December 31, 1946.

The **Honorable Service Lapel Button** sometimes called the **Honorable Service Lapel Pin** was awarded to US military service members who were discharged under honorable conditions during World War II. The award was sometimes slangly called the Ruptured Duck. The button was awarded between September 1939 and December 1946 and was made of gilt brass.

My brother Ken and I took our father to Washington, DC for the Memorial Day 2004 dedication of the **National World War II Memorial.** It is dedicated to Americans who served in the armed forces and as civilians during World War II. Consisting of 56 pillars and a pair of arches surrounding a plaza and fountain, it is located on the National Mall between the Lincoln Memorial and the Washington Monument. It was dedicated by President George W. Bush on

May 29, 2004. Dad got to shake hands with Bob Dole who was overall chairman of the Memorial project.

That same weekend we toured the Capitol building, Ford's Theater where President Lincoln was shot, the National Archives where we saw the Declaration of Independence, Arlington National Cemetery, and Mount Vernon which was the home of President George Washington. That long weekend was a very special occasion for all three of us.

As of 2009, more than 4.4 million people visit the memorial each year. Two of those visitors in October 2010 were your dad/uncle Grant and me. We spent a week in Washington, DC building houses with Habitat for Humanity near Gallaudet University which included meeting and having our picture taken with President Jimmy Carter.

Your great grandfather died on April 11, 2007 at the age of 89. He had significant Alzheimer's dementia and really did not understand very much of what was happening around him or his home in Sullivan, Indiana. Six months earlier Dad and I were spectators at the annual Sullivan County (Indiana) Corn Festival parade on September 23, 2006. There were several thousand spectators watching that parade including several hundred men and boys wearing baseball caps. I want you to know that even though Dad was significantly mentally handicapped at that point, he was the only man present who stood and removed his ball cap each time an American flag passed by in review. Dad was extremely proud of his military service to our country. You can see that in this 2004 photo from Washington, DC.

Love, Granddad

77

Saving War Letters

Dear Will, Kayla, Ava, and Blake,   May 25, 2015

Today is Memorial Day which is a federal holiday for remembering the men and women who died while serving in our country's armed forces. The holiday, which is celebrated every year on the last Monday of May, was formerly known as Decoration Day and originated after the Civil War to commemorate the Union and Confederate soldiers who died in the war. By the 20th century, Memorial Day had been extended to honor all Americans who died while in the military service. It typically marks the start of the summer vacation season, while Labor Day marks its end. Many people visit cemeteries and memorials, particularly to honor those who have died in military service. Many volunteers place an American flag on each grave in national cemeteries.

Last November I noticed an article in the AARP bi-monthly magazine about saving letters written by men and women during times of warfare. I wrote the letter below to Andrew Carroll who had organized the project. Here is our exchange, initially by letter and then by email.

Mr. Andrew Carroll   November 14, 2014
P. O. Box 53250
Washington, D.C. 20009

Dear Mr. Carroll:

I just finished reading your article in the *AARP Bulletin* titled, "Bulletin Readers Share Their War Letters." It was a great article. You are involved in a wonderful project for veterans and their families.

I transcribed about 1,000 daily letters which my parents, Irwin and Mary Reiss, exchanged for 15 months of World War II, all of 1944 and the first quarter of 1945. Dad was in Burma and India. Mom was in California with newborn me who arrived on June 12, 1944. Dad and I met for the first time at my age nine months on Easter Sunday 1945. The letters were published by Author House as <u>From Burma With Love</u>. Here's the cover. It's available at Amazon, Barnes & Noble, etc.

Yours truly,

Stephen W. Reiss

Dear Mr. Reiss,   November 25, 2014

Hello, and thank you so much for sending me information about your book, *FROM BURMA WITH LOVE*. The book looks sensational, and I'll order a copy on Amazon.

I'm not sure if you've already committed to donating the originals somewhere else, but if there is any chance you'd be willing to donate to the Center for American War Letters the original correspondences written by your parents and that you used to create the book, we would be extremely honored to have them. I recognize that this is a huge request to make, but the advantage of donating the letters to an archive is knowing that they will be cared for in perpetuity. Even if you were to donate a handful of originals and keep the rest, that would be phenomenal as well.

Since 1998, when I started this initiative, Americans have shared with us more than 100,000 wartime correspondences from every conflict in U.S. history, including handwritten missives penned during the American Revolution and Civil War up to emails sent from Iraq and Afghanistan. There is no other collection likes ours in the world, and our mission is to honor and remember the men and women who have served their nation through their own words. Nobody, I believe, can tell their story better than they can.

We've been very fortunate in the media attention we've received over the years, and I know you saw the November AARP article, which was actually a follow-up to a cover story the AARP did on us last May for Memorial Day. The Washington Post also did a front page story on our project for Veterans Day (**http://m.washingtonpost.com/politics/war-letter-collector-andrew-carroll-donating-his-trove-for-preservation-and-study/2013/11/09/3af133f8-47bc-11e3-b6f8-3782ff6cb769_story.html**) and "Meet the Press" did a very nice feature on us this past July 4th as well (**http://www.nbcnews.com/meet-the-press/meet-press-finding-history-everyday-places-n149076**). I don't mean to inundate you with material, but in light of what we're asking, I wanted you to have as much information about our organization as possible.

If you would rather not donate any of the originals, I will more than understand, and there's no need to reply.

Again, thank you very much!

Cordially,
Andrew Carroll
Founder & Director,
The Center for American War Letters
www.WarLetters.us

CC: Kenneth I. Reiss, Mary Kay Parnell, Adam Reiss, Grant Reiss

Greetings, Andrew. Thanks for your comprehensive reply. I appreciate learning more about your War Letters Project. You are doing a great service for our veterans and for our country. Thank you very much. I'm going to be windy with my reply below.

I doubt that we'll donate these WW II letters because I have a brother and sister who are co-owners with me. The letters are in my possession but it's all three of us who own them since they were not specifically mentioned in either of our parents' wills. I've copied my brother and sister so they are at least aware of your organization and its objectives. I've also copied my two sons who presumably would continue the preservation of these letters after me.

I do have another book of letters which may interest you. Title is It Takes A Matriarch and it is 780 letters that my great great grandmother (the matriarch) saved from 1852 to 1888. They were written by her siblings and their spouses, her children and their spouses, several grandchildren, and two friends. That book includes about 50 Civil War letters written by her brother Johann Jakob "George" Basler and by her future son-in-law Charles Max Wittig.

George Basler volunteered with the Illinois 22nd Infantry Regiment and was wounded at the Battle of Belmont and at the Battle of Stones River. There is no visitor center for Belmont but we did visit Stones River where I later donated a copy of our book. His letters include a 100-day diary leading up to the battle at Stones River. He mentions foraging 700 wagonloads of hay from the Harding thoroughbred horse plantation just outside Nashville, TN. We visited that antebellum homestead which is now called Belle Meade. George's last years were spent at the National Home for Volunteer Soldiers in Dayton, Ohio which we've also visited. He was buried in that adjacent National Cemetery on the day he died. We may be the only relatives to ever visit his 1897 grave.

Max Wittig volunteered with the Missouri 1st Infantry Regiment and was the leader of their band. He was wounded at Wilson's Creek which we've visited. After that 90-day hitch was up, he volunteered with the Illinois 82nd Infantry Regiment and was wounded at Chancellorsville which we recently visited for the second time. I donated a copy of our book to their visitor center. We found the Wilderness Church near where Max's unit within the 11th Corps was overrun on 5/2/1863 by Stonewall Jackson's flanking maneuver which won the battle. Two of Max's letters from that time are attached. He participated in the first ever Thanksgiving per President Lincoln's proclamation for the last Thursday of November so this week is the 181st anniversary. FDR changed it to the fourth Thursday.

My great grandfather Frank Reiss was drafted into the 31st Illinois Infantry Regiment and served with General Sherman from Savannah on through the Grand March in Washington, DC. He was never wounded and did not write many letters.

Our 50 Civil War letters will probably stay in our family as well but they're all in my second book. I did pay to have 75% of those 780 letters translated from German to English so maybe they are now more mine than my brother's and sister's. Our sons do share my strong interest in both wars and how members of our families served. All of our 1,000 letters and 780 letters are stored in individual acid-free sheet protectors in date order in ten three-ring binders with labels. We have digital copies and book copies as backups.

Thanks again, Andrew, for your reply and outstanding work. Happy Thanksgiving.

Stephen W. Reiss
reiss_steve@yahoo.com

To: WarLetterProject@aol.com   November 25, 2014
Dear Steve,

Hello, and thank you so much for your very thoughtful email. Please excuse the haste of this reply, but I'm heading out first thing in the morning for Thanksgiving-related travel...

I'm actually very pleased to hear that your family's letters are in such good hands. So often, we receive letters by veterans or their family members because no one wants them, and if they didn't send the originals to us, they'd be thrown away. If you ever do come across originals that you're willing to donate, we'd love to have them, but, again, it sounds like you all are doing exactly what's necessary to preserve them. Thanks again, and I hope you have a wonderful holiday as well.

All the best, Andy

Will, Kayla, Ava, and Blake, maybe it's obvious that preserving our two large collections of family letters is a major priority. Both sets are already in book form and available to the general public because they describe significant personal and US history. One of the serendipities in transcribing all these letters for eventual publication is that I got to meet these people as if we were all living and talking at the same time. Now I'm really looking forward to meeting everyone in heaven, assuming I can pass muster.

Love, Granddad

DC Electricity Comes to the Reiss Farm in 1940

Dear Will, Kayla, Ava, and Blake,   December 9, 2013

My Uncle Frank Reiss took this picture in 1948. The caption on his slide mentions the wind charger which is the taller of two electrical poles on the center right. You can make out a large propeller on the top which is turned by the wind to generate 6-volt electrical current that goes to a rechargeable battery inside the house. This home was built in 1940 and was partially wired for DC and then AC electricity.

Our family had traveled from Sullivan, Indiana to the home farm to celebrate Grandma's 60th birthday on March 25. Here are two entries from my Grandma Katie's diary in March 1950.

Fri 24 – Cold winds, fair. Henry and the boys worked on the yard fence, tore down the old brooder house, and set new posts. Irwin & Mary and family came.

Sat 25 – Fair, windy, and getting warmer. Henry, Harold, and Lavern cut down the big wind charger pole and put up a telephone pole for the private line.

I remember this day in 1950 because all the big people wanted all us little people to stand way back when they cut down the pole. That's because the wind charger had not been used since late

1945 when AC electricity was brought to the home farm via the other tall pole in this picture with the connecting wires coming from the left.

By the 1930s windmills were widely used to generate electricity on farms in the United States where distribution systems had not yet been installed. Used to replenish battery storage banks, these machines typically had generating capacities of a few hundred watts to several kilowatts.

The brand name of my grandparents' wind charger was Wincharger. Here's what I found on Google. The most widely-used small wind generator produced for American farms in the 1930s was a two-bladed horizontal-axis machine manufactured by the Wincharger Corporation. It had a peak output of 200 watts. Blade speed was regulated by curved air brakes near the hub that deployed at excessive rotational velocities. These machines were still being manufactured in the US during the 1980s. In 1936, the US started a rural AC electrification program that killed the natural market for wind-generated DC power, since network power distribution provided more dependable usable energy for farms. Funny thing, now we're going back to monster wind farms to help power the grid!

Albers Propeller Company – In 1927, John and Gerhard Albers started experimenting with wind driven generators and eventually established the Albers Propeller Co. in Cherokee, Iowa. They developed a small wind generator called the "Wincharger" to charge 6 volt radio batteries. The Wincharger was a local hit and the company grew to three employees and production increased to 6 units per day.

Wincharger Corporation – In December, 1934 the Albers brothers together with two partners formed the Wincharger Corporation to manufacture their wind chargers at the former Hawkeye Truck plant in Sioux City, Iowa. Later that year, executives from the Zenith Radio Corporation visited Wincharger unannounced, placed an order for 50,000 Winchargers, and took a 51 percent stake in the company. The small Wincharger radio unit would become the most produced wind generator over the next 60 years and the Wincharger name would immediately become an important force in the wind electric plant business. The new larger 30,000-square-foot manufacturing plant had 52 full time employees, the product line was expanded to include larger full home units, and daily production increased to 200 units. Zenith bought the remaining 49 percent of Wincharger, and sales of radio and full home power plants were maintained under the difficult market circumstances resulting from federal rural electrification.

Wincharger Radio Plants – In time, production of the radio charger soared to 2,000 units a day at a price of $44 apiece, or even better at $15 per unit with the purchase of a special Zenith radio with a single rechargeable 6 volt battery. The unit was a two-blade, upwind, direct-drive design.

A tail vane was fixed in place by a length of angle iron to the back of the generator to point it into the wind. A small four-post tower with a turntable, slip ring assembly, and mounting feet for easy installation on the roof of an outbuilding were included. It was not a good idea to mount the Wincharger on the roof of the house since the roof would act as a sounding board to the point of being intolerable. Wires connected the generator to a simple relay panel in the house and to the radio battery. When the wind blew, the battery would charge and the radio would provide continuous entertainment on demand. Since the battery was usually kept charged, the owner would frequently add a few light bulbs to make good use of the abundant wind energy.

Wincharger Power Plants – Before too long, a larger 32-volt, gear-driven "Famous" model with a 10-foot diameter propeller rated at 650 watts was offered to the farm electric plant market. This model was similar to the small model in that it was a 2-blade design with the Wincharger patented air-brake governor. It sold for $69.95, plus tower and battery when it was first introduced.

Will, Kayla, Ava, and Blake, isn't this a fascinating story? The wind made it possible to listen to a radio and do your school homework after dark. In 1940 you would have used a pencil, quill pen, or fountain pen because ballpoint pens we're really perfected until 1943. There were no televisions or computers or heated wet ones. How times have changed!!!

Love, Granddad

AC Electricity Comes to the Reiss Farm on November 17, 1945

Dear Will, Kayla, Ava, and Blake,   December 9, 2013

You know from my other Granddad's Mondays story of today that the Reiss farm home was built in 1940 and was partially wired for DC electricity from a 6 volt rechargeable battery. That battery was charged by a wind charger on a tall pole about 50 feet southeast of the house. You see large wind farms in many places around the country today. It's the same idea as before except that modern wind farms generate AC electricity. The wind charger my grandparents had generated DC electricity which is the same current stored in your car battery. DC stands for "direct current" and AC stands for "alternating current."

Limited DC electricity was the way it was for my grandparent's first five years in their new house until late 1945. Here are entries from Grandma Katie's diary about the coming of AC electricity.

February 1945

Sat 3 – We were at Electric meeting at Waterloo.

September 1945

Fri 7 – The Schilling boys wired our basement today.

Wed 19 – Ludger Schilling was here all day to put in switch box and wire basement and tested all lights.

October 1945

Mon 29 – The Illinois Power men staked off our line today.

November 1945

Wed 7 – The poles for our electric line came today.

Thurs 8 – The electric men brought the hole digger and things.

Fri 9 – The electric men dug the hole for the pole.

Sat 17 – Mr. Lane hooked up our electric this morning. Lights are fine.

January 1946

Mon 7 – Romuald Schilling was here to put in our front porch light.

March 1946

Wed 20 – The boys finished wiring the house and Mr. Dengler brought the pressure pump and connected the sink.

May 1946

Thurs 2 – Rain. Geo was grinding a lot of corn with his electric motor.

July 1946

Tues 30 – Hot. We were at Belleville to get electric stuff for the other house. Towards evening. Ludger came and did the wiring.

March 1948

Fri 12 – Ludger put a light above my sink today.

March 1950

Sat 25 – Fair, windy, and getting warmer. Henry, Harold, and Lavern cut down the big wind charger pole and put up a telephone pole for the private line.

Will, Kayla, Ava, and Blake, now you know the electrical history of our home farm. The tall pole in this picture is DC and the shorter one is AC. The next page shows my grandparents application for AC service. Note my grandfather's robust signature.

Love, Granddad

APPLICATION FOR RURAL ELECTRIC SERVICE

Belleville, Illinois

_____, 19_____

Illinois Power Company

Belleville, Illinois

    The undersigned, hereinafter called "Customer", hereby requests Illinois Power Company, hereinafter called "Company", to supply electric service to Customer upon the following terms:

    1. Company shall supply and Customer shall accept and pay for all electric service required for _domestic_ purposes at premises located in _____ of Section _____, Township _____, Range _____ of the _____ P.M., County of _St. Clair_, State of Illinois, at the rates and charges due and payable therefore in accordance with Company's Rural Electric Service Schedule Ill. C. C. No. 2, Sheet No. 99, Schedule _99P_, with a minimum monthly charge of $_3.00_, and upon the terms and conditions set forth in the Company's Rules and Regulations as now on file with the Illinois Commerce Commission or as reissued and made effective as provided by law.

    2. The acceptance hereof by Company shall constitute an agreement between Company and Customer for a period of _3_ years from the date service is first rendered (hereunder) and thereafter until terminated by giving thirty (30) days notice by either party to the other, and such agreement shall be binding upon the successors and assigns of the respective parties hereto.

Location: _____
P.L. _____ W.O. _____ Docket _____
Contract _____ Acct. _____
Connection Date _____

Geo. W. Reiss
Customer

R.R. #1 Freeburg
Mailing Address

Accepted by the Company this _18th_ day of _April_, 19_45_

ILLINOIS POWER COMPANY

By _A. T. Earley_

A New Water Well in 1944

Dear Will, Kayla, Ava, and Blake,   January 12, 2015

Here's a water story somewhat related to the one I wrote last month that opened with this paragraph – Maybe it's obvious but there is normally no city water when you live on a farm. It's just too far away and too expensive to lay water pipes. Farmers have several options – draw water from a nearby lake or stream, <mark>dig a well to reach underground water</mark>, dig a cistern to save rainwater from roof gutters, or stand in the rain with their mouths open.

This time we're going to dig a well. Here are entries in my Grandma Katie's diary from August 1944. They built their home four years earlier and had only one cistern on the south side of their house for water. Apparently that was not a consistent supply of tasty water, so they decided to drill a well on the same side so they could connect to existing plumbing.

Sat 26 – We were at Henry Lang's and then went to Millstadt to get tile for our well.

Sun 27 – Johnny & Katie and Kleins & Schillings helped us drill our well. It's 31 feet deep. Had 13 feet of water the next day.

Mon 28 – We went to Belleville today and to Millstadt to get more tile.

Tues 29 – Johnny & Katie came in evening to put on the pump.

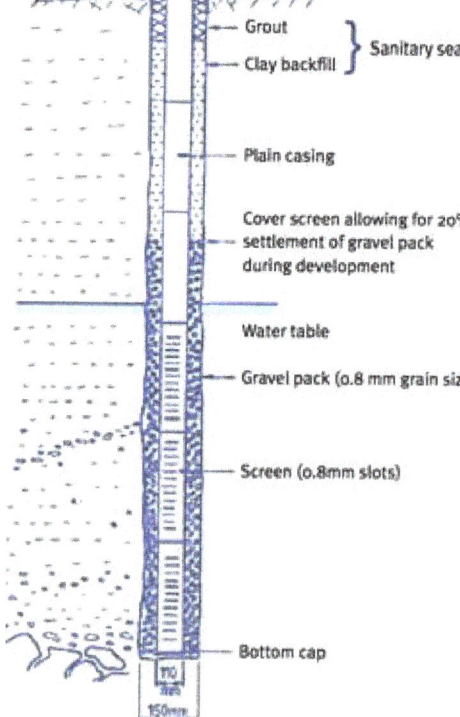

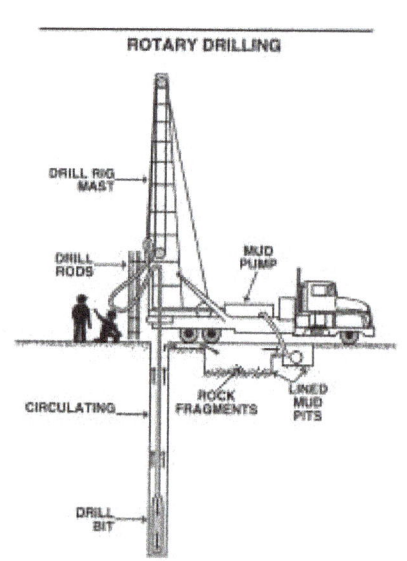

ROTARY DRILLING

Here's how you drill a shallow well using a truck-mounted rig. It works very well for small projects like home wells. You can see where the tile goes to prevent the well from caving in. The submersible pump goes part way down into the water.

Will, Kayla, Ava, and Blake, this water comes straight out of the ground and right into your drinking glass. Normally there are no chemical additives like chlorine or fluorides. Today you have to use your own common sense and maybe a little research to decide whether you'll drink well water, city water, bottled water, or watermelon juice.

Love, Granddad

Growing Potatoes in 1944

Dear Will, Kayla, Ava, and Blake,   January 19, 2015

I don't recall my grandparents growing potatoes on the Reiss family farm, but apparently they did in 1944. Here are Grandma's diary entries. I do remember their tenants, the Joseph family, growing potatoes however in 1950 - 52 in the field just north of the old house. Some of that field today is occupied by grain bins and equipment sheds.

April 1944

Sat 8 – Geo plowed the truck patch.

April 1944

Fri 28 – We planted our first potatoes, first 11 rows of Wolf's cobblers. Then almost 5 rows of his snowflakes. Then our own seed. These potatoes are in the lower patch, started planting at the south end.

Sat 29 – We planted last potatoes.

May 1944

Fri 19 – During the day we worked the potatoes and chopped weeds.

Thurs 25 – Geo plowed the truck patch for second time.

Wed 31 – Dad worked the potatoes.

June 1944

Tues 13 – I also replanted some in the truck patch, also planted sugar melons. Got a letter from Mary, also got word that little Stephen was born.

August 1944

Thurs 17 – We dug our first potatoes today.

Plowing and working the truck patch would have been done by horses. Not only did my grandparents never own a tractor, they didn't even have electricity until 11/17/1945. There would have been no automation for cleaning and packaging potatoes or other veggies for delivery to farmers markets and grocery stores in the area.

I can confirm that cultivating potatoes with animals is not easy. Pictures on the next page show me trying to do just that in Peru with oxen. You can tell that my homemade wooden cultivator is out of the track and digging up potato plants. The farmer is trying to get me back in the groove.

It was very embarrassing as our whole busload of fellow tourists was watching. None of them wanted to take a turn after me.

Will, Kayla, Ava, and Blake, having cultivated with oxen, built my own log cabin, built dozens of Habitat homes, and managed 1350 acres of farmland, I have a totally huge appreciation for what our forebears lived through and accomplished. They were simply amazing. I am totally blown away. We should all be very proud.

Love,
Granddad

Aerial Photo of the Reiss Family Farm, Circa 1941

Dear Will, Kayla, Ava, and Blake,   December 16, 2013

<mark>Happy Birthday, Ava.</mark> You were born yesterday at 3:45 this afternoon. Welcome to your first of many Granddad's Mondays stories.

Here is an aerial photograph of the Reiss Family Farm looking southeast that was taken in the fall of 1941 to 1944. There is no snow and no leaves on the trees which mean it was taken either in the fall, winter, or spring. You can see a white sheet on the ground east of the right side 1940 house which is covering parts of Grandma Reiss' garden against frost which probably means the time is fall rather than spring. There is smoke from a wood-burning kitchen stove or furnace coming up from that roof. The AC electricity lines arrived in late 1945 so this picture was taken before then. The grass yard looks fully established on the 1940 house so at the earliest the picture was taken in 1941.

A month ago I showed the original 11 by 14 colorized print to Lavern and Lucille Lang for their input. They started as our farm tenants in 1954 so everything you see here predates them. They said the angled roof on the west side of the log cabin was a brooder house where hatchling chicks are kept warm and fed. They saw the outhouse but said they always had indoor plumbing. They said the partially visible building on the near right corner was both a hog house and a chicken house during their tenure. You can see hogs at the left end of the dark strip across the bottom.

I also showed the original print to Marcella Klein whose son Al is now our farm tenant. Marcella was born on 2/20/1920 so she is 93.5 years old and still as sharp as a tack. Her parents were Frank and Clara Shilling who lived a quarter mile south on the adjoining farm which you can barely see at the top of this photo. Marcella married Ignatius "Boobie" Klein in 1940 and moved half a mile to the adjacent farm west. The Kleins, Shillings, and my grandparents were all the best of friends. When I showed the print to Marcella, the first thing she immediately said is, "Yes, I can see it." She was referring to a small window box in the north wall of Grandma's summer kitchen (balloon 4) where Pop had built a little rack for short term storage of milk, meat, and cheese since that was the coolest side of the summer kitchen. Here's a fuzzy blow up of that window box.

Here's the same aerial photo but with callout balloons for these captions.

1. Log cabin built in 1838 by Adam Reiss
2. Brooder house for young chickens on the back side of the log cabin
3. Old house built in 1889 by Frank and Anna Reiss
4. Summer kitchen attached to the 1889 house

5. Old chicken and hog house built by Frank Reiss and his son George
6. Outhouse for the 1889 house
7. Log granary built in 1838 by Adam Reiss
8. Two story barn built about 1920 by George Reiss
9. Wooden storage shed
10. Corn crib
11. Machine shed
12. New house built in 1940 by George and Katie Reiss
13. Wind charger which generated 6 volt electricity at about 200 watts
14. Grain grinding shed and single garage for Model T car
15. New brooder house
16. New chicken house
17. Fruit orchard

Besides the photograph, there is significant people history in four of these buildings. Here's a summary using the same balloons.

- 1. This is the log cabin where Adam died in 1849 and his first wife Mary died in 1838. It is where six of Adam's children were born and where the last one died. It is where ten of eleven children born to Adam's son Frank Reiss and his wife Anna were born and where four of them died.

- 1. and 7. These are the log cabin and log granary where Adam Reiss hosted Catholic worship services from about 1838 to 1841. My guess is they switched between buildings depending on the season and number of worshipers. They may be the "church" where Adam married first wife Mary in 1838 and married his second wife Margaret in 1840.

- 3. This is the 1889 house where the youngest child of Frank and Anna Reiss was born in 1890. This home is where Frank Reiss and his wife Anna died. This is where three sons of Frank's son George and his wife Catherine were born. The last of those was my dad Irwin.

- 12. This 1940 house is where George Reiss died.

- There is no callout balloon but the far upper left is the southeast corner of the 160-acre farm as it existed in 1854. That corner is where Margaret Reiss and her second husband Conrad Ebert built a small house such that her son Frank and his expanding family could take over the 1838 log cabin.

Will, Kayla, Ava, and Blake, our extended family is very fortunate to still own this family farm after nearly 180 years and to have lots of original documents and family correspondence. I'm trying to make all that available to relatives through a series of family history books. Hopefully the next milestone event for all of us is a bicentennial family reunion in 2034. You guys are in charge!!!

Love, Granddad

Raising Chickens and Eggs on the Reiss Farm in 1944

Dear Will, Kayla, Ava, and Blake,   February 10, 2014

Do you think the red chickens are roosters and the white ones are hens? If you're in the chicken business, maybe that's an easy way to keep score. You also don't want too many roosters because they don't lay eggs and because they can have turf battles with other roosters. If this picture was taken in 1910 or later, the woman is probably my grandmother, Katie Luetzelschwab Reiss, who lived on the home farm that year working as a domestic helper. She married my grandfather George Reiss on 4/16/1911. If this picture was taken earlier, the woman is probably my grandfather's sister Margaret who married George Dintelmann on 4/22/1908 or his sister Katie who married Philip Petry on 6/2/1909. The chicken house back then was north of the current barn at the edge of the timber.

Which came first, the chicken or the egg? Maybe you can figure it out with twelve months of chicken and egg entries from my grandmother's diary of 1944. The chicken house above was replaced about 1920 with a newer one which still stands in the northwest corner of the 1890 house. George and Katie built their new house in 1940 and four years later built another chicken house in April 1944 as you'll see below. That new chicken house was just east of their home but was removed in the 1970s. We know my grandparents and their crop share farm tenants grew wheat, barley, oats, and corn a portion of which was ground up for chickens. Maybe all of that was for feeding the chickens along with ground up oyster shells from which hens get calcium for egg shells. I remember helping my grandmother gather eggs in the 1950s. When I had to reach under a sitting hen to gather eggs, she would always caution me to not let an unhappy chicken peck at my eyes.

January 1944

Thurs 6 – Pop shelled corn.

Sun 9 – Sanders were to get some roosters.

Tues 18 – We have been getting around 6 doz eggs every day so far.

Mon 24 – Took our first hatching eggs to Smithton today.

February 1944

Thurs 3 – Pop shelled & crushed corn and made firewood.

Mon 14 – We got 150 starter chicks at Luhr's today.

Wed 16 – Geo started to work on the brooder house.

Fri 18 – Geo worked on the brooder house.

Tues 22 – We got 400 chicks at Mascoutah, 300 week olds and 100 three-week olds.

Wed 23 – We were at Smithton to get feed. Then we worked with the chickens and brooder house.

Thurs 24 – We let our chicks in outside shed for the first time.

Sat 26 – We worked outside cleaning up around the brooder house. Were at Brandenburgers in evening.

March 1944

Tues 14 – We put windows in brooder house.

Wed 15 – We worked on the brooder house. It's just about finished.

Thurs 16 – We finished the brooder house and set up the new wood burning brooder. *Electricity did not come to the Reiss farm until November 17, 1945.*

Fri 17 – We moved our chickens into the new brooder house. Pop ground corn.

Wed 22 – 35 degrees. We cleaned the brooder house in morning.

Thurs 23 – We cleaned the brooder house. Pop shelled and ground corn.

Sat 25 – 45 degrees, fair. I cleaned everything and baked bread and coffee cake. Boobe Kleins, Ludger, and Mrs. Mary Klein came for my birthday.

Mon 27 – We took the hatching eggs to Belleville.

April 1944

Sun 2 – We cleaned the brooder houses.

Mon 3 – We took hatching eggs to Belleville. Schillings sewed oats on our land today.

Fri 7 – Sold our first spring chickens today.

Sat 8 – I made garden and cleaned brooder house.

Tues 11 – We cleaned chicken house and ground corn.

Wed 12 – Moved our first chickens into the house by the lane.

Fri 14 – Sold 20 spring chickens again.

Fri 21 – We got 300 red chickens at Belleville. Then Pop plowed while I worked with the chickens.

Sat 22 – Rained all day, thundered. Schillings, Frank Kleins and Margret Merhman & boys were here in evening for Pop's birthday.

Mon 24 – Pop shelled corn.

Tues 25 – Geo crushed corn, mixed feed.

Thurs 27 – We got some feed at Smithton.

May 1944

Mon 1 – George ground corn.

Tues 2 – We finished our rock walk thru the gate by brooder house.

Fri 12 – We cleaned chicken house.

Wed 17 – Geo crushed corn and mixed feed.

Mon 22 – I cleaned the old brooder house and moved the red chicks in it.

Fri 26 – We took eggs to Smithton, got groceries.

Sat 27 – I butchered chickens and prepared for Sunday dinner.

June 1944

Sat 10 – We shelled & ground corn.

Mon 12 – Henry Lang got his combine to start combining barley. Stephen William Reiss was born today in California.

Fri 16 – We took eggs and chickens to Millstadt. Then Pop went to get wheat crushed.

Mon 19 – Schillings & Westerheide started combining today.

Tues 20 – Pop helped the boys unload wheat at the granary.

Wed 21 – Stopped combining for a day & half.

Fri 23 – Schillings finished combining. We got about 500 bu, one third.

Sat 24 – I washed and picked peaches and then we cleaned a chicken house.

Wed 28 – Hottest day so far, 100 degrees by 5 p.m. June fed the small chickens.
Thurs 29 – Schillings combined oats.

Fri 30 – We helped Geo shell corn.

July 1944

Sat 1 – We shelled corn. Geo got some wheat ground and he crushed corn.

Mon 3 – Geo is mixing feed all day.

Tues 4 – Westerheide started combining oats on our place.

Wed 5 – We took 33 old hens to Millstadt.

Thurs 6 – 94 degrees at noon. We cleaned the chicken house and then moved the red chickens in it. Schillings bailed hay here.

Fri 7 – 95 degrees at noon. I cleaned the old brooder house.

Sat 8 – I was at Koerber's. They want to thresh, but it rained too much.

Mon 10 – Very hot. I helped cook for threshers at Koerber's.

Tues 11 – Hot again, still threshing at Koerber's.

Sat 15 – 90 degrees at noon. We finished thresher cooking at Koerber's.

Wed 19 – 88 degrees at noon. I helped cook at Alma's for the thresher. This was the last job.

Sat 22 – Pop mowed grass and then we went to Smithton with eggs.

Wed 26 – 95 at noon, sticky hot. Pop mixed feed.

August 1944

Thurs 10 – Hot. Henry Lang plowed in the eight acres.

Fri 18 – Pop disked the pasture.

Sat 19 – Pop disked his wheat land.

Wed 23 – Pop disked Henry's wheat land.

Thurs 24 – Schillings harrowed our wheat land. Pop disked again.

Fri 25 – Pop disked again.

Thurs 31 – Pop mixed feed.

September 1944

Fri 1 – Pop sowed fertilizer.

Sat 2 – Geo sowed fertilizer and I mowed the lawn.

Mon 4 – John & Katie were here in evening. They got some poulets.

Fri 8 – Geo ground corn.

Tues 12 – Geo mixed feed.

Sat 23 – Geo crushed corn.

Mon 25 – Schillings combined the alfalfa seed. Geo sowed wheat in the hog pasture.

Wed 27 – In morning Bertha Etling was here to get chickens.

October 1944

Mon 2 – Geo sowed wheat.

Tues 3 – Geo & Henry Lang got fertilizer. Geo sowed wheat in afternoon.

Fri 6 – Geo sowed wheat for Uncle Henry.

Sat 7 – I baked cake and butchered chickens for the chicken supper at the Grange. Finished sowing wheat.

Wed 11 – Geo mixed feed and shelled corn.

Sat 14 – Geo shucked corn.

Mon 16 – We shelled corn in morning.

Tues 17 – Pop husked corn.

Fri 20 – Geo husked corn.

Sun 22 – Brandenburger brought us corn.

Mon 23 – Geo husked corn. Westerheide brought us some of our third of the corn.

Thurs 26 – Geo husked corn and I carried in my flowers.

Fri 27 – We blood tested all of our chickens. Geo mixed feed.

Sat 28 – Geo and I were at Millstadt and we also got some cider. Then we moved some chickens.

Mon 30 – I cleaned the hen house in the yard over there. Geo husked corn.

November 1944

Wed 1 – Geo husked corn.

Thurs 2 – Geo husked corn.

Fri 3 – Geo mixed feed.

Mon 6 – Geo husked corn.

Tues 7 – We went voting. Geo crushed corn and mixed feed.

Fri 10 – Pop husked corn.

Wed 15 – Geo husked corn.

Thurs 16 – Geo husked corn and brought in the pumpkins.

Sat 18 – We cleaned a hen house. Then Geo husked corn and I cleaned the house over there.

Mon 20 – Geo husked corn and I cleaned part of the old house.

December 1944

Fri 8 – Pop husked corn and fixed chicken house roofs.

Mon 11 – Geo did the feeding and brought in wood.

Fri 15 – Geo crushed corn.

Fri 22 – Pop is mixing feed and making firewood.

Will, Kayla, Ava, and Blake, you can see that my grandparents worked very hard raising chickens and eggs for sale and for their own table. Grandma was also an exceptional cook. From all their energy, you would never guess that Grandma turned age 54 tomorrow on March 25 in 1944 (age 123 in 2013) and Pop turned age 71 on April 22, 1944. Your great great grandparents were truly amazing people. You come from good stock.

Love, Granddad

Growing Corn and Raising Hogs on the Reiss Farm in 1944

Dear Will, Kayla, Ava, and Blake,   February 24, 2014

Here are my Grandma Katie's diary entries from 1944 which mention these related subjects. Ear corn can be fed directly to hogs or it can be shelled, cracked, and/or soaked overnight in water. It can be shelled, ground, and fed to chickens, or it can be sold to third parties. My guess is the hogs got two-thirds of the corn crop and the chickens the rest. It's readily apparent from Grandma's diary entries that growing and feeding corn was very hard work.

Grandpa George (aka "Pop") did not own a mechanical corn picker. He either harvested individual ears of corn by hand and tossed them into a horse drawn wagon or he cut entire plants and gathered them into shocks like the photo below. Husking or shucking refers to removing the outer plant leaves which surround the ear. You also need to know that:

- Their three sons had homes and families of their own and were unable to help in 1944.

- George (Geo, Pop, Dad) turned age 71 on April 22, 1944.

- Pop plowed with horses. He never owned a tractor.

- The farm did not get electricity until November 17, 1945.

- "Canning" is partially cooking various meats or sausages, putting them into earthenware crocks, and then covering them with hot liquid rendered lard which will further cook the meats and seal them from air. It's a preservation process for longer term storage.

- Katie never learned how to drive a car or farm truck.

Now are you impressed!!!

January 1944

Mon 3 – We butchered a 450 lb hog, made summer sausage. Boobe, Romuald, and Clara helped.

Tues 4 – We rendered the lard today. It made 10 gals. I canned 7 quarts of liver sausage.

Wed 5 – I helped butcher at Klein's.

Thurs 6 – I worked with taking care of the meat.

Tues 11 – I fried in 6 pints of pork sausage.

Mon 17 – I fried down bacon.

Tues 18 – Fried in more bacon.

Tues 25 – We were at Herman's to help butcher.

Sat 29 – We butchered.

February 1944

Fri 4 – We butchered a 300 lb hog.

Mon 7 – I salted and wrapped up the 2 hams and 2 shoulders.

Wed 9 – Fried in sausage and canned ribs in evening.

March 1944

Thurs 2 – Pop & Orville Koerber took hogs to yards.

Fri 10 – We butchered for Willie's hog. Henry Lang helped.

Tues 14 – I salted meat for Bill today.

Tues 21 – We were at Mascoutah first then we got 8 pigs at Herman's. Snow is thawing fast.

April 1944

Tues 4 – Geo husked corn.

Wed 5 – Geo disked corn land.

Thurs 6 – Geo plowed.

Tues 18 – Geo plowed.

Wed 19 – Pop plowed.

Thurs 20 – Pop plowed.

Fri 21 – Pop plowed.

May 1944

Thurs 4 – Geo got corn land ready.

Fri 5 – Geo planted first corn in Schaeffer's place.

Sat 6 – Geo plowed in back of barn for corn.

Thurs 18 – Geo disked the bottom land.

Sat 20 – Geo plowed in the bottom.

Mon 22 – Geo plowed in the bottom.

Wed 24 – Geo planted the long bottom in corn and harrowed it.

June 1944

Fri 2 – Dad finished planting corn.

Thurs 8 – Pop replanted corn in long bottom.

Fri 9 – Pop replanted corn.

Sat 10 – Dad hoed corn.

Mon 12 – Geo worked in corn.

Tues 13 – Pop worked in corn.

Wed 28 – Hottest day so far, 100 degrees by 5 p.m. Geo hoed in the corn.

July 1944

Thurs 13 – Geo cleaned weeds out of the corn.

Fri 14 – Pop plowed.

Sat 15 – 90 degrees at noon. Pop plowed.

Wed 19 – Pop plowed.

Thurs 20 – Dad plowed.

Fri 21 – We got 8 feeder pigs at Oliver Mueller's @ $4.00 a piece. Then Schilling boys helped us put up straw for litter.

Sun 23 – In the evening, we fenced up the hogs to take them away in morning.

Mon 24 – Orville Koerber & Pop took the 8 red hogs to the yards. We got $13.95 for them, weight 243 lbs.

August 1944

September 1944

October 1944

Sat 14 – Geo shucked corn.

Tues 17 – Pop husked corn.

Fri 20 – Geo husked corn.

Sun 22 – Brandenburger brought us corn.

Mon 23 – Geo husked corn. Westerheide brought us some of our third of the corn.

Thurs 26 – Then Geo husked corn.

Mon 30 – Geo husked corn.

November 1944

Wed 1 – Geo husked corn.

Thurs 2 – Geo husked corn.

Mon 6 – Geo husked corn.

Fri 10 – Pop husked corn.

Mon 13 – Romuald Schilling and Geo took 7 fat hogs to the yards today. Then we went to Herman's. Got 7 pigs.

Wed 15 – Geo husked corn.

Thurs 16 – Geo husked corn and brought in the pumpkins.

Sat 18 – Geo husked corn.

Mon 20 – Geo husked corn.

December 1944

Fri 8 – Pop husked corn.

Wed 27 – I was at Schilling's butchering.

Will, Kayla, Ava, and Blake, this photo is your cousin George Reiss at age 2.5 in November 1944 which is somewhat close your ages. He celebrates his 72nd birthday on Wednesday so send him an email birthday wish at george26hi@earthlink.net. Thanks,

Love, Granddad

Here is a 1946 photo of Pop picking individual ears of corn by hand and putting them into a burlap sack for eventual transfer to a horse-drawn wagon and then back to his corncrib for the winter. His straw hat is light weight and keeps the sun off. Long sleeves help prevent rash from the coarse leaves. You can see an unpicked ear of corn at the right center.

Notice these rows are about 3.5 feet apart. Today the standard is 2.5 feet and trending narrower.

Here's Pop admiring his large ears of corn in 1948 in the field west of the orchard. Notice these plants are about a foot apart. Today the standard is 6.6 inches. Notice his straw hat and long sleeves. Pop's corn plants are about eight feet tall. Today corn reaches ten and even twelve feet.

Grandma and Pop's Trip to Their Texas Farm
and to Vista, California in 1946

Dear Will, Kayla, Ava, and Blake,   October 5, 2015

Here are Grandma Reiss' diary entries for their trip to see their son Irwin, his wife Mary, and their two sons Steve (aka me born 6/12/1944) and Ken (born 2/12/1946). It was the first time for grandparents and grandsons to meet. Our sister Mary Kay was not born until 11/1/1947.

August 1946

Sat 17 – Franklin went to St. Louis to get our tickets for our Calif. trip tomorrow.

Sun 18 – Geo, Franklin, and I left for Texas. Henry took us to the station at St. Louis. Train left at 3:30 p.m. *Lamb County, Texas is where George had bought a 160-acre farm in 1907 sight unseen. He will soon see that farm for the first time after 39 years of farming by tenant Brockette and others.*

Mon 19 – Arrived at Texas by 3 o'clock afternoon. Mr. Brockette met us at Farwell Station, light rain by night.

Tues 20 – Mr. Brockette took us out to see our farm and other nice places. At 8 p.m. we took the bus to Clovis, New Mexico.

Wed 21 – Franklin put us on the train at Clovis at 1:30 a.m. Then he took a train back to Kansas City at 2:30 a.m.

Thurs 22 – We were somewhere in Arizona.

Fri 23 – We arrived at Los Angeles by 7 a.m. and Irwin was there to meet us. Then we drove out to his home.

Sat 24 – We were enjoying a nice rest with Mary and the boys after our long trip. We all went to the beach in the afternoon.

Sun 25 – We went out to work around Mary & Irwin's new home. We ate a lot of oranges off their trees.

Mon 26 – We were enjoying ourselves very much, playing with Stephen and Kenneth.

Tues 27 – We went out to Mary & Irv's house to do some work.

Wed 28 – Mary and the boys went to a card party and Geo and I went to a farm meeting with Irwin in the afternoon.

Thurs 29 – We went over to the house again to wash up the rooms and work around.

Fri 30 – We moved some things to the new home. Geo dug in the septic tank hole. This was at Irwin's home in Calif.

Sat 31 – We moved more things and filled up the front yard with ground.

September 1946

Sun 1 – Moving more things and getting ready for our trip to Atascadero. *This is to meet Mary's parents, Andrew and Daisy Stephenson, for the first time. George and Katie had been unable to attend Irv and Mary's wedding on 11/8/1942 in Atascadero due to World War II rationing, etc.*

Mon 2 – We left early for Atascadero. Arrived there by five p.m.

Tues 3 – We were enjoying a nice visit with Mary's folks.

Wed 4 – Irwin, Geo, and I left for our trip to Yosemite Park. Stayed overnight.

Thurs 5 – Left early for San Francisco and came over the skyline to go to Big Basin State Park. Stayed overnight.

Fri 6 – We left Big Basin to go back to Atascadero. Arrived there by 4:30 p.m.

Sat 7 – Spent a nice day with Mary's folks.

Sun 8 – We had another nice Sunday with Mary's folks.

Mon 9 – We left for home to Vista to live in Mary & Irwin's new home.

Tues 10 – We are working around to clean up things. *Here's a penny postcard that Katie sent to her neighbors Frank & Clara Shilling on 9/10/1946. It's of the world largest redwood with a breast height circumference of 44 feet. Tree name is "Santa Clara" and it's still growing strong in Big Basin State Park, CA. Back side appears below.*

Wed 11 – Still working about the place.

Thurs 12 – We worked in the yard today. The men were here to wire the house.

Fri 13 – We washed today. Then we went to the beach. More wiring done.

Sat 14 – We worked about the place.

Sun 15 – We washed, then we all went for a ride to old Mexico. Had a dinner for Irwin's birthday in the evening.

Mon 16 – Mary & I washed and waxed the floors and we

This tree contains sufficient wood to produce lumber for thirty four-room cottages.

Dear Friends: –

How are you all. We are at Mary's folks this week will go back to Vista Monday which is 350 miles from here. Irwin has to go to work again by tuesday. We have had a wonderfull trip so far. yesterday we saw hundreds of acers of head lentuce, radishes carrots, cabbage cellery and mellows and lots more. We walked around this tree.

Love Katie & Theo.

Mr & Mrs Frank Schilling
Freeburg
Ill.
R1.

left for home by 3:30 p.m. Irwin took us to Los Angeles.

Tues 17 – Enjoying our train ride back thru Calif. & Arizona & Texas.

Wed 18 – Arrived at Kansas City by 9:30 p.m. Got on the Wabash by 11:30 p.m.

Thurs 19 – Arrived at St. Louis by 8:15 a.m. Took the bus to Belleville, then Hecker bus to Brandenburger Road.

June 1949

Sun 5 – Fair not so hot, very pretty day. Mr. & Mrs. Stephenson came around 3 o'clock afternoon. We all went to Elsie Hesse's wedding.

Mon 6 – Rained quite a bit. I worked in the house. Mr. & Mrs. Stephenson left for Indiana in the morning. *to visit Irv and Mary and children.*

Will, Kayla, Ava, and Blake, this was a big trip in 1946 for my grandparents 69 years ago. Pop had been 650 miles from home when he took his son Irwin to Fort Benning, Georgia in 1941. This trip to Vista was 1870 miles from home. It was great that the grandparents could meet again in 1949. Lots of memories. Clara Shilling Klein gave me this postcard when I visited with her on October 22, 2013. She was born on the next farm south of the Reiss home and now lives on the next farm west. Post card stamps now cost $.34.

Love, Granddad

The Floraville Grange

Dear Will, Kayla, Ava, and Blake,   January 6, 2014

Here's more unique history about our family farm in St. Clair County, Illinois and how some of those farm residents were active in the Floraville Grange and other Granges in the county. Let's start with the letter below from 1948 where my grandmother Katie Reiss is trying to establish a Grange in Floraville. You'll notice in the table below that the Floraville Community Grange was indeed established less than a month later on 3/8/1948. That village of 200 folks is 1.7 miles west of our family farm.

Bonnie Dale FARM

BREEDER OF PURE BRED
ABERDEEN ANGUS CATTLE

Orville W. Helms * R. F. D. 1, Belleville, Illinois * Just Off Route 13, South of Belleville

Feb. 15, 1948.

Dear Mrs. Reiss:
Received your letter in regard to organizing a New Grange at Floraville and will say that I will, down your way one of the first days after this weather gets a little better.
It would be best if one of you would go along with me some day, we might visit your prospects then call a meeting some evening.
Yours truly,
Orville W. Helms
Co. Deputy.

Here's what I found on Google.

Fast forward 40 years to an article below retyped from the 2/22/1989 *The Millstadt Enterprise* newspaper – Floraville Community Grange has been remodeling the Grange Hall and the Grange will be getting a new look with siding to be installed when weather permits. New ceiling fans and lights were purchased with Memorial money given by the Reiss family in memory of their parents, Mr. and Mrs. George Reiss. Mr. and Mrs. Reiss were the co-founders of the Floraville Community Grange. A plaque will be hung in the hall in their memory.

So now let me tell you national history about the Grange and then bring it back to St. Clair County.

The Grange, officially referred to as **The National Grange of the Order of Patrons of Husbandry**, is a fraternal organization in the US which encourages families to band together to promote the economic and political well-being of the community and agriculture. The Grange, founded after the Civil War in 1867, is the oldest American agricultural advocacy group with a national scope. Major accomplishments credited to Grange advocacy include passage of the Granger Laws and the establishment of rural free mail delivery.

In 2005, the Grange had a membership of 300,000, with organizations in 3,600 communities in 37 states. It is headquartered in Washington, DC in a building built by the organization in 1960. Many rural communities in the United States still have a Grange Hall and local Granges still serve as a center of rural life for many farming communities.

History – After the Civil War ended in 1865 President Andrew Johnson commissioned Oliver Kelley to go to the Southern States to collect data to improve Southern agricultural conditions. In the South, poor farmers bore the brunt of the civil war and were suspicious of northerners like Kelley. Kelley found he was able to overcome these sectional differences as a Mason. With southern Masons as guides, he toured the war-torn countryside in the south and was appalled by the outdated farming practices. He saw the need for an organization that would bring people from the north and south together in a spirit of mutual cooperation and after many letters and consultations with the other founders, the Grange was born. The first Grange was Potomac Grange #1 in Washington, D.C. which continues to this day.

Paid agents organized local Granges and membership in the Grange increased dramatically from 1873 (200,000) to 1875 (858,050). Many of the state and local granges adopted non-partisan political resolutions, especially regarding the regulation of railroad transportation costs. The organization was unusual at this time because women and any teen old enough to draw a plow were encouraged to participate. The importance of women was reinforced by requiring that four of the elected positions could only be held by women.

Rapid growth infused the national organization with money from dues, and many local granges established consumer cooperatives, initially supplied by the wholesaler Aaron Montgomery Ward. But poor fiscal management, combined with organizational difficulties resulting from rapid growth, led to a massive decline in membership. By the turn of the 20th century, the Grange rebounded and membership stabilized.

The Granger movement lobbied successfully for legislation regulating the railroads and grain warehouses. The birth of the Cooperative Extension Service, Rural Free Delivery, and the Farm Credit System were largely due to Grange lobbying.

Other significant Grange causes included temperance, the direct election of Senators, and women's suffrage (Susan B. Anthony's last public appearance was at the National Grange Convention in 1903). During the Progressive Era of the 1890s to the 1920s political parties took up Grange causes. Consequently, local Granges focused more on community service, although the State and National Granges remained a political force.

In the 20th and 21st centuries, the position of the Grange as a respected organization in the United States was indicated by a membership that included Presidents Franklin D. Roosevelt and Harry S. Truman, and artist Normal Rockwell. The monument to the founding of the Grange is the only private monument on the National Mall in Washington, D.C.

Grange membership has declined considerably as the percentage of American farmers has fallen from a third of the population in the early 20th century to less than two percent today. In the last

15 years, the number of Grange members has dropped by 40%. Washington has the largest membership of any state, at approximately 40,000.

The Grange today –The Grange is nonpartisan, and only supports policies, never political parties or candidates. Although the Grange was originally founded to serve the interests of farmers, because of the shrinking farm population the Grange has begun to broaden its range to include a wide variety of issues, and anyone is welcome to join the Grange. The Junior Grange is open to children 5-14. Regular Grange membership is open to anyone age 14 or older. The Grange Youth is a group created within the Grange and consists of members 14-35. The Grange provides opportunities for individuals and families to develop to their highest potential in order to build stronger communities and states, as well as a stronger nation. The impressive motto of the Grange is: In essentials, unity; in non-essentials, liberty; in all things, charity.

Back to St. Clair County – Our cousin Lynnette Lang Schaeffer was the Illinois State Grange Historian so she provided the summary below of the Granges in St. Clair County. There have been 1,941 Granges altogether in the state and they are numbered as they were organized.

Grange	Location	Number	Year Started
Badgley			1874
Bethel Star			1883
Bluff	Millstadt	1826	12/1/1922
Bob White		1809	1921
Broad Hollow	Hecker	1806	1/18/1921
Central			1874
Choctaw			1874
Country Friends		1941	1998
Dutch Hill			1874
Emerald Mound	Lebanon	1813	11/29/1921
Enterprise	O'Fallon	1929	3/10/1956
Flora			11/1873
Floraville Community	Floraville	1918	3/8/1948
High Prairie			1874
Locust Grove			1874
Mississippi Valley		1834	1/1/1925
Oakland		1740	1904
Pleasant Valley			1874
Point Lookout		1749	1/13/1908
Progressive	New Athens	1811	3/16/1921
Richwood			1875
Ridge Prairie		1825	1922
Shiloh Valley	Shiloh	1807	1/27/1921
St Clair			1874
Turkey Hill	Belleville	1370	4/9/1874
Valley		1046	2/1874
Wheatland			1874
White Star			1874
Whiteside			1872
Woodland	Mascoutah	1736	5/25/1901

The photo below was taken in 1948 shortly after the Floraville Grange was organized. They met in the building behind which was originally built as the Flora Hotel and later became the hall of the Modern Woodmen of America, a fraternal insurance group. Some of this building history appears below from a 1965 brochure by Edward Wirth. My grandfather George Reiss is at the far left and my grandmother Katie is third from the right with the sash.

Seated from left to right seated are: Clara Mehraman, Mrs. Emma Barthel, Arthur Barthel, Ida Gasser, Mrs. Eliza Koerber, Eileen Klein Grau Assistant Steward.

Standing from left to right standing are George Reiss, Alma Metzger, Anna Franke, Oscar Probst, Orville Koerber, Michael Mueth, William Kempf, Richard Gasser, Frank Klein (back partially hidden), Gus Metzger (behind Mrs. Emma Barthel), John H. Wiegand, Mamie Wiegand (front of Mamie) Laura Muskopf, Leroy Muskopf, Robert Schneider behind Mamie, Betty Klein Beckerle (standing in front) Mazrie Koerber, Harry Franke (behind Marie), Virginia Mehrman, Theo "Teddy" Klein, Helen Klein, Irene Griebel (behind Helen), Norman Barthul behind next to Irene G. Martha Mueth front standing Katie Reiss, Nora Kempf, Robert Griebel, Walter Mehrman back between Martha & Katie, Bill Schneider (behind Walter) partial face don't know man for sure behind Nora Kempf, Cletus Mueth, Henry Griebel. The Grange had its first meeting in March 1948. Then they had two meetings each month 2nd and 4th Thursdays

This is Floraville, Illinois
by Edward H. Wirth of Belleville, Illinois in 1965

Floraville had two hotels: The Green Tree Hotel operated by Christ Lindauer and the Flora Hotel operated by Mr. Hartmann. (Mine – that Mr. Hartmann may have been William Hartmann of nearby Millstadt who founded Post 684 of the G.A.R. there on 9/22/1889 which included my great grandfather Frank Reiss as a charter member.) In connection with the hotel they also conducted a saloon, beer, and whisky establishment. The main source of revenue for the hotels was obtained from traveling salesmen, in those days called Drummers. They were out drumming up business for large establishments in East St. Louis, St. Louis, and Belleville. These salesmen traveled by horse and buggy and called on the merchants in the southern part of Illinois and could not make the trip home on the same day. There were trips that took several days to complete.

The Floraville Community Grange

Floraville Community Grange No. 1918 was organized March 8, 1948. The first meeting took place at what is now the Modern Woodman Hall. The building was owned by St. Paul Church of Floraville. Orville Helms, St. Clair County Grange Deputy, was in charge of the first meeting.

Mr. and Mrs. George Reiss and Mr. and Mrs. Arthur Barthel were members of the Broad Hollow Grange. They were responsible and instrumental in bringing the group together. Through their knowledge of Grange work, the idea of Grange work spread through the community. It took hold and the organization was formed, 52 charter members were signed. The first master was elected. He was Arthur Barthel who served for seven years followed by Orville Koerber for two years, John Weigand for one year, Lavern Lang for two years, Theodore Klein for one year, and again Orville Koerber for two years, and again Arthur Barthel in his third term. On October 23, 1952 the Grange held its first meeting in its new hall.

I bought the photo above on eBay from Randy Hutsch (phonetic spelling) at 618 303 1688 who had a bunch of Millstadt and Floraville stuff. It is an event at the Flora Hotel in about 1890. It's only men and boys and a maybe two dozen rifles. My guess is that it was a G.A.R. function maybe to celebrate an anniversary from the Civil War. The photo below was probably taken the same day in 1948 as the first photo above as this building transitioned from a Woodmen Hall to a Grange Hall. I remember going to a Grange function in this building about 1950 when I was six years old. I also remember falling/rolling all the way down the stairs from the second floor to

the first floor which would have been at least 16 steps. A lot of adults came to my rescue at the bottom. Fortunately I wasn't hurt but I definitely remember being embarrassed.

At right is the Golden Sheaf Certificate my grandmother Katie Reiss received on 12/22/1971 for being a 50-year member of the Grange. She and Pop had joined the Broad Hollow Grange on 12/22/1921 which is 11 months after it was established so they were almost charter members in that Grange as well. My grandfather George died on 8/19/1964 so he was almost a 43-year member of the Grange. My grandmother Katie died on 10/17/1986 so she was almost a 65-year member of the Grange. I remember Lavern Lang speaking at her funeral about the Grange connection.

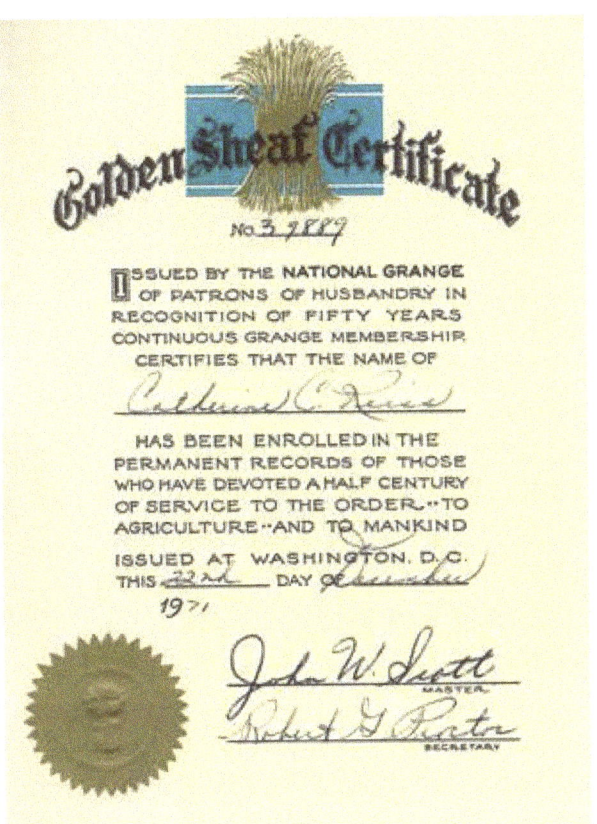

Will, Kayla, Ava, and Blake, check out the next page. Your cousin Lynette Lang Schaeffer was elected president of the Illinois State Grange on 9/20/2013 for two years. Can you imagine how pleased Grandma Katie would be!!! The Reiss and Lang families are so proud. Lynette will do an outstanding job.

Love, Granddad

Illinois State Grange Elects New President

On Friday, Sept. 20, Lynette Schaeffer was elected President of the Illinois State Grange during their 142nd Annual Convention, held in Rockford.

Schaeffer, of Lebanon has been a member of the Grange "since I can first remember," noting that her parents were active in the Grange before she was born and remain members today.

She has held several offices at the Subordinate and Pomona levels and most recently served as Historian of the Illinois State Grange. She is a member of Floraville Community and Shiloh Valley Granges and St. Clair County Pomona Grange. She was also a member of the Junior Grange.

"I look forward to serving the Grangers in IL to the best of my abilities. As past ISG Historian I hope to incorporate some of the old ideas in a new way to keep IL Granges and Grangers going strong," Schaeffer said.

Schaeffer and her husband, Don, have been married for 38 years after having met at a Grange Youth event. They served as Illinois State Grange Young Couple in 1983, representing the state at National Session that November.

They live on a farm where they raise cattle, corn, soybeans and hay. She also provides IT support to USDA service center agencies in ten southern Illinois counties.

The couple has two children and three grandchildren. Their son, Justin, serves as

Lynette Schaeffer

Illinois State Grange Steward and their daughter and her family are active at the local Shiloh Valley Grange.

Immediate Past Master Lyle Lee, of Belvidere, stepped down after four years as President. His wife, Patti, serves as the National Grange Flora.

Contact Information:
Lynette Schaeffer
10647 Rieder Road
Lebanon, IL 62254-2509
Tel: (618) 537-4837 * Email: schaeffr@att.net

Pop's Pine Woods

Dear Will, Kayla, Ava, and Blake,   October 15, 2012

Here are three paragraphs which your great great uncle Frank Reiss wrote 61 years ago yesterday on Sunday October 14, 1951 after returning from a visit to the Reiss Family Farm 12 miles south of Belleville, Illinois.

We just returned from a trip down to the home farm. We arrived down there on Friday evening. Mother, Dad, and I immediately went to the Floraville Grange Booster Night. Saturday morning we all went to look at the new lake on Gundlach's land. It is really nice. About 5 – 6 feet of water in it already at the lower end.

We stopped in the long bottom and got two big sacks full of walnuts. They are large size and heavy this year. Took pictures of Dad and his planting of short-leaf pines. He planted them as seedlings in the spring of 1940.

Gerry and I drove the car back to the 8 acres and gathered hickory nuts. We found the ground just covered on top of the hill in the mailbox woods where the pigs used to be. We gathered about ½ bushel of shelled nuts. I have never seen them so plentiful.

This edition of Granddad's Mondays will concentrate on the middle paragraph which mentions your great great grandfather's planting of short-leaf pines. That was something that Pop, as we called him, was very proud of. That grove is about 200 yards northeast of the mailbox at the end of the woods lane. That new lake on the Gundlach land that he mentions is what we now know as the first lake at the Smithton Sportsman's Club. From the photos below we can estimate these trees were on 10-foot centers and the rows were on 15-foot centers which is about 280 trees per acre and there is at least one acre of them. The spring of 1940 is also when Grandma and Pop broke ground for their new house. Perhaps there is a connection between the two projects or maybe Pop had long term plans for those trees. Here's what I found on Google about that species:

Shortleaf Pine is a species of pine native to the 3astern US from southern New York to northern Florida and west to eastern Texas. The tree reaches heights of 65 to 100 feet with trunk diameters of 1.5 to 3 feet. The leaves are needle-like, in bundles of two and three mixed together, and from 2.7 to 4.3 inches long. The cones are 1.5 to 2.8 inches long.

I remember walking through "Pop's Pine Woods" dozens of times. One time when I was about 12, we found one particular tree with lots of white bird droppings under it. We looked up and saw a great horned owl looking down at us. This was obviously his home.

Over the years, some of these trees were harvested for fence posts and other farm uses. Some of the land was returned to farming so today Pop's Woods is about 40 trees. We call it the George Reiss Memorial Grove which we would like to preserve well beyond its current 72 years.

So, Will, Kayla, Ava, and Blake, trees are beautiful creations of nature. You can admire them from a distance, walk through them for special smells and discoveries, climb them for better views, or even build a tree house as we did in our back yard. Remember when walking through a woods to look in all directions including down and up. And thanks to Uncle Frank, we're finding it greatly helpful to future generations if you take pictures and keep a daily diary. A recently found photo album included the picture below from 1945 when Pop's trees were about five years old.

Love, Granddad

Quilter, Granger, Grandma, Matriarch

Dear Will, Kayla, Ava, and Blake,   February 23, 2015

In 2009 I transcribed my Grandmother Katie Reiss' daily diary and had it published as a book by this title. It covers the years 1949 through 1953. During those five years her diary shows she was quilting or "patching" on 31 days in 1949, 58 days in 1950, 93 days in 1951, 61 days in 1952, and 43 days in 1953. Patching is her word for sewing subassemblies of individual pieces into one- or two-foot squares or shapes which would then be sewn together into the overall top layer of the quilt. Some quilters identify this "patching" step as "piecing."

The first step is to assemble all the "patches" or "pieces" together to form the top sheet. The next step is to lay that top sheet face down on a large table or the floor, then add the "batting" layer which was usually bonded cotton, and then add the bottom or "backing" layer face up. That sandwich is then smoothed out very flat and held together with a series of safety pins or special quilting pins so none of the layers can move. The two long edges of that sandwich are then partially rolled around the outside poles of a quilting frame like the second picture below. There are ratchets which pull in all four directions to keep everything taught for effortless hand stitching. The choice of batting and other layers must consider water laundry, dry cleaning, warmth, possible wall hanging, shrinkage, etc.

Here are Grandma Katie on the right and her sister Lottie quilting in 1962. Both have their right hand on the underneath side with a raised-edge thimble to carefully detect the needle coming from above so it can be turned around and carefully pushed back up with that thimble to complete one stitch. They are assembling the overall quilt at this point with the "patched" top layer, middle batting layer, and bottom backing layer. Their work is held flat, in position, and in a bit of tension by the quilting frame. These sisters are smiling for the camera and look like they are having lots of fun. Katie's son Frank took the picture.

Grandma typically assembled her quilts with a series of diamond stitch patterns in rows about two inches apart. Sometimes her assembly stitches also followed the patterns of the top sheet. Her choice of thread colors was another decision.

Pieced quilts are also known as Patchworks. They consist of geometric shapes taken from different fabrics that are sewn together. After that process, it is referred to as a quilt top. The quilting patterns generally follow the design of the geometric patterns. The quilt ends up being a mixture of different fabrics and geometric designs and shapes that are organized in some fashion.

Here is a typical quilting frame. The central area below the quilt is left open for needle access to the bottom side of the quilt. I remember my grandma having her quilting frame set up in her living room on some of our visits. She was a real artist and took great pride in her work. She made quilts as gifts to relatives and for fundraiser auctions at their Grange. She even made a few custom quilts for a fee.

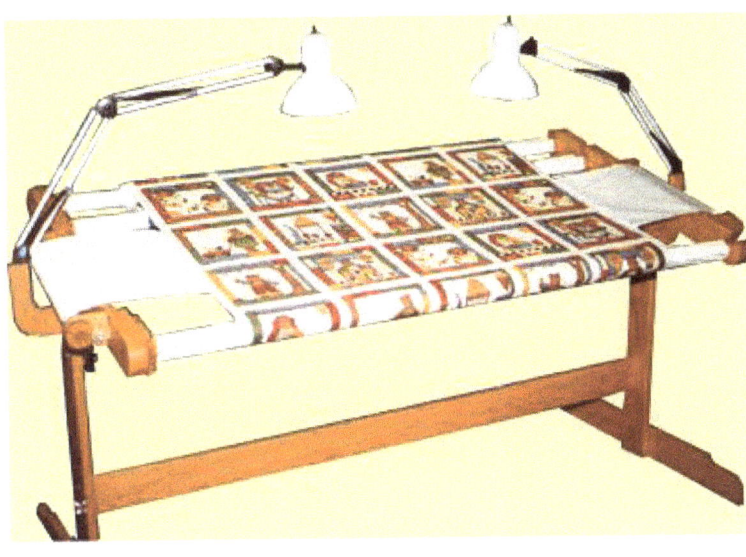

I have five of Grandma's quilts in our family collection. Here is a close-up of a "patch" that was repeated over and over with different cloth scraps and then sewn together to make the top layer in the quilt on the next page. Notice all the sewn joints. I measured all that and came up with 26.75 interior inches per patch. That does not include the exterior edges of a patch since those stitches are shared with its neighbor.

This quilt has 88 patches from 11 rows and 8 columns. So altogether there are 2,354 inches of interior stitches plus another 528 inches of stitches joining patches together. Grand total is 2,882 inches or about 28,000 stitches. That just blows my mind. This is my favorite quilt of the five by far. It's a treasure. See if you can find where I took the close-up picture.

Check out all five quilts. Sometimes you'll see the same cloth in more than one quilt. The last one is all corduroy which is fairly uncommon.

This is Grandma's treadle sewing machine which she may have used for some patching but its throat is way too small to assemble top layers of quilts. This sewing machine now resides in our log cabin. I have an upcoming story about it on August 3, 2015.

Will, Kayla, Ava, and Blake, you'll recognize this last quilt below from our basement wall. I had it made about eight years ago for Grand DD's birthday by a woman with a long-arm, computer-controlled sewing machine. The colored squares were cut from twenty of my most favorite T-shirts. There are shirts from high school sports, travel, church, Habitat, running, Race for the Cure, and Boy Scouts. Pretty neat don't ya think . . . . . but not nearly as neat as those made by my Grandma Katie.

Love, Granddad

Croquet and Ayrshire (1947)

Dear Will, Kayla, Ava, and Blake,   June 4, 2012

Do you know who this cute three-year old boy is? Well, it's me in 1947. I'm trying to figure out how to play croquet at the Reiss family farm south of Belleville, Illinois. My dad and I had taken the train from Los Angeles, California to St. Louis, Missouri to visit his parents on the home farm. I stayed there for a few days with my grandparents while Dad traveled on to Indianapolis, Indiana for a job interview with Ayrshire Collieries.

In the United States, United Kingdom, and South Africa, a coal mine and its structures are called a "colliery" so Ayrshire was a company with about five coal mines in Indiana, Illinois, and Kentucky. The primary owner and chairman of the board of Ayrshire was a man named Pierre Goodrich. He was a very smart man with a law degree from Harvard. He also had lots of money. Pierre was the only child of James Goodrich who was governor of Indiana 1917 – 1921.

Pierre Goodrich wanted to grow his company with better management of the farmlands above his underground coal mines as well as do a better job of reclaiming surface land that had been strip-mined. The normal practice back then was to leave acres and acres of tall dirt ridges called spoil banks, plant them with pine trees, create a few lakes, and then more or less abandon all that to the forces of nature. There were no attempts back then to use Caterpillar bulldozers to flatten out all those spoil banks, put the rich top soil back on top, and turn that reclaimed land back into productive farming. So Goodrich's plan was to hire a recent college graduate with a degree in Agricultural Economics to manage the surface farming and to do a much better job of reclamation after strip-mining was complete.

Goodrich visited Purdue University and asked for names of recent Ag Econ graduates. He either didn't get any good recommendations or none of those names were interested. So he next visited the University of Illinois and asked for the best Ag Econ alumnus in the last ten years. That's how he got my dad's name. We were living in Vista, California so Goodrich wrote a letter to my dad inviting him to Indianapolis for an interview, all expenses paid. Since the home farm twenty miles southeast of St. Louis is almost on the route from Los Angeles to Indianapolis, Dad decided to visit his parents and leave me with them while he went on to Indianapolis.

The interview went very well with Ayrshire, Dad met a lot of key people, visited several mines and farms, and was offered a job at a salary of $480 per month. He retrieved me from the home farm and we took the train back to Los Angeles and to Vista where we lived in north San Diego County. Mom and Dad talked over the offer and decided to turn it down. Mom had grown up in

California and wasn't interested in cold winters in the Midwest, uprooting our family, moving away from her parents in Atascadero, etc.

Well that winter, San Diego County had a heavy frost and lost a lot of the avocado and citrus trees that Dad was helping to manage as a field man for Calavo Growers which was a combination name from "<u>Cali</u>fornia" and "<u>avo</u>cado." Other economic factors like thousands of former World War II soldiers looking for jobs, etc. caused Mom and Dad to rethink their "no thanks" position on the job offer from Indianapolis. So they sent a large box of avocadoes to Pierre Goodrich in Indianapolis with no return address and no note inside. It was pretty much anonymous but nevertheless Goodrich drew the right conclusions. He sent a thank you letter to my parents with a sweetened job offer of $600 per month. Dad accepted the new offer and so our family relocated to Sullivan, Indiana in September of 1948. Sullivan is where the headquarters of the Ayrshire Collieries' farming subsidiary, Meadowlark Farms, was located.

A starting salary of $600 a month may not sound like very much but it really was an excellent figure. Some 18 years later my starting salary at Caterpillar in 1966 was $670 a month which was pretty normal for our college class of graduating engineers.

Sullivan is where my brother, sister, and I all went through twelve years of public education. My sister and her husband still live there. Our parents have since passed to their greater rewards and are buried there. It's also where we have our lake house and several farms that we inherited from our parents plus more that Grand DD and I bought on our own.

Will, Kayla, Ava, and Blake, we started this edition of Granddad's Mondays by talking about croquet so now I want to invite you both to a game of croquet in our front yard. It's a lot of fun and it can be quite challenging when you have teams of players who take turns railroading the other team's wooden ball off the course.

Love, Granddad

Wall Telephones

Dear Will, Kayla, Ava, and Blake,   July 22, 2013

Here is your great great grandma Katie Reiss in 1960 demonstrating how to use one of two old wall telephones they had at the home farm. You can see that white disconnect switch about six inches above the phone which owners would open during lightning storms for fear of damage.

The crank on the right side would allow the owner to create "short" rings of about one second or "long" rings of about two seconds for calling neighbors. I think the Reiss Farm number for crank phones was "long short long." You can see the black mouthpiece for speaking into. The hearing piece is in Grandma's left hand at her ear and out of sight. The ring sound came from those two black bells at the top.

I have ten of these old phones in our collection of antiques of which nine are oak and one is walnut. Only the latter still had a disconnect switch. A few of them still ring so I'll teach you all about that on one of your next visits.

Notice these phones are huge compared to modern cell phones which fit in your pocket. These wall phones are also not portable like cell phones and there was no texting, no voice mail, no built-in cameras, and no monster collection of apps. There were also no robocalls or telemarketers back then and timeshares hadn't yet been invented.

Neighbors could call neighbors through a series of short and long rings. For longer distances the customer would do one real long ring and the switchboard operator would come on and say "number please." You would tell her that number and she would take a few seconds to connect you to whoever you wanted to call. There is more on how that worked in two more pages. Sometimes the operator lady was a friend and instead of saying "number please," she would say, "Hi, Will or Kayla, how are your today?" Sometimes the operators would listen in on the conversation they had connected and thereby keep up on the latest news. Operators were often a good source of the latest news that was spreading within a community. Our "number please" phone number when I was growing up in Sullivan, Indiana was 1025.

I can remember many times at the home farm when my mom wanted to call her parents in California. We would drive 1.7 miles to the telephone office in Floraville and those people would make the necessary connections. Those calls were more complicated and a quality connection wasn't always easy from the home phone. It might take five minutes or more for those calls to go through. It wasn't at all like today where you can call anyone in the world from your cell phone within five seconds.

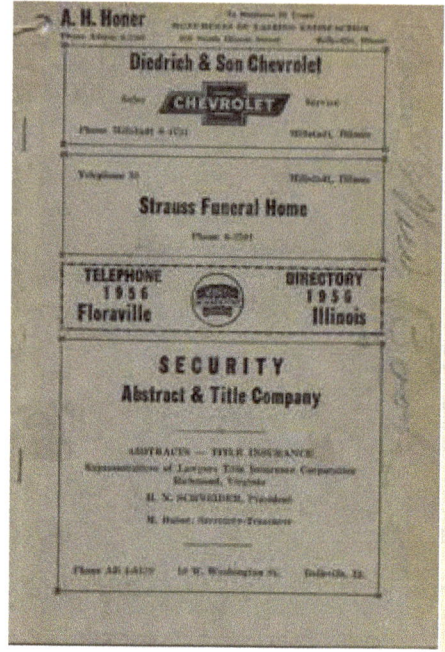

Here is the 1956 Floraville phone book. You can see in the right margin that Grandma had written "Floraville New Book." The first page was this list of instructions and etiquette. The book had only 8 pages, 158 names with phone numbers, and 30 advertisements. Most phone numbers had an "R" and a number behind each name which was probably the mail delivery route. There were 13 numbers in Belleville, 46 in Freeburg, 13 in Millstadt, 26 in New Athens, 4 in Smithton, and 73 in Waterloo. None of these

FLORAVILLE

FLORAVILLE RURAL TELEPHONE CO.
R. R. 3, Waterloo, Illinois
H. Campe, Secretary

1. In case of fire call Floraville Central and the operator will notify the Fire Department (State Which One).

2. You must not engage the operators in conversation, as this is strictly against the rules of the company and detracts from the operator's work.

3. If you want a long distance call sent collect you must tell the operator when you place the call.

4. This company assumes no liability for suspension of service caused by accidents, weather conditions, or conditions beyond its control. This company or publisher is not responsible for errors or omissions in this directory.

5. Subscribers are held responsible for all toll messages originating at their telephone.

6. On all toll calls, three minutes is the limit of the first charge. Extra charge will be made for each minute after the first three.

8. Call by number only. When through talking, ring off.

9. Obscene or profane language must not be used under any circumstances.

10. Conversation on party lines should be limited to five minutes.

11. Answer your call promptly. The subscriber is a part of the telephone system and by proper use of his telephone, can do much to promote the general efficiency of the service.

12. If you desire to make a number of calls in succession, notify the operator and she can do much to save time.

13. "Line busy" or "They don't answer" may at times be annoying, but the subscriber must bear in mind that it requires no more exertion on the part of the operator, and is much more agreeable to make the connection at once than to have to report a busy line.

14. Operators are instructed to treat subscribers with respect and courtesy, and telephone users are requested to be equally courteous and respect them.

15. Do not allow the children or disinterested parties to use or tamper with your telephone.

16. Do not use the telephone during electrical storms.

17. "Trouble" occurs constantely in all telephone systems. The management can only remedy it when they know it. Let us have the first complaint.

18. Nine short rings calls everybody on the line at once.

phone numbers was longer than three digits. My guess is that these were primarily rural customers and that Floraville numbers appeared under Waterloo. The customer whose phone number was "1" was the Floraville Telephone Office on Waterloo Route 3.

Here is the "R" page from the Floraville phone book showing the phone number for George Reiss was 324. Notice that they show our farm attached to the village of Freeburg because that is where the nearest post office was in 1956. Now it is attached to the village of Smithton which got its post office later.

The Floraville Rural Telephone Company was organized in 1905-1906. The Board of Directors was Louis Eckert, Otto Etling, Geo. Hoffmann, Dr. Emery Holcomb, John Sauzeck, Philip Wirth, and Louis Zimblemann. This company sold stock certificates to all people who were interested in the new venture.

The setting of the poles and the stretching of wire was all done by members. Telephone poles were young trees of the local forests. The system used was the Ground System which operated on one wire line. The telephone wall unit was large and somewhat bulky. A set of wet batteries was used to produce enough amperes to ring the bell. This bell was rung by cranking the phone.

This company had its switchboard in a general merchandise store in Floraville. Later it was moved to a series of private homes. There were twenty trunk lines to the switchboard, each line had a capacity of taking care of twenty subscribers. The people on each line could call their neighbors by ringing their number and did not have to go through the switchboard. However, to call persons on any of the other lines, you had to place your call with the operator, who in turn rang the number on the other line.

The rings were made up of long and short rings, not exceeding four rings like Long, Short, Long, Short and the different variations. The switchboard closed for the night at 9:00 p.m. and gave the signal on all lines, five long rings. People were urged not to use the switchboard after 9:00 p.m. except in an emergency. The telephone also served to notify the people on their respective lines about emergencies, such as fires, family in distress, etc. This signal was given by the operator and consisted of six long rings. The subscribers took the receiver off the hook and learned, from the operator, what unusual happening had taken place.

Pfannebecker Edgar Waterloo R3		808
Pfannebecker Marvin Waterloo R3		226
Phillips Cyrus Freeburg R1		109
Probst Chas New Athens R2		114
Probst Elmer Waterloo R3		64
Probst Henry Waterloo R3		70
Probst Monroe Waterloo R3		173
— Q —		
Quirin Dr Chas Smithton		53
Quirin Floyd Millstadt R2		330
Quirin Oliver Millstadt R2		331
— R —		
Rapp John Freeburg R1		327
Reheis Jacob Waterloo R3		130
Reinhardt Clem Waterloo R3		251
Reiso Mrs Amanda New Athens R2		210
Reiss Geo Freeburg R1		324
Rosenberger Hy Waterloo R3		69
Rosenberger Louis Waterloo R3		78
Ruhmann Irwin Waterloo R3		63
— S —		
St Michael's Rectory Waterloo R3		83
Schaefer Clarence New Athens R2		280
Schaefer Paul Freeburg R1		273
Schaefer Sylvester New Athens R2		278
Schilling Frank Freeburg R1		192
Schilling Roman Waterloo R3		143
Schneider Louis Waterloo R3		32
Schwaegel Bros Store Smithton		61
Sense Rev Edmund Waterloo R3		83
Sensel Levi Waterloo R3		136
Shoemaker James Freeburg R1		115
Skaer Geo New Athens R2		279
Skaer Louis New Athens R2		103
Skaer Orlando Waterloo R3		307
Skaer Orlin Waterloo R3		319

Will, Kayla, Ava, and Blake, you can see that telephone technology has advanced significantly from the days of wall telephones with hand crank ringers. Now you don't have to stand on a stool to reach the ringer and mouthpiece to make a call. You can simply click on the numbers stored in your cell phone and call Grand DD and me any time you have a few minutes. We're waiting!!!

Love, Granddad

1950 – 1959

1950 Population of St. Clair County is 205,995.

1950 States total 48, national population is 152.27 million. Alaska and Hawaii were added in 1959.

1950 President is Harry Truman. Dwight Eisenhower is inaugurated in 1953.

1953 The description of a double helix DNA molecule is published.

1953 Color television sets go on sale.

1954 The first large scale vaccination of children against polio begins in Pittsburgh.

1954 Racial segregation in public schools is declared unconstitutional by the US Supreme Court in Brown vs. the Board of Education.

1955 Ray Kroc incorporates McDonalds and opened his first franchise in Des Plaines, Illinois.

1955 Disneyland opened in Anaheim, California.

1956 The Interstate Highway System began with the signing of the Federal-Aid Highway Act.

1957 Gordon Gould invented the laser.

1958 Jet airline passenger service inaugurated in the US.

1959 Alaska and Hawaii are admitted to the US as the 49th and 50th states.

1959 The St. Lawrence Seaway is opened allowing ocean ships to reach the Great Lakes.

Grandma's Flower and Vegetable Gardens

Dear Will, Kayla, Ava, and Blake,   March 23, 2015

I wish you could have met my Grandma Katie. She was a wonderful woman. She lived to age 96.5 but would be age 125 this Wednesday. We are blessed to still have hundreds of memories, hundreds of pictures, hundreds of farm documents, and two of her five-year diaries which are now in book form. Here's a picture from about 1965 of Grandma walking out from her sun porch to admire her vegetable and flower gardens. All those east-facing windows on her sun porch made that room into a winter greenhouse for geraniums. Their easily recognizable smell is another memory. Below are entries from her 1953 diary about working in her gardens.

April 1953

Mon 27 – I spaded garden, planted peas.

Tues 28 – I spaded garden & planted sweet corn & pickles, also peas & tomatoes & cabbage seed.

Wed 29 – I planted more sweet corn & cucumbers also sugar melon.

May 1953

Fri 1 – I planted more cucumbers & a few watermelons.

Wed 6 – I spaded some and planted more potatoes also flower seed.

Thurs 7 – I spaded some.

Fri 8 – I worked in the garden all day, planted flower seeds, cucumbers, and sweet corn.

The picture above is 1952 and below is 1953

Sat 9 – I planted more cucumbers & watermelons.

Mon 11 – I hoed my garden.

Fri 15 – I spaded in the garden, planted more sweet corn & watermelons.

Wed 27 – Spaded the garden.

Thurs 28 – I spaded garden & hoed a lot of weeds out.

July 1953

Thurs 2 – I dug some potatoes.

August 1953

Mon 31 – We peeled tomatoes for canning.

Thurs 24 – I potted flowers.

Fri 25 – I potted flowers and brought them on the sun porch.

Mon 5 – I potted more flowers.

The picture above is 1956 and below is 1960 with great niece Lynette Lang.

Will, Kayla, Ava, and Blake, here is my favorite picture with Dad and Grandma from about 1975. Dad was still working and would visit his employer's farms in southern Illinois once a quarter. He would always visit or stay overnight with his mom on those trips. Pop had died in 1964 after which their mother/son bond was stronger and more comforting for both. Dad was more than practicing that old idiom . . . . . take time to stop and smell the roses.

Love, Granddad

"GRANDMA'S GARDEN"
I remember Grandma's garden
The beauty and the grace
Of all the lovely flowers
In that dear, sweet place
I remember Grandma's smile
As she planted, pruned, and tilled
Laboring with love and laughter
As this world with joy she filled
I remember Grandma's patience
When we ran amid the flowers
With her beauty all around us
We would spend those precious hours
I remember Grandma's garden
And I'm happy in the knowing
That when she knelt there in the soil
It wasn't just flowers she was growing.

Grandma's Stove

Dear Will, Kayla, Ava, and Blake,   March 23, 2015

As a kid, my favorite way to wake up on cool mornings at the Reiss family farm was to the smell of Grandma Katie building a fire in her kitchen stove and starting breakfast. Her fuel was corncobs and kindling that Pop had cut during the previous weeks. My favorite breakfast was pork sausage, scrambled eggs, and cottage fries which you learned about in my Granddad's Mondays story of 7/8/2013.

I remember Grandma's first stove which was totally a wood burner for the right and left sides of the top and the oven. There was a flue with a damper for the smoke and heat going out the top. I'm not sure how she would have controlled the oven temperature except by frequent inspections.

Her new combination stove was delivered on 6/29/1953 by Schneiders in Waterloo. It burned wood on the top left but the top right and oven were both electric. That sounds more practical but still allowed the tradition, fun, and smell of burning wood – especially in making memories for grandchildren.

Belleville is 12 miles north of our family farm. It's the eighth largest city in Illinois outside of the Chicago area. After the failure of the German Revolutions in 1830 and 1848, many of the educated people fled their homeland. Belleville was the center of the first important German settlement in Illinois. By 1870, an estimated 90% of the city's population was either German born or of German descent.

After the Civil War, Belleville became a manufacturing center for nails, printing presses, gray iron castings, agricultural equipment, and wood/coal burning stoves. The number of stoves produced and wealth generated from the stove foundry industry gave Belleville the moniker, "Stove Capital of the World." Belleville continues to produce high-quality stoves and heating products for today's market. It is believed that industrialists of Belleville enameled the first stove in America and came up with the idea of the "Jacketed Stove." Another tidbit – in 1868, Gustav Goelitz founded his candy company in Belleville which you know today as "Jelly Belly" for the world's best gourmet jelly beans.

An immense deposit (400,000 acres) of bituminous coal was found in St. Clair County. By 1874, some farmers had become coal miners. One hundred shaft mines were in operation in and around Belleville. Coal was consumed by over fifty local iron foundries making parts for stoves, etc. Coal also brought the steam railroad to town, which allowed for the transport of many tons of coal to be shipped daily from Belleville to St. Louis. Later, Belleville would have the first electric trolley in the state.

The **Labor & Industry Museum** on North Church Street in Belleville displays 26 different stoves dating from 1881 to 1940, including a wide range of heating and cooking styles - all made in Belleville. Several look like the stoves I remember from Grandma's kitchen but unfortunately I don't recall any brand names.

My grandparents moved 50 yards from their 1889 house to their new house built in 1940. Their old house had a summer kitchen which had a diagonal corner connection to the main house. Just as the name implies, it was for cooking meals during the hot summer. I don't know if they moved their wood burning stove from the house kitchen to the summer kitchen or simply had two stoves. Anyway, that switch allowed the heat of summer cooking to not make the rest of the house too hot. In other words, Grandma was the only one who had to endure all that cooking heat year round. How fair is that? Grandma lived to age 96.5 so maybe all that heat was a blessing. She would have been age 125 this Wednesday.

Will, Kayla, Ava, and Blake, the old sawn wood on my log cabin door, gables, and porch ceiling came from a 150-year old summer kitchen in West Peoria. Good thing I'm at the end of this story. It's time for breakfast for all five of us. Enjoy!!!

Love, Granddad

Grandma's Sausage and Eggs

Dear Will, Kayla, Ava, and Blake,   July 8, 2013

My grandmother Katie Reiss would be your great great grandma. She was the matriarch of our extended family even before she married my grandfather George "Pop" Reiss on April 16, 1911. That's because she was a domestic housekeeper living on the Reiss farm with the Frank Reiss family (including bachelor son George) when the Federal Census was taken on April 25, 1910. They misspelled her last name as Luietcelschwab instead of Luetzelschwab. That's how/where she met Pop in the first place. They married a year later and raised three sons who married and raised six grandchildren. Grandma was a saint to all those descendants. You have two of her five-year diaries in book form as <u>Granger, Quilter, Grandma, Matriarch</u> (1944 – 1948) and <u>Quilter, Granger, Grandma, Matriarch</u> (1949 – 1953).

Grandma's world-class breakfast that we had almost every morning during our quarterly visits was pork sausage and scrambled eggs. Yummy, yummy, yummy!!! She cooked that on a kitchen stove which burned corncobs and small bits of wood that Pop cut and split. Later on Grandma got a new stove but still one half of it was a wood fire and the other half was electric. She preferred the wood side.

I remember we occasionally had Cheerios for breakfast on the home farm. I thought they were tasty and special but my mom apparently didn't care for them and never bought them back home in Sullivan, Indiana. So I grew up thinking Cheerios was a local breakfast cereal available only in the Belleville and St. Louis area. Wrong!!!

Anyway, I remember making trips to two butcher shops in Belleville and later to one in Millstadt to buy pork sausage, summer sausage, blood sausage, head cheese, and other German meats to be eaten at the home farm or taken back to our home in Sullivan. My favorite butcher shop was Weyhaupt's and then Streck's, both in Belleville. My ranking was based on the smells, sawdust on the floors, and the friendliness of the butchers rather than on the quality of their German meat products. Decades later Schubert's in Millstadt became my favorite.

I couldn't find any history on Weyhaupt's other than their address of **Weyhaupt Brothers Packing Company** at 1510 Lebanon Avenue, Belleville, IL 62221.

Streck Packing Company is at 401 W. Washington Street, Belleville IL, 62220. Not much history here either except this advertisement in the 1956 Floraville Telephone Directory. Three brothers, Ernest, Clarence and Adolph Streck, many years ago entered into a partnership to engage in the meat packing business in and about Belleville, Illinois. On January 31, 1928 the three brothers, together with their wives, executed a written partnership agreement that provided for the partnership to continue in case of the death of one of the brothers. Well one of the brother's wives died and he remarried. Then he died and that second wife initiated a lawsuit which got kinda messy. No thanks.

MR. FARMER:
Bring Us Your
CATTLE — CALVES — HOGS

STRECK BROS.

Manufacturers of None Better Meat Scraps
Protein Food For Hogs and Chickens
Telephone 2450   401 W. Washington St.   Belleville, Illinois

Schubert's Packing Company is at 700 S Breese Street, Millstadt, IL 62260. Their website has the following paragraph – Schubert's Packing Co., Inc., Millstadt Illinois owners Larry and Marlene (Mabel) Schubert have been in the meat processing business for 29 years. Their wholesale and retail operation starts at slaughtering and includes fresh and cured meats, homemade sausages, German style specialty meats and sausages, and deer processing. State and national award winning products include country style smoked hams (bone-in and boneless) and bacon, summer sausage, smoked jerky, bologna, braunschweiger, smoked turkey, bratwursts, and Schubert's Smokies. Their Hermann, Missouri Wurstfest award winners include braunschweiger (2 time winner of the Best of the Show), head cheese, liver sausage, blood sausage, smoked jerky, bratwurst, summer sausage, and Schubert's bockwurst (an old German favorite). As a result of Larry's achievements, in the summer of 2004, Larry and his son Bryan, were invited to Gross Bieberau, Hessen, Germany to prepare meat products such as bratwurst and cut pork steaks for an 'American Festival in Germany'.

Here's another tidbit from the obituary of Larry Schubert's father, Walter: Walter Kermit "Red" Schubert, 88, of Millstadt, IL, born Sept. 29, 1923, in Millstadt, IL, passed away Thursday, July 26, 2012, at his residence. Walter had worked for 40 years as a foreman/meat cutter at **Streck Packing Company in Belleville, IL, then he worked at Schubert Packing Company** in Millstadt, IL. Walter was a member of the Meat Cutters Local 545, Modern Woodmen, and Zion Evangelical Church in Millstadt, IL. Walter was an avid coon hunter. He and his friends were the charter members of the Millstadt Coon Hunters Association. He loved gardening and nurturing his pecan and walnut trees, and if you needed a well "witched", "Red" was the one to call. He enjoyed watching the St. Louis Cardinals and he loved visiting with his grandchildren and great-granddaughters.

Maybe it's obvious now that good German pork sausage was the foundation of Grandma's special breakfasts. She taught me how to use a fork to make lots of holes in the pork sausage as it was cooking so the oils could drain out. She taught me how to make scrambled eggs by not turning them until bubbles half an inch in diameter started rising from the egg/milk slurry. She was adamant that stirring or turning scrambled eggs too soon would lead to watery eggs that kinda looked like yellow cottage cheese. Not good. I have followed Grandma's scrambled egg advice for 60 years now and received lots of compliments, mostly from friends who didn't think I could do anything in a kitchen, let alone make good looking and tasty scrambled eggs.

So, Will, Kayla, Ava, and Blake, that's my story and I'm sticking to it. I'm very pleased that Grandma taught me how to make great sausage and scrambled eggs breakfasts and that I paid good attention as an eight-year old. An hour after I sent this Granddad's Mondays this morning, Will and I were busy on his first lesson cooking scrambled eggs. The photos below tell the story.

Love, Granddad

Grandma's Custard Fruit Pies

Dear Will, Kayla, Ava, and Blake,   July 28, 2014

By now you know that my grandma Katie Reiss was an outstanding cook. My previous stories have mentioned her scrambled eggs and sausage, morel mushrooms, and even her store-bought Cheerios. Well, this story is about her very healthy fruit pies made with apples, cherries, plums, strawberries, gooseberries, blackberries, dewberries, or raspberries which also included custard filling. I don't know what happened to her recipe file, if she even had one, so I looked on Google for custard pie filling which made her pies both tasty and healthy. Here's what I found:

GRANDMA'S PLAIN CUSTARD PIE FILLING

1 c. white sugar
1/2 tsp. butter
1 tsp. vanilla
1/4 tsp. nutmeg
1 tbsp. white flour
4 lg. eggs
2 c. scalded milk

Heat milk in a saucepan to just scalding (do not boil). In bowl combine the sugar, flour and butter. Beat until well mixed. Add vanilla and eggs and beat hard for 3 minutes. While beating, add milk very slowly.

GRANDMA NORMA'S CUSTARD PIE FILLING

4 eggs, beaten
2/3 c. sugar
1/2 tsp. salt
1/2 tsp. nutmeg
2 2/3 c. scalding hot milk
1 tsp. vanilla

Mix in order given and pour into unbaked crust. Bake at 450 degrees for 15 minutes. Reduce to 350 degrees for 10 more minutes. Test for doneness with table knife - should come out clean when done.

AUNT HATTIE'S CUSTARD PIE FILLING

3 c. milk
4 eggs
1/2 c. sugar
1 tsp. vanilla

Heat milk to scalding, beat eggs, add sugar and vanilla. Pour hot milk over mixture. Pour in pie shell. Sprinkle with nutmeg.

These ladies aren't Reiss relatives but it's obvious they wanted to bake healthy pies for their own grandchildren. Notice that all their ingredients are good for youngsters and oldsters except perhaps the sugar content and even that is reduced as you go down the page.

Here are a few pictures of fruit pies with custard filling. Notice that pouring in the custard is the last step before baking so you can pour shallow so the fruit is on top or you can pour deep so the custard is on top. You can mix fruits together like the lower right which is a combination of apples, strawberries, and blueberries. Notice also that the cast iron skillet pie in the lower left which has no crust so it's probably the healthiest of them all. If you baked that skillet pie over a campfire, you could toss the emptied skillet back into the hot embers upside down which slowly converts the pie crumbs to a light grey dust that brushes off. No scrubbing or washing. That's the way the Boy Scouts do dishes but it only works on cast iron.

Will, Kayla, Ava, and Blake, we can make our custard fruit pies even more healthy by harvesting our own fruit or buying it at a farmers market rather than buying cans of small fruits at Krogers which probably contain corn starch or sugar syrup. If we bought fresh sweet Bing or Rainier cherries rather than traditional tart pie cherries, we could probably take all of the sugar out of our custard filling. To further authenticate our pie-making process, you three could each choose different cherry pitters from my basement museum of antique kitchen contraptions. You could de-seed the cherries for our pie but you might want to leave a seed or two as proof our cherries were not from a store-bought can. Just be sure to not bite down hard on a seed. I don't remember my grandma using any table mounted cherry pitter like the above left. Maybe she used a hand held pitter or a small knife.

Will, Kayla, Ava, and Blake, I looked for poems about grandmas like mine and their fruit pies. The best poem by far came from the <mark>Peoria Poetry Club</mark> just down the road from us. That's further confirmation that the five of us need to pool our talents to hand make a very healthy custard fruit pie for our families. We could even use an iron skillet, probably with a lid, on the cast iron stove in our log cabin. It would be so healthy that it could be our entire lunch. Whaduyasay?

Love, Granddad

Grandma's Apple Pie

Of childhood recollections
Amid scenes that linger on,
Fondest thoughts (I need not lie)
Recall our Grandma's apple pie.
Black cast-iron coal stove
With radiant tended glow,
And heated baking oven
Warming just below.
Grandma in her flowery garb,
With apron dusted white with flour,
Porcelain mixing bowl with
Wooden spoon in this exciting hour!
Crisp Courtland apple slices,
Cinnamon-covered crumbly crust,
Pipe hot from the oven
With Grandma's smiling trust.
Patiently waiting in that Heaven-bound
Awesome line (and pray I'm not too late),
Amid God's blue celestial sky, to reach the Pearly Gate.
As St. Peter stands on high I'll humbly beg
For one more slice of Grandma's apple pie!

Grandma's Apron

Dear Will, Kayla, Ava, and Blake,   December 8, 2014

This is one of my favorite subjects. I sat down to write this story and was hoping to find a poem that would be a good start. This is the first poem I found. It was so great and so perfectly matched my memories of my grandma, that I stopped looking and pretty much stopped writing. Here it is:

I don't think our kids know what an apron is.

The principal use of Grandma's apron was to protect the dress underneath,
because she only had a few,
it was easier to wash aprons than dresses and they used less material,
but along with that, it served as a potholder for removing hot pans from the oven.

It was wonderful for drying children's tears,
and on occasion was even used for cleaning out dirty ears…

From the chicken coop, the apron was used for carrying eggs,
fussy chicks, and sometimes half-hatched eggs to be finished in the warming oven.

When company came, those aprons were ideal hiding places for shy kids.

And when the weather was cold grandma wrapped it around her arms.

Those big old aprons wiped many a perspiring brow, bent over the hot wood stove.

Chips and kindling wood were brought into the kitchen in that apron.

From the garden, it carried all sorts of vegetables.

After the peas had been shelled, it carried out the hulls.

In the fall, the apron was used to bring in apples that had fallen from the trees.

When unexpected company drove up the road,
it was surprising how much furniture that old apron could dust in a matter of seconds.

When dinner was ready, Grandma walked out onto the porch, waved her apron,
and the men-folk knew it was time to come in from the fields to dinner.

It will be a long time before someone invents something that will replace
that 'old-time apron' that served so many purposes.

Grandma used to set her hot baked apple pies on the window sill to cool.
Her granddaughters set theirs on the window sill to thaw.

They would go crazy now trying to figure out how many germs were on that apron.
I never caught anything from an apron…But Love.

Here is my Grandma Katie in 1956 with her year old grand niece, Lynette Lang. It's no surprise that Lynette grew up to be the current state president of the Illinois Grange. Her Aunt Katie deserves some of that credit. Notice Grandma's apron.

Below is Grandma in 1951 at Hoelscher's sawmill on the northeast corner of her farm. She is with grandsons George and Richard. They are about a mile from the homestead. Notice Grandma's apron.

Below is an interesting article about aprons and a farm wife named Esther Duncan which appeared in the 9/1/2006 Danville, Illinois newspaper called "Commercial News." The author visited the Farm Progress Show in Amana, Iowa, which is something Grand DD and I will do in a few more years with all you young farmers.

Woman keeps history of aprons alive; farm wife accessory popular again

AMANA, Iowa — While most farmers spent the 2006 Farm Progress Show exam-ining new seed varieties and test driving the latest in farming machinery, Esther Duncan of Veedersburg, Ind., drew many of their wives to the arts and crafts tent.

Among dozens of booths boasting jewelry, cosmetics, and country crafts, Duncan, a seasoned Farm Progress exhibitor, showcased and sold her specialty: replicas of farm women's old aprons.

"I'm not trying to bring the apron back, it's more of a nostalgia trip," she explained of her passion for the garment that once was a staple on every farm.

Apron History

Duncan has spent countless hours researching the history of aprons and listened to farm women everywhere tell the stories of their aprons.

"I'm more interested in the person who wore the apron than the apron itself. I want to hear the apron talk when I look at it, and how the apron was worn — the rips and tears in it — gives it a voice," she said.

It all started in 1996, when Duncan replicated her mother's old apron and told stories about it at a family reunion.

After that, people began contacting her about copying their old aprons and she started to give talks about the garment's history. The phone never stopped ringing and today she travels to farm shows all over the country with her business Farm Woman's Apron.

Duncan, whom some have branded "the apron lady," is not only driven by her company's success, but also by the resolve to rectify the fact that a woman's work on the farm rarely was recognized, even though the success of the farm depended on it.

In her booth at the Farm Progress Show hung a sign declaring that "Women's handwork is no longer considered women's work. Women's work shall be classified into a new category called ART," which is something Duncan feels strongly about.

Wanda Weber of Cedar Rapids, Iowa, visited Duncan's booth while her husband watched field demonstrations with 24-row corn planters and received a history lesson while admiring Duncan's work.

"It was really interesting," she said. Weber especially liked Duncan's farm daughter's apron line.

"If I'd had a little granddaughter I would've bought that," she said and pointed at a small orange-and-white checkered apron.

The times when every farm woman owned at least three aprons — one for every-day use, one to wear when she had company and one for Sundays — may be long gone, or as Duncan jokingly puts it, "When women burned their bras, they burned their aprons as well," but she thinks the apron still has a place in modern society.

"Today, most women never wear an apron, but they want to be country chic and hang it in their kitchen. I think aprons are very collectible today and people follow that trend."

Will, Kayla, Ava, and Blake, it looks like I'm not alone in appreciating the traditional farm apron or the wonderful women who wore them. There is great significance and history in farm aprons that you don't see much of today. The memories of Grandma's aprons have stuck with me for over 60 years.

Love, Granddad

The Indian Mound

Dear Will, Kayla, Ava, and Blake,   August 10, 2015

That rise on the far end of this field is what our family has always called "the Indian mound." It's near the northeast corner of the Reiss family farm and just west of the bridge where Knab Road crosses over Richland Creek. This formation rises out of a flat valley and is next to a year-round stream which may imply that it is manmade. At the same time it seems too big and un-steep for a traditional Indian mound. It does not appear on any local or state maps as an Indian mound. So we'll never know for sure but for the purposes of this story, let's assume it is real.

Our family looked here for arrowheads and anything manmade on dozens of occasions. The best time was after spring plowing and before the crops got very tall. There is too much corn stover and volunteer weeds in this picture to make this a prime time season for looking. You need newly turned dirt and a few good rains to make "rocks" easily visible on the surface. Over the

years we found a dozen complete arrowheads, maybe 100 broken arrowheads or bits of flint, and this fine tomahawk.

I remember the day in 1954 when about ten of us were tramping the mound and my brother Ken came up to our dad and said, "Dad, is this anything?" Dad was blown away because this was a perfect granite tomahawk. Looks like the round end had

seen more use by its owners than the pointed end. A few years later, Ken also found this beautiful discoidal stone on the Indian mound. Here's what I found on Google.

Mississippi Discoidals: Ancient Sports Collectibles?

One of the most popular Mississippian artifacts today is the discoidal. What is a discoidal? The easiest answer is that a discoidal is a round Mississippian game stone that was used in the ancient Native American game known as chungke or chunkey. No description of discoidals would be complete without some description of the game itself. In 1775, James Adair, in his 18th Century English, wrote a description of the game. The language seems rather difficult to follow in places, but the message seems clear enough:

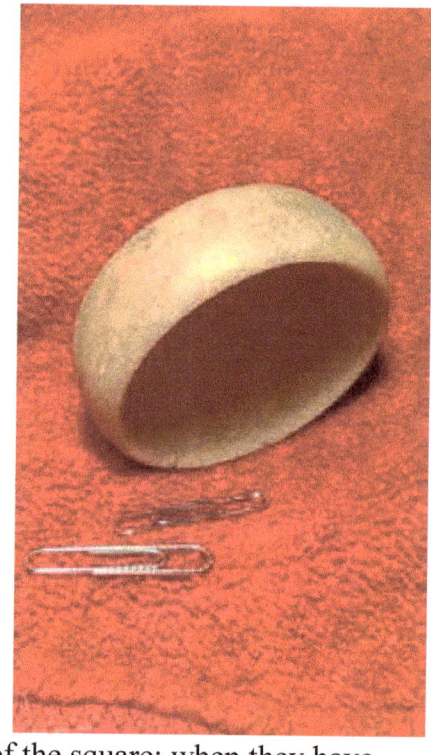

The warriors have another favorite game called chungke, which, with propriety of language, may be called 'running hard labor'. They have near their state-house a square piece of ground well cleaned, and fine sand is carefully strewed over it, when requisite, to promote a swifter motion to what they throw along the surface.

Only one or two on a side play at this ancient game. They have a stone about two fingers broad at the edge, and two spans round; each party has a pole of about eight feet long, smooth and tapering at each end, the points flat. They set off abreast of each other at six yards from the end of the playground; then one of them hurls the stone on its edge, in as direct a line as he can, a considerable distance toward the middle of the other end of the square; when they have run a few yards, each darts his pole anointed with bear's oil, with a proper force, as near as he can guess in proportion to the motion of the stone, that the end may lie close to the stone; when this is the case, the person counts two of the game, and, in proportion to the nearness of the poles to the mark, one is counted, unless by measuring both are found to at an equal distance from the stone. In this manner, the players will keep running most part of the day, at half speed, under the violent heat of the sun, staking their silver ornaments, their nose, finger, and ear rings; their breast, arm and wrist-plates; and even all their wearing apparel, except that which barely covers their middle. All the American Indians are much addicted to this game, which it seems to be of early origin, when their forefathers used diversions as simple as their manners. The hurling-stones they use at present were, time immemorial, rubbed smooth on the rocks, and with prodigious labor, they are kept with the strictest religious care, from one generation to another, and are exempted from being buried with the dead. They belong to the town where they are used, and are carefully preserved.

Discoidals, sometimes called discs, were treasured tribal possessions throughout the Mississippian world. They have been found across all of the great Mississippian lands including the states of eastern Oklahoma, Missouri, Arkansas, Illinois, Indiana,

Discoidals began appearing at late Woodland sites in eastern Missouri and southern Illinois around 700 A.D. By Mississippian times, chunkey's popularity had spread throughout the Mississippian world.

Our grandfather Pop Reiss always told us about his boyhood practice of finding arrowheads on this mound and then tossing them among the spokes of an old wagon wheel that lay nearby. Eventually he gathered all those arrowheads together and stored them in a cigar box in his 1889 house and then in his 1940 house on the homestead. He would show us his collection during the 1950s which further energized our looking for more arrowheads on the mound.

Fast forward to October 2008 when my cousin George Reiss was cleaning out his mom's apartment at Clark Lindsay Village in Urbana, Illinois following her passing on 9/8/2008. He had sold, stored, and given away everything from her place except several large furniture items he was donating to CLV. He gave them the apartment keys and flew back to California. The CLV folks went inside to clean and paint but soon found a box which had been overlooked under one of the furniture items. It was full of arrowheads. They called George who immediately recognized them. He called me and said, "They're yours and will be waiting at the CLV front desk." I was thrilled. Here's what they look like now in my den.

Will, Kayla, Ava, and Blake, looking for arrowheads was a frequent family outing when I was growing up, not just on our Illinois farm, but near our home in Sullivan and elsewhere. I found one on an island in Long Island Sound, New York. I've found them when walking to work at Caterpillar in Mossville. I look forward to showing each of you how to look and where to look.

Love, Granddad

Brooder Houses

Dear Will, Kayla, Ava, and Blake,   August 10, 2015

A brooder house is a structure for raising young chickens or other hobby and commercial fowl from the day they hatch until six weeks later when they no longer need heat and fulltime shelter. Brooders can be as small as a card table and as large as a 50-foot building. They can be heated by electricity, oil, gas, or wood. They can have dirt or concrete floors or can be totally portable. They need ventilation, water, food, and a means of regular cleanup.

The brooder house I remember is in the background of this 1953 picture of us three kids with our grandparents. This brooder house is about 10 feet square, had a concrete floor, and got a little free solar heat from the windows on the right or south side. That kid in the back row is not paying attention.

The inside of this brooder house looked something like the next two pictures where the central shelter or brooder heated the underneath area as well as the whole room. Chicks were free to scurry about for food, water, exploring or to gather together for additional warmth and social networking.

155

Here's a bright-eyed chick, a small kerosene brooder heater, and an old photo when turkeys were raised on the Reiss family farm. That's the 1889 house in the background.

Right in the middle of this picture is the 1838 log cabin on the Reiss farmstead with a brooder house attached to its left or west side. Again, note the south-facing window. Those are white sheets drying on the clothes line further left of that brooder house. Those two buildings were demolished in 1957. There may have been other brooder houses on the home farm over the years but these are the only two I'm aware of.

Will, Kayla, Ava, and Blake. Here are the two hobby brooders I had built for your homes in Chicago and Springfield. We may want to add a little house like the other picture to give your pets some privacy. You could raise chickens, pheasants, ducks, geese, turkeys, quail, carrier pigeons, or maybe even rabbits, mink, chinchillas, guinea pigs, or mongooses. Or is that plural – mongeese or polygoose or polygeese? Let me know when your mom's say it's okay!!!

Love, Granddad

Clay Marbles

Dear Will, Kayla, Ava, and Blake,   November 3, 2014

I remember playing with clay marbles like these when we visited Grandma's farm in the mid-1950s. I thought the colors were really pretty and that there might be lots of history attached to her marbles. Did Grandma buy them for her six grandchildren or were they left over from when her own sons played with them in the 1920s? We'll never know.

This grouping of clay marbles recently sold on eBay for almost $.60 each. There are about 250 clay marbles in my basement museum. I'm sure they sold for less than a penny when new.

A marble is a small spherical toy usually made from clay, glass, steel, plastic, or agate. They vary in size but most commonly are about 1/2 inch to 1 inch in diameter. Marbles can be used for a variety of games called marbles. They are often collected, both for nostalgia and for their aesthetic colors.

Uncle Ken and I used to play marbles on our living room floor in Sullivan, Indiana. We did that for ages about 10 to 14. Our parents had an oriental rug with an elliptical pattern in the center

HOW TO HOLD YOUR MARBLE.

which was our marble ring as compared to outdoor circles drawn in the dirt. Our ellipse was about three feet by five feet where outdoor rings were about three feet in diameter and drawn with a stick. We would "knuckle down" on that elliptical rug ring just like you would around a dirt ring outdoors. There were two ways to hold your "shooter" marble – with the thumb and one finger (at left) or with the thumb and two fingers. Most boys were more accurate with the thumb and two fingers.

Most boys took their marbles to school for grades four through seven or eight. We would play marbles in groups of two to four at recess and sometimes after school. We would play "keepsies" which meant each player got to keep the marbles he knocked out of the circle. Sometimes we would also play "quitsies" which allows any opponent to stop the game without consequence like when recess was over. The most popular marbles were clear colored glass that you could see through and were called "clearsies." Others had a colored eye inside the clear glass and were called "cats eyes." Sometimes we would play with metal ball bearings called "steelies."

Another marble game involved a brick wall rather than a circle in the dirt. Half a dozen or more boys would play at the same time. The game started by placing a single recognizable marble about a foot short of that brick wall or building foundation. There was a line drawn in the dirt about ten feet away that no one could cross. The boys then took turns "lagging" one marble at a time through the air to hit that target marble. Whoever hit it first, got to claim all the marbles that had been lagged which was often 25 or more. Many times our junior high social studies teacher, Bob Spencer, would join in that game. He would usually win because he really aimed for that target marble rather than just being fairly casual about it like most of the boys. He would save his winnings and every month give them to boys at the Gibault School in Terre Haute which was a school for troubled kids. None of us minded losing to our teacher because he was a good person with a good cause.

World championship – The British and World Marbles Championships have been held at Tinsley Green, England every year since 1932. Marbles has been played in Tinsley Green and the surrounding area for centuries. "Time" magazine traces its origins to 1588. Traditionally, the marbles-playing tournament started on Ash Wednesday and lasted until midday on Good Friday, playing after that brought bad luck. More than 20 teams from around the world take part in the championship, each Good Friday. German teams have been successful several times since 2000. The first championship in 1932 was won by Ellen Geary, a young girl from London.

Manufacturing locations – There were a lot of businesses that made marbles in Ohio. One major marble manufacturing company today is Marble King in Paden City, West Virginia which was featured in the television show "Made in America" staring Cliff the mailman from "Cheers." Currently, the world's largest manufacturer of playing marbles is Vacor de Mexico which makes 90 percent of the world's marbles. Over 12 million are produced daily.

I asked Uncle Ken to preview this story. Here is what he wrote: "Great story, Steve. My strongest memory was being intimidated by those who were so much better at marbles than I was. Gary Alexander was one. It was an early education on not betting "all your marbles" which I guess is where that expression came from. I would not play keepsies when the other guys were so much better. There are probably all kinds of life lessons in that game. I was unaware of the Bob Spencer story. Could be that Charles Manson played with some of our marbles since he was at the Gibault school for a while before running away."

Well, kids, I was unaware of Uncle Ken's comment about Charles Manson being at the Gibault School so I Googled that. Turns out Manson is still in a California prison for his involvement in seven Hollywood murders in 1969. Manson was born in 1947 and sent to the Gibault School at age 12 for stealing. That makes it 1959 when I was in grade 9 and past the marbles stage. So maybe he did play with some of our marbles!!!

I asked John Hays to preview this story. He was a church friend, neighbor three blocks away, and four years ahead of me in public school. Our parents were good friends. Grand DD, Aunt Carol, and I had dinner with John in Honolulu in January 2010 where we talked about marbles among other things. First time I had seen him in 50 years. Here's what John wrote:

"I do have a marbles memory. Jerry Bennett, who was the best marble player, always seemed to have an inexhaustible supply of "steelies." They were heavy ball bearings which most of us considered unfair (mostly because we did not have them). The

Manson story which you're remembering is my wife Susan's incredible story about their school bus. When her family moved from Shelburn and Sullivan to California (after her dad's factory burned to the ground), they bought a school bus - a Wayne brand, from Wayne County, Indiana. It worked fine, and when they got to California it was superfluous, and very soon after advertising it, they had a visit from a couple of women who, we would later learn, were part of the Manson "family." They came back and bought it for cash, and it must have been "the Manson bus" for several years. Doesn't have anything to do with marbles, but it is an interesting anecdote."

I tried to find Bob Spencer to get his input as well. Sadly, I learned he had recently died at age 84 on 7/26/2014 leaving a wife, two sons, two daughters, and seven grandchildren.

Will, Kayla, Ava, and Blake, someday I'll teach all of you and your dads how to play marbles. It takes some practice to develop your shooting technique but after that, it's a lot of fun. Plus you get to keep your winnings, trade marbles with friends, and eventually write stories to your grandchildren about olden times. Check out these paintings by Norman Rockwell that were covers for the "Saturday Evening Post" magazine in 1925 and 1939. My favorite is on the left where the girl is winning all the marbles.

Love, Granddad

Smithton Sportsmen's Club

Dear Will, Kayla, Ava, and Blake,   August 17, 2015

These two entries from July 1951 appear in your great great grandmother Katie Reiss' daily diary which is also in book form as <u>Quilter, Granger, Grandma, Matriarch</u>. These are the initial meetings between the Smithton Sportsmen's Club members and the extended Reiss family to discuss a long term lease of 40 acres on the east edge of the Reiss Farm where the Sportsmen's would eventually build three lakes and a clubhouse for their meetings and recreation.

> Mon 16 – Fair hot. Franklin & Gerry and boys & I were at Belleville to meet with the Sportsmen's Club & Otis Guyman lawyer.

> Tues 17 – Fair hot. Franklin, Gerry, George, Richard, June Ann and I were on the boat excursion. In evening the Sportsman Club and Bill & Franklin met here.

After the next picture are the suggested agenda and lease details which my uncle Frank Reiss prepared for that meeting. He was a professor of agricultural economics at the University of Illinois and specialized in farm leasing.

Here's what the finished project looked like in 1980 with a clubhouse in the bottom center, first lake just north of it, second lake at the left, and third lake in the upper right. Over the last 60 years our family has enjoyed lots of fishing, ice skating, walks, persimmons, photography, horseshoes, and reunions on these 40 acres. Memorials to Frank and Gerry Reiss are in the trees to the right of the clubhouse overlooking the first lake.

Suggested Addenda to Lease to Smithton Sportsmen's Club

1. The area under lease shall be increased to include all land in the SW ¼ of the NW ¼ of Section 8, Twp. 2S, R 8W except for approximately 4 acres of bottom land on either side of the branch running through the northwest corner of the tract.

2. The terms of the original lease shall apply to this extended area except for provisions stated in the following clauses.

3. All tillable land on the tract (estimated to be 10 acres) may be put to such use as is in harmony with the objectives of the lessee provided that it shall be kept as tillable land and under good husbandry and soil conserving practices.

4. The lessee agrees to keep any fence rows free of undesirable growth, including the border between any multi-flora fence and the public roads.

5. Rent for the extended area shall be paid annually by the lessee to the lessors as follows: A lump sum of ten dollars ($10.00) plus a one-third share of any grain, hay or seed crop harvested, plus a cash rent per acre on tillable land not harvested for grain, hay or seed equal to the value of 2.5 bushels of wheat at the average price for the year previous. The average price shall be the price received by Illinois farmers as determined and published by the Illinois Cooperative Crop Reporting Service.

6. The lessors agree to furnish agricultural limestone for the tillable land according to needs indicated by soil tests. The lessees shall furnish all other fertilizer materials and all labor and expenses in growing and harvesting crops on the tillable land.

An agreement was eventually reached pretty much along the lines proposed by Uncle Frank. It exists like this today except that rent is now a dollar figure instead of a formula. It's about $1600 per year with an automatic 1% annual increase. Our objective is to maintain outstanding two-way relationships rather than maximize the income. The Sportsmen's and the Reiss family have been great friends for 64 years and one month since the initial meetings.

The next two photos are from 1951 with the first lake under construction.

Then there are two photos from 1952 with Uncle Bill offering a boat ride for June Ann, George, and Richard. The other is the entrance from Knab Road.

The frozen lake picture is from 1953 and shows George, Richard, Ken, and yours truly trying to stand up.

The two fishing pictures are from 1954 with George and Richard testing their patience.

The last two pictures are the clubhouse in 1954 and the Frank/Gerry Reiss Memorial in 2013.

Will, Kayla, Ava, and Blake, isn't this a great story. How did you like all those old pictures? We'll have to take lots of our own pictures on future visits. The Sportsmen's gave me a key to their clubhouse but still we should call ahead to make sure our visits are known and don't conflict with any of their programs. Below is a chart the Sportsmen's made of their grounds. And following that is a detailed history of those 40 acres going all the way back to August 15, 1836 when a land speculator named Thomas Houghan first bought it from the Federal Government. That was 179 years ago this past Saturday. My grandparents bought this land on October 11, 1917 which is almost 100 years ago. They are the 13th owners!!!

Love, Granddad

Round Slingshots in 1957

Dear Will, Kayla, Ava, and Blake,   January 12, 2015

Here's the Reiss Cousins Army at Christmas 1957. On the left are my brother Ken and me and on the right are my cousins Richard and George from Urbana, IL. Our weapons of choice (actually they were gifts) were round frame slingshots. Ammunition was clay pellets which exploded on impact and left a really neat grey circular mark kinda like a bullet hole without the hole. You see them now sometimes as small decals on cars. We were at the Reiss farm for the holidays. Don't you think your dad/uncle Grant looks totally like my brother Ken.

In the garage at back is our 1956 DeSoto which Chrysler discontinued after 1961. The other half of that building was Pop's grain storage and feed grinding for his chickens. It always smelled "farmy" inside partially due to lots of cobwebs and a few mice.

Here's what our ammo looked like except it was grey instead of red. We ran out of ammo within an hour and resorted to rocks from the gravel driveway in the back. They could do a lot more damage than a clay pellet.

Here is the round frame slingshot. That small site at the top is for aiming but of course you had to allow for wind and gravity if your target was very far away. We had a lot of fun.

169

A few years later my Stephenson grandfather Andrew taught my brother and me how to make and use slings like the David and Goliath story in 1 Samuel 17 in the Old Testament. Here's what Google says about slings: A **sling** is a projectile weapon typicxally used to throw a blunt projectile such as a stone, clay, or lead "sling-bullet." It is also known as the **shepherd's sling**.

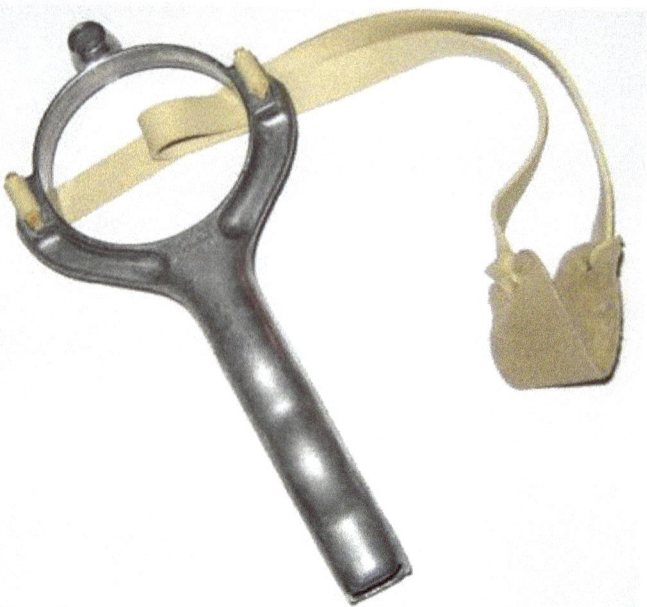

A sling has a small cradle or *pouch* in the middle of two lengths of cord. The *sling stone* is placed in the pouch. The middle finger or thumb is placed through a loop on the end of one cord, and a tab at the end of the other cord is placed between the thumb and forefinger. The sling is swung in an arc, and the tab released at a precise moment. This frees the projectile to fly to the target. The sling essentially works by extending the length of a human arm, thus allowing stones to be thrown much farther than they could be by hand.

The sling is inexpensive and easy to build. It has historically been used for hunting game and in combat. Film exists of Spanish Civil War combatants using slings to throw grenades over buildings into enemy positions on the opposite street. Today the sling interests sportsmen as a wilderness survival tool and as an improved weapon.

Granddad made our slings so the loop end tied around our wrist. Our center pouch was made of scrap leather. It was fairly easy to use our slings but it took a lot of practice to send your projectile in the right direction. I'm impressed by what David accomplished against Goliath.

Will, Kayla, Ava, and Blake, here's a question. If a sling is roughly twice as long as a person's arm, could a professional baseball pitcher who can throw a strike at 100 miles an hour use a sling to "throw" a ball at 200 miles an hour? Whadoyathink? The answer is at https://submissions.scholasticahq.com/supporting_files/7302/attachment_versions/7312 thanks to cousin George's research. Anyway, I'm looking forward to helping each of you make a slingshot from a forked tree branch. We'll carve your initials into the handle. When my brother and I made slingshots, the rubber straps were scrap catheters which had been rejected by the American Latex factory in our town. How's that for ingenuity but honestly we didn't know what they were at our ages. Some day I'll also help you graduate to homemade slings.

Love, Granddad

Adam Reiss Log Cabin Demolished in 1957

Dear Will, Kayla, Ava, and Blake,   August 17, 2015

One of my books is titled, <u>Highlights of 40 Years of Diaries by Franklin J. Reiss</u>. It includes 95,000 words or 2.3% of the 4.2 million words Frank wrote in his daily diaries from 1951 to 1991. Frank was my dad's next older brother and a very intelligent man. He made frequent visits to the home farm where he was born to see his parents and also as manager for about 25 years. He took lots of pictures including several of this cabin.

These are the only diary entries in 40 years which mention this cabin –

"**3/1/1957** – Another beautiful day at the home farm. George and I drove to Belleville to pick up Dr. Lawson Culver, Extension Forester, for a visit to our plantings of pine trees. It was a very successful day. Culver recommended delaying thinning for 3 or 4 years. The trees should be pruned of dead branches now, however."

"I made final decisions with Lavern to go ahead on the new garage. George and I walked to the new pond. It is within 18 inches of full. They had 3" of rain last week. Bill & Nita came out in the evening. So did Uncle John and Ella."

"**4/20/1957** – Very warm last night at the home farm. Gerry, Richard, & I took a walk in the woods. Irwin and family came from Sullivan in mid-afternoon. Will & Rose and Bill & Nita, June & Jim came for dinner."

"Lavern came over to work on the new lease. I asked Irv to sit in, but he excused himself. He feels, I think, that I have gone contrary to his judgment on the new garage. Lavern is putting in a lot of work on cleaning up the farm. We have to give him some things he wants. Lavern told me Ted Klein was moving to the Wirth farm because he was getting no cooperation from his landlord, Bill Klein."

To make way for a new concrete block garage, Frank and Lavern unilaterally agreed to demolish this log cabin. I can easily agree with "cleaning up the farm" but not with destroying such a significant family structure. It contained tons of Reiss DNA. Here is a summary –

- Built by Adam Reiss in the fall of 1838 from logs he felled and dragged from the nearby woods.

- Place where Adam's son John was born on December 11, 1838 and where his wife Anna Maria died that same day in childbirth.

- Adam hosted Catholic church services in this cabin and/or the adjacent log granary in 1839/40.

- Adam's church is probably where/how he met Margaret Basler who became his second wife on September 10, 1840. Maybe they were married in this log cabin.

- Five children were born to Adam and Margaret in this cabin – Frank in 1841, Charles in 1843, Martin in 1845, Catharine in 1847, and Barbara (stillborn) in 1849.

- This cabin is where Adam Reiss died of cholera on May 23, 1849.

- This cabin was home for Margaret Basler Reiss and her second husband Conrad Ebert following their marriage on April 2, 1850.

- Three daughters were born to Margaret and Conrad in this cabin – Anna Maria in 1851, Louisa in 1853, and Margaret in 1856. This is where their first daughter died.

- This cabin was home for Frank Reiss and his wife Anna Sybilla Feder following their wedding on April 9, 1866 until 1889 when they built a new modern home next door.

- Ten children were born to Frank and Anna Sybilla in this cabin – Charles in 1867, Adam in 1869, Catharine in 1871, George in 1873, Anna in 1875, John in 1877, Henry in 1880, Louis in 1882, Louisa in 1884, and Elizabeth in 1888. Four of these ten children died here – Catharine in 1872, Charles and Adam both in November 1874, and Elizabeth in 1889.

- This cabin was the artwork logo for the Reiss Reunion in 1984 celebrating 150 years since Adam Reiss bought his first farm.

This cabin is where 19 of our relatives were born, where 8 died, where 30 lived, and where church has held. I think a more appropriate plan from those 1957 family meetings would have been something like this – You know, folks, we have something really significant in this cabin. We can always tear it down at a later date, if desired. We can build a new garage in several alternate locations. Why not develop a plan which preserves this cabin for another 100 years for generations to come and as a tribute to the man who started it all – Adam Reiss.

Will, Kayla, Ava, and Blake, this story was very difficult for me to write because I didn't walk in the shoes of the men who debated this cabin's future in 1957. I have to respect their thought process and priorities back then even if I disagree now. At the same time this awkward history makes me even more determined to save the remaining log granary which was also built in 1838 by the strong hands of our patriarch, Adam Reiss.

Love, Granddad

Here's Pop cutting up the log cabin where he was born in 1873. Those timbers still look pretty good to me. Note for Model T Ford in the background.

Feather Blankets

Dear Will, Kayla, Ava, and Blake,   November 23, 2015

If you must resort to sleeping at night, the most comfortable way to do that is under a feather blanket. It also helps greatly if the outside temps are below freezing and that you're upstairs at Grandma and Pop's farmhouse. Uncle Ken and I usually shared the double iron bed in their upstairs northeast corner. But sometimes when the house was full of relatives, Ken and I were on the opposite southwest corner with a feather blanket. The only problem with that second bed is that it was across from the one Uncle Frank and Aunt Gerry shared. Her snore often exceeded the 85 decibels threshold above which the Occupational Safety and Health Act requires hearing protection. Really loud!!!

Here's what an iron bed with a feather blanket looks like. Grandma's iron beds weren't this fancy but you can get the idea.

I Googled "feather blanket" and learned that they are also called duvet, continental quilt, or comforter. In some cultures, sleepers lay on top of one feather blanket and under a second one. Besides feathers, they can be filled with wool, silk, or synthetics. They often have a removable outer cover so it can be laundered instead of the whole thing. A cloth bag full of wet feathers would take forever to dry.

In 1985 three of us businessmen were in Baden, Switzerland visiting Brown Boveri Corp. on turbochargers for a new diesel engine Caterpillar was developing. The two engineers with me were very pleased with their technology. My objective as the purchasing guy was to get them to private label their turbos with just our Caterpillar name rather than their company name. That's so we could control the aftermarket parts business. BBC was founded in 1891 and our project was the first time in their company history where they agreed to private labeling. Anyway, we stayed in their company hotel for three nights. There were no screens on the windows because there were no bugs. I remember their feather blankets which were sometimes too warm. Grandma Reiss' heritage was Swiss so it was nice to enjoy that ongoing feather blanket connection.

In 2007 Grand DD and I were in Mongolia for a week building houses with Habitat for Humanity. They had arranged our lodging which turned out to be a very clean but also very basic one-star hotel. The beds were so hard that we resorted to sleeping on top of our feather blankets rather than under them. I was the leader of our nine-person team so at breakfast on day 2, I suggesting making a list of "negatives" that we would laugh about six months later. Very quickly our list also included missing shower curtains, questionable hot water, and an unfriendly restaurant waitress we called "Smiley." Well, guess what, we were laughing about our list of negatives within 30 minutes. It was my best ever job of spinning lemons into lemonade and it all started with feather blankets.

174

This past October Grand DD and I visited a silk store in Shanghai, China. They had a small factory exhibit on silk worm technology which was interesting. They explained that a significant percentage of silk worm cocoons are doubles or misshapen such that they cannot be unwound into filaments. Those are processed in a different fashion to save the silk exterior which then becomes stuffing for duvets. They are lighter weight and just as comfortable as old fashioned feather blankets. So your choice is either chickens or worms to keep you warm at night.

Will, Kayla, Ava, and Blake, I'm sorry to say we don't have any authentic feather blankets in our home. What we'll have to do, especially when sleeping overnight in our tree house, is to unzip two sleeping bags. One goes under and one goes over. Will, his dad, and I did that last year and without a tent. That night we heard crickets, tree frogs, two kinds of owls, and a deer walking underneath. It was awesome. Who's next?

Love, Granddad

The Old Corn Crib

Dear Will, Kayla, Ava, and Blake,   January 19, 2015

Here's Lavern Lang emptying the old corn crib which was across from the old barn. The barn dates from about 1920 but the corn crib in the background of this 1955 picture may date from well before the 1880s. It sat on a stone foundation just like the 1838 log granary still does today. It was made of rough sawn native oak which was nailed vertically with narrow gaps to allow air circulation but not wide enough to allow mice to help themselves. Lavern is removing ear corn from the crib and putting it into the orange shelling machine which sends seeds to his truck and

cobs and husks to the old wagon with a percentage of that ending up on the ground.

Illinois law back then required that all pickup trucks have the owner's name, address, and phone number on both doors. I've had five pickups over the years and there were times when I had a magnetic door sign even as a non-business city guy before the law was changed.

In 1956 a 1,000-bushel grain bin was added to store shelled corn. More were added in later years, all to the north of the 1889 house. Here's Lavern in 1958 loading that bin with very little help from my cousin George Reiss who is working hard stabilizing the wagon.

Here's a 1960 picture of a new crib for storing ear corn next to that still newer grain bin for storing loose corn seeds. Newest of all is that green wagon which may be holding corn for the first time. Lavern had a cattle operation so he needed both storage systems.

Will, Kayla, Ava, and Blake, here's your great grandfather Irv Reiss talking farming with Lavern in 1958. They are first cousins because their two mothers were Luetzelschwab sisters, Katie born in 1890 and Edna born in 1905. Dad was born in 1917 and Lavern in 1928. A lot of people have told me that I look like my dad. I take that as a compliment.

Love, Granddad

Pop's Grindstone Sharpening Wheel

Dear Will, Kayla, Ava, and Blake,   July 20, 2015

This tattooed young man wanted to grind an old railroad spike into a throwing knife. He could use that overhead can which held water to keep his work piece cool. The wheel could rotate in either direction depending on which way you initially pushed it by hand to get it started. Only problem for our young operator was that he couldn't reach the foot pedals to keep the wheel in motion. He also needs eye protection.

I have fond memories of sharpening my pocket knife on Pop's wheel. My brother and I would have contests on who could pedal the fastest. These wheels were outstanding for sharpening axes, hatchets, splitting wedges, garden hoes, stakes to play horseshoes, making bolts shorter, and just about anything you wanted. On the next page is an advertisement from 1910 by a company in Aurora, Illinois. We don't know the brand name of Pop's wheel.

I typed "pedal grinder" into eBay and got a dozen hits. Most were $150 to $250 but one was $850 and had 46 people watching. They also advertised "free shipping" which may have been a big perk. There was another internet story where a Boy Scout camp was looking for someone to donate their old wheel so the boys could have some unique fun and learn more about farm times. Will, Kayla, Ava, and Blake, I don't want you to grow up too quickly because I enjoy you all so much just as you are. But if you do happen to grow taller such that your legs can reach these pedals, then we'll have fun sharpening and grinding something. But maybe not your moms' Cutco kitchen knives.

Love, Granddad

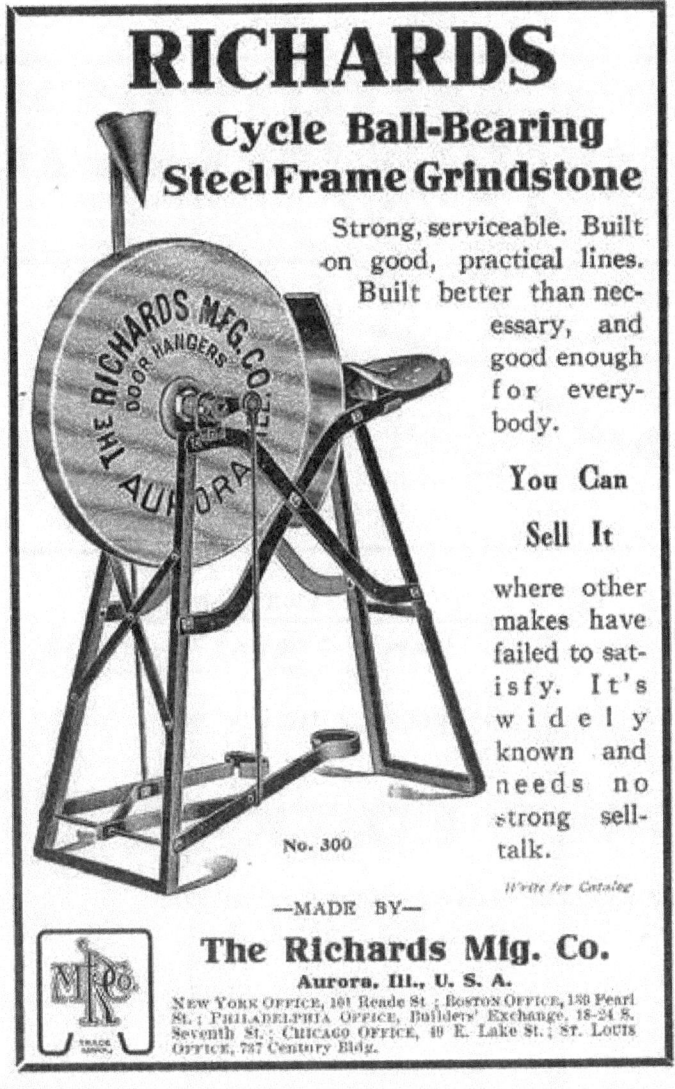

179

St. Louis Cardinals Baseball

Dear Will, Kayla, Ava, and Blake,   April 20, 2015

Are you sports "fans" yet? Do you realize that word comes from "fanatic" or "fanatical?" Do you know the Chicago Cubs hold the world record for the most number of years without a world championship in any sport, not just baseball? They have not won the World Series since 1908. That's over a hundred years!!! How bad is that???

I remember going to my first professional baseball game. It was in St. Louis about 1954. They were hosting the Pittsburg Pirates. I was age 9 or 10. Here's the stadium whose name had been Sportsman's Park. It was changed to Busch Stadium in 1953 when Anheuser-Busch bought the St. Louis Cardinals Baseball Team. Our seats were in right field under the overhang.

That game progressed without a lot of action despite all the flag waving and cheers by a loud and slightly obnoxious Pittsburg fan right in front of us.

In the bottom of the ninth inning, the score was tied at 1 to 1 and the Cardinals were up as the home team. The first two batters grounded out before left-handed Stan "The Man" Musial came to bat. At that point, the Pittsburg fan in front of us stood up and left. He said, "I'm going out to catch Stan's home run on Grand Avenue." Pretty soon Musial had a full count of 3 balls and 2 strikes. Well, guess what, the next pitch was just what he wanted and he knocked it high over our heads and outside the park onto Grand Avenue. I doubt that Pittsburg fan ended up with the ball but it makes a nice story.

Sportsman's Park / Busch Stadium was replaced early in the 1966 season by Busch Memorial Stadium, during which time much was made of baseball having been played on the old site for more than a century. A helicopter carried home plate to the new Busch Memorial Stadium after the final Sportsman's Park game on May 8, 1966.

We went to several more games in that new stadium which was really neat with its full round architectural design. The Gateway Arch was nearby and it was a great location. My favorite time there was twenty years ago on March 25, 1995 when 40 boys and dads from our Boy Scout Troop 88 camped overnight in center field. I just made a note to myself to write that story as a future Granddad's Mondays.

But that beautiful stadium was replaced in 2006 with the current Busch Stadium. I remember going there for a game with you, Will, your parents, and Grand DD. It was the day the Cardinal players received their World Series championship rings from the previous season. All the visitors in the stands received awesome replicas of that championship ring. All that is in my Granddad's Mondays story of April 16, 2012.

As I write this story, Las Vegas has posted odds for the 2015 baseball season. They have the St. Louis Cardinals, the Chicago Cubs, the Boston Red Sox, and the Seattle Mariners all at 14 to 1 odds to win the World Series. That's the best the Cubs have looked in decades so this might be their year.

Will, Kayla, Ava, and Blake, let's do this. First of all, I strongly encourage you to root for the Cardinals since historically they have proven to be the better team. But it's okay if you want to root for the Cubs to just kinda suck up to your dads so they will let you stay up late. However, if the Cubs and the Cardinals both make the playoffs, then you simply have to embrace the Cards out of common sense and family tradition. Let's make this a little more exciting. I'll give you each a $100 bill if the Cubs win the World Series but you have to spend it in April 2016 going to the Cubs home game where their rings are awarded and all visitors receive replica rings. Whaduyasay?

Love, Granddad

Our Grapevine Swing

Dear Will, Kayla, Ava, and Blake,   April 14, 2014

Here is the extended Reiss family on the Friday after Thanksgiving in 1954 working off a big meal from the day before. The photo is by Frank Reiss. The head scarf ladies are Gerry Reiss at center and Grandma Katie Reiss at the lower right. George Reiss is on the swing, Ken Reiss has already swung across, Richard Reiss and I are next in line. Location is the east side of the woods lane halfway from the homestead to the mailbox on the Reiss family farm.

The only negative about making a grapevine swing is that you have to cut the grapevine off near ground level so it's free to swing out from a hillside or across a creek like this picture. That cutting kinda kills the vine such that it will only last another two or three years for safe swinging.

That cutting also stops the vine from making hundreds of pea-size grapes like this picture. These little grapes are quite small so it takes a lot to make a dozen. On top of that they are mostly skin and seeds such that you can't munch on them like the seedless kind your moms bring home from Krogers. These wild grapes however are good for making old fashioned wild grape jelly. Grapes ripen in late August. Get them ahead of the birds. Here is the recipe.

3 lbs wild grapes, stemmed
3 cups water
4 1/2 cups sugar. That's a lot of sugar to look into using honey.
1 (85 ml) package liquid pectin

Directions:
- In large saucepan, crush grapes with potato masher; pour in water and bring to boil.
- Reduce heat and simmer, covered, for 10 minutes or until fruit is very soft.
- Transfer to jelly bag or colander lined with a double thickness of fine cheesecloth and let drip overnight.
- Measure juice (you should have 3 cups) into a large heavy saucepan; stir in sugar.
- Bring to boil over high heat, stirring constantly.
- Stir in pectin.
- Return to full boil and boil hard for one minute, stirring constantly.
- Remove from heat and skim off foam with a metal spoon.
- Pour into sterilized jars, leaving 1/8 inch headspace.

Practicalities:
- Don't de-stem the grapes. It takes too much time and your fingers get all blue. Just pick out the unripe grapes and most of the spiders.
- Don't let your first slurry drip overnight. Just use that same potato masher to gently push the liquid through the cheesecloth and continue with the directions.
- That foam during the second and third boilings can be eliminated with a pinch of butter to break the surface tension. We know that from making maple syrup.
- If you made only enough jelly for one or two jars, keep it in the fridge for use over the next few months rather than messing with a water bath canning process.
- If even this practicalized jelly-making process sounds like too much work, make grape wine instead of grape jelly!!!

One question I try to answer when I see real old and loose grapevines is how they grew so high without being attached to anything closer to the ground. There might be 20 feet before their smaller tentacles attach to nearby tree canopies. I think the answer is that both the vine and the tree started out small and grew up together. Maybe the tree died and rotted away.

Will and Ava, one time your dad and I sawed through a poison ivy vine that had grown up a white oak tree in our front yard. We counted the growth rings and found there were 35 that were each less than 1/16th of an inch thick. That vine was about 1.5 inches in diameter. Those numbers would also apply to grape vines.

Will, Kayla, Ava, and Blake, we have lots of grapevines in our yard for harvesting grapes and making jelly. I don't recall any, however, that are on a hillside for making a swing. Plus I'm not real keen about cutting them off because that would make the grapevine sad. We'll make rope swings on those hillsides instead. Check out the grapevine swing poem on the next page.

Love, Granddad

Here's a poem from 1892 by Samuel Minturn Peck from his book of poems called <u>Rings and Love-Knots</u>. He was Alabama's first poet laureate. It's written from a southern perspective about plantations and cotton but it does a good job expressing the fun and unique memories of swinging on a grapevine swing.

Swinging on a Grapevine Swing

When I was a boy on the old plantation,
Down by the deep bayou -
The fairest spot of all creation
Under the arching blue -
When the wind came over the cotton and corn,
To the long, slim loop I'd spring
With brown feet bare, and a hat-brim torn,
And swing in the grapevine swing.

Swinging in the grapevine swing,
Laughing where the wild birds sing,
I dream and sigh
For the days gone by,
Swinging in the grapevine swing.

Out o'er the water lilies bonny and bright
Back to the moss-green trees;
I shouted and laughed with a heart as light
As a wild rose tossed by the breeze.
The mocking bird joined in my reckless glee;
I longed for no angel's wing;
I was just as near heaven as I wanted to be
Swinging in the grapevine swing.

Swinging in the grapevine swing,
Laughing where the wild birds sing -
Oh, to be a boy
With a heart full of joy,
Swinging in the grapevine swing!

I'm weary at noon, I'm weary at night,
I'm fretted and sore of heart,
And care is sowing my locks with white
As I wend through the fevered mart.
I'm tired of the world with its pride and pomp,
And fame seems a worthless thing.
I'd barter it all for one day's romp,
And a swing in the grapevine swing.

Swinging in the grapevine swing,
Laughing where the wild birds sing -
I would I were away
From the world today,
Swinging in the grapevine swing.

Indian Ball

Dear Will, Kayla, Ava, and Blake,   July 15, 2013

How do you play baseball with just five cousins and three cows? Well, you play a version called Indian Ball. Here's my cousin Richard Reiss at bat and my sister Mary Kay cheerleading. In the field are my brother Ken, cousin George Reiss, and myself. I don't know the names of the cows.

Indian ballgames have no pitchers or infielders. Instead the batter tosses the ball in the air and then hits it as far as possible. If an outfielder catches the ball in the air, he is the next batter. If the outfielder retrieves the ball from the ground, he throws it toward the batter who has laid his bat on the ground perpendicular to the throw. If that throw hits the bat on the ground, that thrower is the next batter. If it misses, the same batter hits another ball toward the outfield. And so it goes on an on with no one keeping score. The game is over whenever Grandma calls everyone to lunch or supper. This picture was taken on the Reiss Family Farm in St. Clair County, Illinois in 1958.

The size of the field you need is determined by the size of the kids. So, Will, Kayla, Ava, and Blake, your yards and ours are very adequate for the next few years. After that we'll have to walk to the soccer field or parking field at the German American Society festival grounds around the corner on Hickory Grove Road. Unfortunately there are no cows in those fields which removes the excitement and challenge of watching out for cow pies on the ground!!!

Love, Granddad

Cedar Christmas Tree (1953)

Dear Will, Kayla, Ava, and Blake,   December 17, 2012

This is a cedar tree growing in our front yard next to the street. It's a volunteer meaning it came up by itself. It probably sprouted from a seed dropped there by a bird. It's about 4' tall now. Each December I decorate it with red and silver balls so folks driving past can enjoy a Christmas tree in the wild. But there is another reason for my decorations.

Starting in 1948 my family of five always celebrated Christmas at my Reiss grandparent's home on the family farm twelve miles south of Belleville, Illinois. My parents (your great grandparents) would load us three kids in the station wagon along with all our suitcases, Christmas gifts, two cats, and a parakeet in a cage and drive 186 miles from Sullivan, Indiana to the farm.

We kids, from as young as I can remember, would help our grandma Katie decorate a cedar Christmas tree that she had cut from the pasture where it had grown up as a volunteer. They didn't have any wild pine trees, so she always used a cedar tree. Plus it was free, unlike going into Millstadt or Smithton to buy a normal pine tree. Anyway, those cedar trees were always very scratchy to decorate. We would wear long sleeve shirts but still our hands would get all scratched up. Plus hanging tinsel icicles was difficult because the branches were all close together as you can see. Cedar trees are a challenge.

We celebrated Christmas on the home farm for about 20 years beginning in 1948. We would go to St. Paul UCC Church in Floraville which was always special. My grandfather (we called him Pop) died in 1964 and then my grandmother started spending winters and Christmases with her son Frank in Urbana.

186

Grand DD and I got married in 1971 so we would spend Christmas Eve in Peoria with her relatives and then drive 217 miles on Christmas Day to Sullivan, Indiana to spend the holiday with my parents. We never missed a year except 1987 – 1992 when we lived in South Korea and Hong Kong. My dad died in 2007 and my mom in 2010 so we no longer make those trips.

I remember we bought a new 1976 Datsun station wagon but didn't realize until a few days later that it had only an 8-gallon gas tank. Since we got only 20 miles to the gallon, we had to fill up every 150 miles. So, those Christmas Day trips meant that we had to find a gas station that was open on the holiday. There was usually one in Urbana.

Will, Kayla, Ava, and Blake, being with family for Christmas is a big deal. Decorating a scratchy cedar tree is also a big deal because it's a reminder of grand times with my grandparents. Here is what our tree looks like today. ==Maybe you two can help decorate our cedar tree next year and appreciate a few scratches as a unique memory.==

Love, Granddad

187

Cisterns and Saturday Night Baths

Dear Will, Kayla, Ava, and Blake,   December 15, 2014

Maybe it's obvious but there is normally no city water when you live on a farm. It's just too far away and too expensive to lay water pipes. Farmers have several options – draw water from a nearby lake or stream, dig a well to reach underground water, dig a cistern to save rainwater from roof gutters, or stand in the rain with their mouths open.

Here are Grandma Katie's diary notes from 1953 when a new cistern was dug on the north side of their farmhouse. They already had a well and a cistern on the south side from when the house was built in 1940. Jakie and Johnny are Grandma's brothers Jacob and John Luetzelschwab. Lavern is the new tenant on the Reiss farm and Henry is his dad. George is Katie's husband and Bill is their son. Henry's wife is Katie's sister Edna so all of these people are relatives except Raymond who is a neighbor.

If this new cistern was 10 feet in diameter and 6 feet deep, that would be 471 cubic feet or 3,500 gallons of water. The house is 28 by 32 feet so with 1-foot eaves, the roof area is 1,020 square feet. That means it would take 41" of rain to fill the cistern. Average annual Illinois rainfall is 48" in the south to 32" in the north. A more likely scenario is that the cistern was maybe 8 feet in diameter and 4 feet deep which means it would fill on just 18 inches of rain. I called Lavern who dug the cistern and he said it was about 8 feet in diameter and 10 feet deep so it would take 45" of rain. In other words, it was probably never full, especially when rainwater was also diverted to the cistern on the south side of the house.

April 1953

Fri 17 – Jakie brought all the bricks for our new cistern.

June 1953

Mon 1 – Johnny & Jakie came to start on the cistern.

Tues 2 – Henry & Lavern Lang helped ½ day with the cistern. Raymond helped in the afternoon.

Wed 3 – Johnny, Jakie and Geo & I worked on the cistern.

Thurs 4 – Langs, Jakie & Johnny all worked on our cistern. All dug and started to lay bricks.

Fri 5 – Langs, Jakie & Johnny bricked the cistern today.

Mon 8 – Johnny & Jakie made the concrete slab for the cistern top.

Mon 15 – Lang's, Jakie & Johnny came and plastered the cistern & laid the slab on top.

Tues 16 – Johnny & Jakie finished the spouting for cistern.

July 1953

Sat 18 – Bill & Johnny set up our water system.

Rainwater is naturally "soft" because is has not touched the ground where it could absorb calcium and other elements which make it "hard." Hard water tastes "normal" but soft water is better for laundry and baths because it makes soap bubbles faster, easier, and bigger.

Here's my cousin George Reiss in 1945 taking a bath in cistern water that sat in this tub all day so it could be warmed by the sun. That means this is the south cistern which is in the sun instead of the new north cistern which is in the house shadow. I remember taking lots of these cistern baths in the 1950s. The real challenge was to figure out which of us three kids went first because the same water was used for all. Maybe we flipped a coin or maybe whoever was dirtiest always went last.

Will, Kayla, Ava, and Blake, this coming summer we'll put our laundry tub on our back deck and let you fill it from the garden hose. There is lots of privacy there just like on Pop and Katie's farm so you four can take Saturday night baths. We'll let you figure out who goes first. Whaduyasay?

Love, Granddad

Pop's Farm Scale

Dear Will, Kayla, Ava, and Blake,

April 6, 2015

This small platform scale belonged to my grandfather George "Pop" Reiss. He used it on the home farm several times a week for decades to weigh corn, wheat, and other grains before and/or after grinding. He also weighed to maintain the blend ratio of various grains and other ingredients like ground oyster shells in preparing feed for his chickens. Young chicks took one kind of food mix and mature hens took another. The oyster shells were a source of calcium to build strong egg shells. He was also known to weigh grandchildren on several occasions.

The brass beam on this scale is marked "U. S. Standard" which I think that means that it meets certain federal standards for accuracy rather than being a brand name. I've seen "U. S. Standard" on other small platform scales and on large commercial pitless platform scales made by Fairbanks, Howe, Chicago Scale, and others.

Pop's scale is on display in my log cabin. You can see the logs and chinking in the background. The floor is sycamore. The scale can weigh up to 700 pounds. There is a steel rod which links the lower central platform to the brass beam above just left of the square slide for every 100 pounds.

Will, Kayla, Ava, and Blake, the picture on the next page is my collection of brass beams in our basement museum. They were all purchased at antique shops from someone who had disassembled a non-functioning wooden scale which had not been properly maintained against the weather. The small ones on the left and top right came from scales like Pop's. The larger ones on the floor and bottom right came from pitless platform scales.

Love, Granddad

Pop's Bucksaw

Dear Will, Kayla, Ava, and Blake,   March 2, 2015

This is the bucksaw that my grandfather George "Pop" Reiss used forever and then some to cut kindling for Grandma's kitchen stove. He also cut wood for the stove in his 1838 log cabin, the furnace in his 1889 house, and the furnace in his 1940 house before the latter two were converted to propane and oil. You don't heat your house year-round but you do have to cook almost every day which means continual firewood. We could have the lower right handle of this saw tested for his sweat DNA.

Tightening that turnbuckle on top adds tension to the blade across the bottom so that it cuts smoothly both pulling and pushing. The long lower handle is for one-man sawing. A second person like a grandchild could grab onto the other side and help cut more firewood while Grandma was in the kitchen baking cookies over a fire with the wood that was cut yesterday. That's kinda like a firewood-to-cookie assembly line, don't ya think?

A sawhorse was normally used to hold the wood that was being cut. Here is a sketch of what the whole setup looked like.

A **Bucksaw** is a hand saw generally used to cut logs or firewood to length (bucking). It usually has a metal frame ("H" or "C"-shaped) and a removable blade with coarse teeth held in tension by the frame. Lightweight portable or foldable models used for camping or back-packing are also available. It is often referred to as a bow saw in the North American hardware market, but that term traditionally refers to a different type of saw with a wooden frame.

192

Will, Kayla, Ava, and Blake, here's a poem for the occasion. I remember Pop cutting kindling for Grandma's kitchen stove well into his late 80s. He died at age 91. Keeping the kitchen supplied with kindling helped with his fitness and with his sense of contribution.

Love, Granddad

Shsh, Zzzzz; Shh, Zzzzz:
from behind the stone house the hissing
of the bucksaw's blade in rhythm
as though the day is drawing breath—
there, at a sawhorse between two rows of cordwood
stacked five feet high and longer than the house is,
he, at ninety seven, is sawing, sawing
a twisted gnarl of maple
—of course I grab the other end and pull....

St. Paul United Church of Christ in Floraville, Illinois

Dear Will, Kayla, Ava, and Blake,   August 31, 2015

This church holds a lot of history for our Reiss family. It's where my grandfather **George William Reiss married Catherine Charlotte Luetzelschwab** on 4/16/1911. Here's a summary of our family baptisms and confirmations:

William George Reiss was born on 5/6/1912 and baptized on 6/2/1912. He is the first son of my grandparents George and Katie Reiss. Sponsors were his parents Frank and Annie Reiss. William was confirmed in 1925.

Royal Wright Reiss was born on 5/23/1911 and baptized on 6/2/1912. He is the son of Louis Philipp Reiss and Harriet Francis Wright Reiss. Sponsors were his parents Frank and Annie Reiss. Looks like a double ceremony.

Franklin Jakob Reiss was born on 10/31/1915 and baptized on 4/9/1916. He is the second son of George and Katie Reiss. Sponsors were Mr. and Mrs. George Dintelmann and Mr. and Mrs. Jakob Weihl. Franklin was confirmed in 1927.

Ervin Hermann Reiss (should be Irwin Henry Reiss) was born on 9/18/1917 and baptized on 10/14/1917. He is the third son of George and Katie Reiss. Sponsors were Hermann Friedrich Luetzelschwab, Caroline Luetzelschwab, and Henry W. and Emma Reiss. Irwin was confirmed in 1931.

June Ann Mabel Willet Reiss   was born on 12/2/1936 and baptized on 3/28/1937. She is the daughter of William G. and Anita Hesse Reiss and granddaughter of George and Katie Reiss.

George Henry Irwin Reiss was born on 2/26/1942 and baptized on 4/24/1943. He is the son of Franklin J. and Geraldine Hulet Reiss and grandson of George and Katie Reiss. Sponsors were Mr. and Mrs. William G. Reiss.

I remember going to St. Paul Church on numerous Easter Sundays when our extended family gathered for worship. There was always a lady in the choir with a fairly shrill voice which was really apparent during the "Alleluias" of the hymn, "Christ the Lord Is Risen Today." It's one of my favorites and dates from the 14th century. St. Paul celebrated its centennial on 9/27/1959.

Will, Kayla, Ava, and Blake, below is what St. Paul looks like today. You can see from the first picture to this one that the original church was enlarged with a fellowship center and classrooms on the east side. That round window in the steeple was replaced during this renovation. The new one was funded by my grandparents so they were given the previous window which was removed and stored in the barn on our family farm.

Love, Granddad

1960 – 1969

1960 Population of St. Clair County is 262,509.

1960 States total 50, national population is 180.67 million.

1960 President is Dwight Eisenhower. John Kennedy is inaugurated in 1961, Lyndon Johnson in 1963, and Richard Nixon in 1969.

1961 Construction of the Berlin Wall began.

1962 John Glenn became the first American astronaut to orbit the earth.

1962 Sam Walton opened his first store in Bentonville, Arkansas. He incorporated in 1969 as Wal-Mart Stores and now has 11,526 stores in 28 countries under 65 banners.

1963 The Civil Rights march on Washington, DC with Dr. Martin Luther King's famous "I Have a Dream" speech.

1963 President Kennedy is killed in Dallas, Texas.

1966 Medicare began.

1968 Civil rights leader, Martin Luther King, is killed in Memphis, Tennessee.

1969 Astronauts Neil Armstrong and Buzz Aldrin land on the moon.

1969 The Internet, called Arpanet during its initial development, is invented by the Advanced Research Projects Agency at the U.S. Department of Defense.

Pop's Hands

Dear Will, Kayla, Ava, and Blake,   September 29, 2014

My grandfather, George "Pop" Reiss, had the largest and strongest hands of any person I ever met. You can see that in the next two pictures below where he is holding his first surviving grandson, George Henry Irwin Reiss, who was born on 2/26/1942. The first picture of the two was taken about 72 years ago. The second picture of them was taken less than a year later. Grandma and Pop did have an earlier grandson, William George Reiss, Jr., who was born on 11/4/1938 but he did not survive the day. That sad news made the 1942 birth even more special. Both grandsons had "George" in their name.

Pop was born on 4/22/1873 on the Reiss Family Farm and lived there until he passed away on 8/19/1964 at age 91.3 years. Here he is about age three in 1876 which is the oldest picture we have of him. I remember him telling me a story which happened when he was age five or six. He was at a general store with his dad, perhaps the one that used to be in Floraville 1.7 miles west of their farm. The storekeeper asked young George and other kids if they wanted some free candy. You know their immediate answer, but George had to first empty rocks and sticks out of his pants pockets to make room for that candy. George was eagerly throwing those sticks to the side and did not realize that he was standing close to an old German sword which was lying on top of a wooden barrel. The end of the middle finger on his right hand struck that sword with enough impact to split the fingernail back into the quick. From then on, George had two fingernails on that finger. You can see that in next picture below.

Pop and Grandma bought the 180-acre family farm from his parents in 1921. They had already bought 180 acres of adjacent farmland in 1917 so now he was farming 360 acres just as his three sons were born in 1912 thru 1917. So Pop and Grandma had their hands very full with three sons, church, one-room school, crops, chickens, pigs, horses, wood heat and cooking, no tractor, and no electricity until 1945. He worked as a farmer until age 75. No wonder Pop developed large, strong hands. Can you imagine!!!

Will, Kayla, and Ava, there is absolutely no greater joy for an adult than holding a new family baby, especially when it's your own grandchild who is named after you. Will, I know that feeling very well myself since you have been a huge joy in our lives for 4 years, 8 months, and 8 days. I'm also thrilled that you share your first name with your other grandfather, "Ba" Pottgen.

I have Pop's wedding ring which shows very little wear. I took it to a jeweler who measured it as size 13 which is the largest standard size available. Anything larger would have to be custom made for really big people like Shaquille O'Neal.

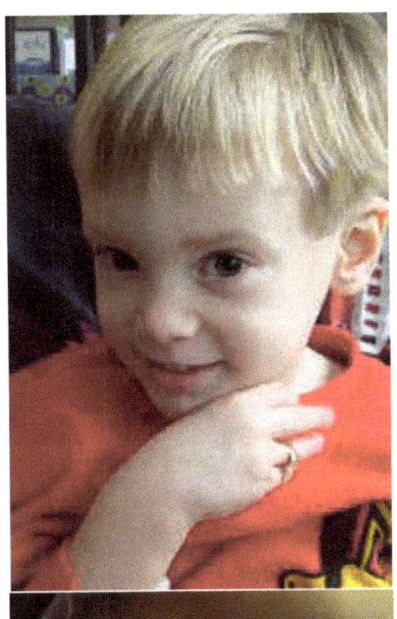

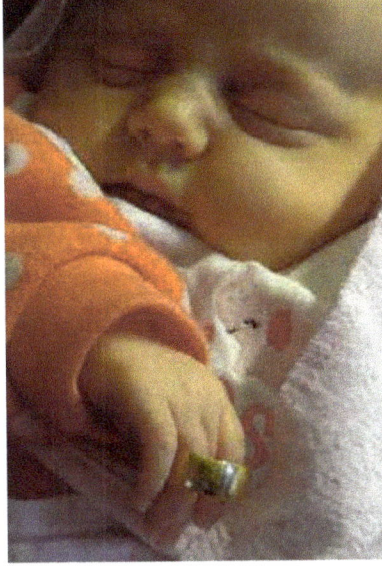

I don't see that ring on Pop's finger in this 1943 picture. Perhaps he didn't wear it because it was too small and his ring finger was actually larger than size 13!!! Here are Pop's great great grandchildren, Will and Ava, "wearing" his ring on two fingers and three fingers.

Will, Kayla, Ava, and Blake, here's a poem I found titled "My Grandfather's Hands" which is very appropriate for this Granddad's Mondays story. The poem even mentioned 91 years which exactly matched Pop's life.

Love, Granddad

My Grandfather's Hands

Funny the things we recall.
Images that flash through our brain.
Some most vivid for me were of an old man.
Skin like creased parchment paper,
Lined and yellowed with age.
The veins visible just below the surface,
of a thin nearly transparent veneer.
Liver spotted flecks of red,
Charted paths from the toil of many years,
Palms callused forever from a life time of labor.
Big fingers knotted and misshapen.

Looking at those old hands, one could hardly guess
That still there remained gentleness in their caress.
For an old dog, or a little grandson in need of some
Companionable affection or parental love.

Those aged hands could also make things,
Toy sailboats, and wooden trains, complete with caboose.
A cool flute whistle that actually worked,
He said it was like the Indian's used out Oklahoma way.
And he would know, he'd cowboyed there.

His hands taught me to tie my shoes,
Open and close my first pocket knife.
Those same hands could become birds,
rabbits, butterfly's, all sorts of things.
When projected up on the wall,
Silhouetted by a naked back light.
His hands knew magic too,
Could pluck silver coins right out of my ears.

His tired face matched his hands,
visual weathered, creased, and wrinkled road maps,
Of 91 years of rugged life traveled.

Yet, his lively pale blue eyes remained
forever fraudulently youthful prisms,
Eyes and spirit of a much younger man within.

But it is his hands most of all I shall remember,
Their imposing look and their reassuring
touch of tenderness.

I shall never forget my Grandfather's hands.

Cousin Richard's 1968 Letter to Grandma

Dear Will, Kayla, Ava, and Blake,   February 4, 2013

GrandDD and I were in Oxford, England this past September to visit Christ Church College which is one of 39 colleges that make up the University of Oxford. That's where John Wesley was a student before he became a famous preacher and founded the Methodist Church about 1750. We were on a pilgrimage of Wesley sites in London, Bath, Bristol, Oxford, and Epworth. It was a fascinating tour and we learned a lot about Wesley and the Methodist Church which we joined in 1976.

In Oxford we also walked past Queens College where my cousin Richard Reiss was a student for a year or so in 1968. He was a smart guy and already had a degree in economics from Yale University, a year as a Fulbright Scholar in Berlin, and eventually most of a doctorate from Rockefeller University in New York. While he was at Oxford, he wrote the letter on the next page to our Grandmother Katie Reiss at the family farm south of Belleville, Illinois.

Here's what I found on Google about Oxford and Queen's College. The **University of Oxford** is the second oldest university in the world after the University of Bologna founded in 1088 in Italy. Although its exact date of foundation is unclear, there is evidence of teaching as far back as 1096.

Most undergraduate teaching at Oxford is organized around weekly tutorials at self-governing colleges and halls, supported by classes, lectures and laboratory work organized by University faculties and departments. Oxford consistently ranks among the top five universities in the world. For more than a century, it has served as the home of the Rhodes Scholarship, which brings students from a number of countries to study at Oxford as postgraduates or for a second bachelor's degree. Famous American alumni include President Bill Clinton and NBA basketball star and US Senator Bill Bradley.

Queens College was founded in 1341 by Robert de Eglesfield, chaplain to Queen Philippa, the wife of King Edward III of England, hence its name. Two of their more famous alumni are Edmund Halley who discovered the comet that bears his name and King Henry V of England. It has a beautiful campus with several old buildings.

February 6, 1968

Dear Grandma,

Sorry I've been negligent in my letter writing. I certainly did get your birthday present and letter. Thanks.

I like England very much, and the English people have been very nice to me. I know several families and have been often invited to dinner, etc., so I have been able to get a change of pace from straight school work all the time.

Oxford is a very demanding school and I have to work very hard. The school system is very different from ours in America, and it took me a while to adjust to what they wanted. There are few regular classes and lectures. I'm studying philosophy and psychology and I have one teacher for each subject for which I must write one essay a week. I have to take the essay and read to my tutor, as the teacher is called here, and then we discuss what I've written for an hour or so. To write this essay, I have to read many books and articles, which means that I have to spend lots of time in the library.

Oxford is a very lovely town and very old. My college, the Queen's College, was first started in 1341, more than six hundred years ago. Consequently they have lots of old traditions, like you're supposed to wear a robe each time one goes to the tutor or when one eats dinner in the college. Most of the students live in the college itself, but since I already have a degree from an American university, I don't; so I'm living now in a house with two other Americans, one of which I knew when I went to school at Yale. I like Oxford very much and I'm very interested in what I'm studying, so I don't really mind having to work so hard. I'm actually working harder, I think, than I've ever worked before, even at Yale.

The town Oxford is not so big and has lots of lovely countryside around it, so I can get to go out and take walks and things through lovely farm villages. Some friends of mine from London were here last weekend, and we drove out and saw a beautiful old English castle.

I can't write much more now, as I'm still in process of moving into this house and I also have to write an essay in philosophy for my tutor tomorrow.

I hope things are all right with you and the farm. Mom and Dad have been writing me about it and all the traveling you are doing. I think that's wonderful. I hope I can do that when I'm your age.

Love,
Richard

So, Will, Kayla, Ava, and Blake, never underestimate the value of a good education from a good school. It opens many doors for career opportunities as well as eventual networking with high-end fellow students and professors. The other lesson here is to write fairly often to your grandparents so you don't have to start your letters with an apology.

Love, Granddad

Richard Reiss in Yale Alumni Magazine

Richard Franklin Reiss was born November 21, 1944 and raised in Urbana, Illinois. He graduated from Yale University in 1966 with a degree in economics. He studied in Berlin for a year on a Fulbright Scholarship and then graduated from Oxford University with a degree in philosophy. Richard was working on his PhD at Rockefeller University in New York when he discovered and embraced the writings and philosophy of the Church of Scientology. He devoted himself fulltime to that ministry in 1973 and eventually became the senior minister of the church's headquarters in Clearwater Florida, a position he held for a quarter of a century. His primary duty was to oversee the spiritual counseling by church ministers worldwide. He was personally known and loved by tens of thousands. Richard died on March 4, 2011 and is survived by his wife of 36 years Cala, son Jesse, and daughter Rebecca.

Painting Grandma's House

Dear Will, Kayla, Ava, and Blake,   December 15, 2014

About June 1961 our family drove from Sullivan, Indiana to the Reiss farm for a weekend visit. I had volunteered to paint the exterior of Grandma and Pop's home so this trip was to drop me off there for two weeks. Their house is a story and a half so we needed to borrow a 16-foot ladder from Marcella Klein at the next farm west. I remember Grandma and me walking that ladder back to her house. Grandma was on one end and I was slightly past the middle so she would have way less than half the weight.

The first task was scraping off the flaking parts of the previous paint job. I was using oil based paint so that was a little heavier and tougher to clean up after than the latex water-based paints that nearly everyone uses today. Lunch that first day was one hot dog and a drink. Lunch the second day was two hot dogs. Grandma got all the way up to five hot dogs per lunch before I asked her to level off at three.

I listened to lots of Cardinal baseball games on the radio during those two weeks. That's when I really learned the names of various players and their positions. I learned the other team names which helped me remember which were in the National League versus the American League.

I helped Grandma hang the wash out to dry on her clothesline. There was usually enough low-humidity wind to dry the starting end of her line by the time you finished hanging the other end.

Folks don't use clotheslines much these days except for your next door neighbor, Will and Ava, in Springfield. Maybe the Mapes family will let you help them sometime.

The job was completed on schedule thanks to a few finishing touches by my mom below. I really enjoyed my two weeks on the farm. I helped Lavern with a few chores and got to drive his tractor. I rode my bicycle on an eight-mile loop along gravel roads. It was a great summer vacation. Grandma paid me $100 for painting her house which I thought was too much. Mom and Dad picked me up to drive back to Sullivan.

About June 1968 my Caterpillar friend Gene McKay and I drove to the home farm for a weekend to hunt rabbits, shoot groundhogs, and paint Grandma's kitchen a pale blue. We succeeded on all three objectives. Grandma got to meet Gene and vice versa. The kitchen was slow to paint because there was lots of window, door, and cabinet trim to mask off to insure a good job. We shot two or three rabbits which Grandma cleaned, dressed, and cooked for our evening meal. I remember spitting out at least one buckshot that she missed.

About June 1970 Diane Peterson and I drove my Corvette to the home farm to paint Grandma's living room and to drive into St. Louis for a Saturday night date. You know Miss Peterson better as Grand DD. We did a good job painting her living room but it was slow also because there was a lot more trim work to paint around than in the kitchen. Miss Peterson did a very good job and really impressed Grandma. Actually I think that was her objective from before we arrived and Grand DD succeeded wonderfully. Our evening in St. Louis was at the Playboy Club which was also nice due to the unique scenery.

Love, Granddad

1970 – 1979

1970 Population of St. Clair County is 284,931.

1970 States total 50, national population is 205.05 million.

1970 President is Richard Nixon. Gerald Ford is inaugurated in 1974 and Jimmy Carter in 1977.

1971 Disney World opened in Orlando, Florida.

1971 English teacher Jerry Baldwin, history teacher Zev Siegl, and writer Gordon Bowker formed Starbucks to sell roasted coffee beans and equipment in Seattle. They started selling brewed coffee in 1986 and now have 23,132 stores worldwide. Starbuck was the first mate aboard the whaling ship Pequod in Moby Dick published in 1851.

1972 President Nixon made first visits to Beijing and Moscow and met with respective leaders.

1974 President Nixon resigned from office.

1976 The Bicentennial of the United States is celebrated throughout the country.

1976 Microsoft becomes a registered trademark, one year after its name for microcomputer software is first mentioned by Bill Gates.

Franklin Reiss – US Senate Testimony (1979)

Dear Will, Kayla, Ava, and Blake,   July 9, 2012

Below is testimony your great great uncle Frank Reiss gave before a U. S. Senate Committee 33 years ago tomorrow. He was your great grandfather's older brother and was a college professor in agriculture for 40 years at the University of Illinois for his first professional career. He was born on the Reiss family farm in Southern Illinois so he was a farmer in his amateur career and then manager of that home farm for 20 years in his second professional career.

I typed his name into Amazon.com and found 31 publications listed, of which only 2 were still in print. Those two dealt with farm leasing in Southern Illinois and East-central Illinois and are probably actual books. I think the rest are pamphlets. I typed his name into Google and found 84 hits on the first ten pages. Pretty impressive, don't you think?

Frank's grandson, Jesse Reiss, provided several photos for me to choose from for this edition of Granddad's Mondays. I really had to laugh at this one because it shows Uncle Frank is his weekend clothes – a white shirt and tie with jeans or bib overalls. This was his normal garb for weekends in the 1950s and 1960s when we'd all gather at the home farm and go for walks in the woods or to the Sportsman's Club a mile away. I was always curious about the white shirt and tie for such outings and then it donned on me. Much of Frank's career at the U of I involved the Farm Extension Service where he would travel all over the state making presentations on his papers to groups of farmers gathered at Farm Bureau or FSA offices. I never went to any of those meetings but I imagine (you guessed it) he was wearing a white shirt and tie for his professor image and jeans for his farmer image. Probably a very effective combination.

Frank's specialty was farm leasing. That's what the vast majority of his professional writings and Amazon.com titles indicate. One of his early papers was titled "Farm Operating Agreement" published in 1957. It dealt with the Reiss Family Farm where your great great grandparents owned the land, their nephew tenant Lavern Lang provided the labor, and a guy named George Ziebold provided the dairy cows. Here's a photo below of Frank's son Richard feeding a Holstein calf in 1956. Maybe you can see this is a boy calf so his future is in a veal factory rather than as a dairy cow.

Frank was always taking pictures on our outings at the home farm and on vacations with his family. He often showed those vacation slides at family gatherings as the evening entertainment. He took most of the photos which appear in two of our six family history books, Granger, Quilter, Grandma, Matriarch and Quilter, Granger, Grandma, Matriarch. Those books are the five-year daily diaries written by Frank's mother, Katie Reiss, for 1944 – 1948 and 1949 – 1953. Both are subtitled, "Life on the Reiss Family Farm."

Frank kept a comprehensive daily diary for 1956 through 1994. His son, George, gave me all those diaries in 2010 for safe storage. Frank's entry for July 10, 1979 reads as follows:

Mild and pleasant and partly cloudy in Washington, DC. I ate breakfast at Ho Jo's across the street from the Watergate Hotel. Walked over to the Kennedy Center for the Performing Arts. Then got my bag and walked to the Foggy Bottom Metro Station. Took the Blue Line to Capitol South. Walked 1st Street To Russell Senate Office Building. The Hearing on Agriculture by the Select Senate Committee on Small Business got started about 9:45 a.m. when Senator Gaylord Nelson of Wisconsin arrived. Two U.S.D.A. people testified first. I came on about 11:30 third from last. A young woman asked me to have lunch with her in the cafeteria in the Dirksen Senate Office Building so she could ask me about the farmland market in Illinois. After lunch I walked around the Capitol Building and took pictures. It was cloudy and very hazy. Arrived back at Willard Airport where Gerry met me at 8:20 p.m.

Introductory Statement by Franklin J. Reiss before the U. S. Senate Select Committee on Small Business in Washington, D.C. on July 10, 1979

Ownership is only one of several ways to gain operating control of farmland. However, given the means to achieve ownership, it is generally the preferred method. The other major way to gain operating control of farmland is by renting it. We are, thus, concerned with two independent but highly interrelated markets, the farmland ownership market and the farmland rental market.

Ownership generally provides the greater degree of tenure security, but renting allows control of land without the high capital costs of ownership. Under Cornbelt or Midwest agricultural conditions, typically the highest-priced land tends to be tenant-operated while the lowest-priced land tends to be owner-operated. Also typically, ownership of land is more common among the older, financially established farm operators, while tenancy is the most common method of operating control of land among young, beginning farmers. In the State of Illinois there is actually more rented than owner-operated farmland by a ratio of 55 to 45 according to the 1974 Census of Agriculture.

My own evaluation is that the present system, and particularly the Illinois situation, has worked quite well. There are, however, some questions I want to raise, and some developments that, if they continue to develop, are likely to create some problems.

My first area of concern is the question of what is an optimum level of land ownership by farm operators for Midwest agriculture? For example, I see no need to try to make owner-operators out of all farmers. But, on the other hand, how far below 45 percent can we go without losing politically, socially, and economically? The problem is not acute yet. I predict that the 1978 Census of Agriculture may record an increase in farm owner-operation from the 1974 level. But I also predict that, given present farmland prices, the relatively low rates of return on farmland, and high interest rates, we will experience an increase in farm tenancy.

A second area of concern is the probability that we are experiencing the beginnings of a change in the nature and distribution of farmland ownership. It is quite clear that most current purchasers of farmland are individuals who already own other farmland which they use as an equity base and the income from which helps to amortize the new land acquired. Is this leading to a concentration of ownership in fewer hands?

My third area of concern is a potential decrease in the market supply of farmland, in both the short and long run, and in both the land rental and the farmland purchase markets. The aggregate supply of farmland, in spatial terms is more or less fixed, as every farmer knows when he tells you "they aren't making any more land" as a justification for his most recent purchase. My concern is about the annual availability of land to the beginning farmer and to those who seek to expand their existing operations into more efficient or more effective units.

The most frequently cited reason for buying land has been to enlarge an existing operation. The current rate of turnover is only 3 to 4 percent annually, and much of that is not available in the open market, being transferred preferentially within families. If land ownership is being concentrated into fewer and stronger hands; if alien owners of land contemplate long-term ownership; and if corporations (including farm family corporations) acquire more land and thus remove the human lifetime turnovers, will there be an adequate market supply of land to permit farm enlargements?

I submit that this problem requires study and more information about the sources of market supply. If, as I suggest, the problem is one of supply, then programs to increase demand on the part of selected buyers would only aggravate the problem and tend to bid up the price of land.

The farmland rental market, which has previously provided an alternative source of land, is likely to be similarly affected. How will increased alien ownership of farmland affect the annual supply of that land in the rental market? Is corporately owned farmland likely to come into the open rental market? Will the use-values under paragraph 2032a (the 1976 Tax Reform Law) for federal estate tax purposes diminish the market supply of land through the required 15 year holding period?

As I see the present situation, we need more information about current changes in farmland ownership, and we need to know more about the sources of the annual market supply of farmland. My own profession seems to have overlooked the importance of the latter. We have already experienced a "seller's market" in farmland since 1973. Can we, or should we, accept changes that could lead to still higher farmland prices relative to the earnings from such land?

At the roots of these questions are value judgments. Farmers as a group resent the price competition from foreign buyers of U. S. farmland. But they appear to have no hesitation about farming that land if it is offered as rental property at reasonable rents and terms.

I, personally, feel that the system of individual proprietorships that characterizes Midwest agriculture has served us extremely well. The opportunities for and benefits from farmland ownership that have been associated with it have attracted and motivated competent people as managers and operators of the individual farm firms in the system. I doubt very much that this level of competence and the productivity of the industry would be maintained without the element of land ownership.

The dominant tenure group in Midwest agriculture is the part-owner operator group. These are essentially family operations, but they own part of the land they farm and they rent the rest of it. The proportion rented has gradually increased relative to the part that is owned. Ownership, by the operator, of the land with the buildings on it provides the best solution to an otherwise difficult leasing problem. The combination of owning and renting provides the best opportunities for growth as personal competence and capital accumulations grow. We need to know more about how the supply side of this system works in order to maintain its effectiveness and vitality.

Solutions are not automatic. The process is complicated. Among 134 buyers of Illinois farmland in 1978-79, the average buyer bought 105 acres of which 93 were tillable. The property bought was located an average of 2.7 miles from the buyer's base of operations or from other land that he controlled. Less than 40 percent of the tracts purchased had buildings on them. The average price paid was $2,253 per acre, or $236,552 in total. The buyer estimated he would get a gross income of about $260 per acre from the purchased tract. He estimated his net income would be about $125 per acre, but that was the net income when only about half the full cost of machinery depreciation, interest on machinery investment, and his own labor and management were charged against the income from the land purchased.

The buyer's financing arrangements require annual payments of about $185 per acre for the next 23 years to amortize his borrowing of $1,834 per acre. The $185 is more than twice the true net earnings from the property, and $60 more than the estimated $125 "net income." Clearly, only supplementary income from other land or off-farm sources could make the purchases possible.

The five major reasons cited most frequently for buying the land were: (1) Farm enlargement, (2) Inflation hedge, (3) Bring a son into the farm business, (4) Tenure security, and (5) Invest savings. Income tax savings ranked 7th or 8th among the reasons for buying land. This relatively low ranking on income tax savings may help to explain why farmers feel an unfairness about competition in the purchase of land from non-farm buyers who are in higher tax brackets and have more to gain from this source.

In closing I wish to emphasize again the importance of recognizing the two markets that deal with farmland, and the critical role that I see emerging in the factors that affect the annual supply of farmland in these markets. A study on growth among large Illinois farm firms that I did in 1970 indicated that these farms added 30 acres through renting for every acre they added through purchase.

I shall be happy to respond to your questions.

Franklin J. Reiss, Professor
Land Economics and Extension Specialist
College of Agriculture
University of Illinois

Will, Kayla, Ava, and Blake, this is most impressive, don't you think. There are a lot of smart people in our family including the four of you. Always remember that nothing is out of your reach as long as you continue reaching.

Love, Granddad

This is (Flora) Floraville, Illinois
by Edward H. Wirth of Belleville, Illinois in 1965

Dear Will, Kayla, Ava, and Blake,   November 16, 2015

Here's a fascinating and comprehensive history of Floraville. It's 1.7 miles due west of the Reiss family farm. It's where the Reiss family attended St. Paul United Church of Christ and where the Reiss boys all went to a one-room school. I remember a telephone exchange there for making long distance calls, a general store, and both the old and new Grange buildings. What follows is by Edward Wirth except for my highlights and ending.

This town of Floraville is located about six and one-half miles southeast of Millstadt. In the year 1860, a United States Post Office was established here, hence the necessity of changing the name from Flora to Floraville. At that time there was a town in eastern Illinois known as Flora.

The exact year in which the present town of Floraville was founded has not been determined. According to history in 1848 a church, protestant, was founded. This congregation erected a frame building for their church. In 1858 a man named Frederick Horn and surveyor named Frederick Cramer plotted and laid out the town in 50 lots. This plot had all streets named. The main road to Millstadt was Frederick St., to the east of Frederick St. was Buchanan St., to the west of Frederick St. was Douglas St. Intersecting streets running east and west were School St., Koerner St., Cass St., Franklin St., and Humboldt St. At the turn of the century Floraville had a population of about 200 people. Among the early settlers were the families of John Vogel 1828, Adam Reiss 1834, William Skaer 1834, John Probst 1834, J. S. Just 1836, Jas. Fleckenstein 1834, Fred Horn 1840, Peter Etling 1848, Geo. Lengfelder 1850. The Wirth family settled in Stookey Township north of Millstadt in 1846. A member of this family moved to the Floraville area in 1863.

Religion

According to the earliest church record, in January 1859, a group of forty-six men organized the Evangelical Society of Flora of St. Clair County. The first church of brick construction was dedicated September 1859. The first pastor was Rev. Theodore Horn. The first child baptized in the church as Geo. Wiegand, November 6, 1859. The first confirmation class was that of 1860. Continued progress was made by this congregation. In the year 1894 a new church was erected, which still serves the people of the Floraville area. During the 100 years of its existence, in 1959, the church records show that 765 persons were consecrated to God in Holy Baptism, 600 persons committed themselves to God in the Rite of Confirmation, 158 marriage ceremonies were conducted and 305 persons received Christian burials.

Education

The State of Illinois and St. Clair County have no record of the first school established here, but we do know that Frank Reiss, born in 1841, attended Floraville School. We also have the record that a former Catholic Church at Floraville was sold in the early 1860s to the District School. The enrollment at this school in the 1890s was about 60 pupils. Teachers of wonderful ability taught these rural pupils. Included in the course of study was a course in bookkeeping for eight grade pupils. All teachers during these early days were men teachers. These teachers were an inspiration to the youth of the Floraville area. This fact is brought out by the fact that between 35 and 40 boys and girls went to college, and many became teachers. Among these students a large number became public school teachers. Five from this area attained the honor of receiving the degree of Doctor of Philosophy. Many others received degrees in Bachelor of Science and Master of Arts. Also from this group three people became nurses, several were school administrators. Two former teachers of the Floraville School, Leonard Niess and Fred Vogel, became medical doctors. Several became college instructors, several took positions in banking, and one was President of the Board of Directors of a large St. Louis Bank. One of the Floraville students became a famous historian and wrote several text books for both high schools and grade schools.

The Craftsmen

Many of the craftsmen of Floraville learned their trade in the land of their birth and all were skilled workers. Gotlieb Opitz was a wagon maker by trade and had a very flourishing business in this village. He made these wagons in their entirety with the exception of putting on the steel or iron rims on the wheels. All woodwork and painting was done in his own shop.

Louis Metzger was a shoe and boot maker, and did general repairing of boots and shoes. This man had a very good business, although he was interrupted in his work by the Civil War, his business was a huge success. He reared a family of ten children.

Andrew Franke was a blacksmith and was kept busy sharpening plow shares and working on farm equipment and shoeing horses and mules. He also put the rims on the wagon wheels manufactured by Gotlieb Opitz.

William Dill was the saddler of the town. He made harnesses for the farmers' horses as well as fly nets to protect the horses and mules against the pesky flies. He also made repairs on harnesses.

Mr. Fischer was the stone-mason and brick layer. He lined the wells that were dug in the community and also made stone foundations for buildings.

Floraville also had three general merchandise stores: The Sensel's later Zimbelman's, Klein's, and Lengfelder's. Floraville had two hotels: The Green Tree Hotel operated by Christ Lindauer and the Flora Hotel operated by Hartmann. In connection with the hotel they also conducted a saloon, beer and whisky establishment. The main source of revenue for the hotel was obtained from traveling salesmen, in those days called Drummers. They were out drumming up business for large establishments in East St. Luis, St. Louis, and Belleville. These salesmen traveled by horse and buggy and called on the merchants in the southern part of Illinois and could not make the trip home on the same day. There were trips that took several days to complete.

Co-operative Enterprises

The Floraville Creamery was established west of Floraville in the year 1890. This was a farmers' co-operative and did a flourishing business for 40 years. The farmers brought their milk to the creamery where the cream was separated from the milk, the cream was then placed in a huge churn. This churn, with a rotary motion was propelled by steam power. This butter was sold at wholesale price. It was placed in tubs of about 30 pounds per tub and hauled to Waterloo. It was then loaded on the M & O Railroad and shipped to St. Louis. Butter was also printed; that is, made into one pound packages and placed in butter cartons. Much of this butter was sold at retail in local stores and at the Creamery.

Mr. Fred Metzger was one of the early butter-makers. Next to the creamery there were two large ponds. The creamery also had an ice house, the construction of this building was rather unique. There was an air space of about eight inches between the outer and inner walls. This space was tightly packed with sawdust to keep out the heat. The winters usually were cold and when the ice on the ponds reached a thickness of ten inches or more, a crew of men, owners of the creamery, cut the ice into blocks about two and one-half feet square, loaded it on the sled or wagon and hauled it to the ice house.

Here the ice was packed with sawdust. The supply was usually all used up by August and then commercial ice was purchased from the Schorr Brewery, Waterloo, and hauled by wagon to Floraville. Early trips were made so the ice would not melt. It was then stored in the ice house number two, inside the creamery. The Floraville Creamery was sold to the Waterloo Milk Company on June 18, 1930. Another creamery owned by Henry Vogel operated for a number of years.

The Floraville Rural Telephone Company was organized in 1905-1906. The Board of Directors was Louis Eckert, Otto Etling, Geo. Hoffmann, Dr. Emery Holcomb, John Sauzeck, Philip Wirth and Louis Zimblemann. This company sold stock certificates to all people who were interested in the new venture.

The setting of the poles and the stretching of wire was all done by members. Telephone poles were young trees of the local forests. The system used was the Ground System which operated on one wire line. The telephone unit was large and somewhat bulky. A set of wet batteries was used to produce enough amperes to ring the bell. This bell was rung by cranking the phone.

This company had its switchboard in the general merchandise store. Later it was moved to private homes. There were twenty trunk lines to the switchboard, each line had a capacity of taking care of twenty subscribers. The people on each line could call their neighbors by ringing their number and did not have to go through the switchboard. However, to call persons on any of the other lines, you had to place your call with the operator, who in turn rang the number on the other line.

The rings were made up of long and short rings, not exceeding four rings, as an illustration: Long, Short, Long, Short, and the different variations. The switchboard closed for the night at 9:00 p.m. and gave the signal on all lines, five long rings. People were urged not to use the switchboard after 9:00 p.m. except in an emergency. The telephone also served to notify the people on their respective lines about emergencies, such as fires, family in distress, etc. This signal was given by the operator and consisted of six long rings. The subscribers took the receiver off the hook and learned, from the operator, what unusual happening had taken place.

This Floraville Concert Band was organized October 2, 1913. Richard Probst was the organizer and Chas Hill from Hecker, Illinois was the Instructor and Director. The charter members were: Arthur Etling, Louis Etling, Walter Etling, Harry Franke, Otto Gasser, Adam Gerhardt, Arthur Kuhn, Adam Probst, Oliver Probst, Oscar Probst, and Richard Probst. Walter Etling is the only surviving charter member. This band was very popular in Floraville and the surrounding areas. Their services were very much in demand, especially during the summer months. They played for the Floraville Church Picnic and the School Picnic.

Military Service in the Civil War and Two World Wars

Many people from this area served their country in the military services from the Civil War of 1861 – 1865 and to the present time. It is impossible to list all the names of people who served in World War I, World War II, the Korean War and the conflict in Vietnam.

The following people from Floraville area served in the Civil War: Louis Kleber, Menninger, Christian Fischer, Henry Fischer, Louis Metzger, Berth, Fred Wagner, Gotlieb Opitz, Jac Lauth, Andreas Franke, Liellich, Karl Probst, Frank Reiss, Henry Koerber, and Schwab.

Pvt. Edwin L. Hoffmann, son of Mr. and Mrs. George Hoffman born November 3, 1893 died November 13, 1918 of pneumonia while serving as an Infantryman with the American Expeditionary Forces in France. His final resting place is Floraville Cemetery.

Clifford Franke was born May 20, 1922 and died February 22, 1944 during the heavy action at Anzio. Wilbur Krupp was born June 4, 1919 and lost his life on February 2, 1944 in Italy. Both men are buried in Belleville.

The Floraville Community Grange

Floraville Community Grange No. 1918 was organized March 8, 1948. The first meeting took place at what is now the Modern Woodman Hall. The building was owned by St. Paul Church of Floraville. Orville Helms, St. Clair County Grange Deputy, was in charge of the first meeting.

Mr. and Mrs. George Reiss and Mr. and Mrs. Arthur Barthel were members of the Broad Hollow Grange. They were responsible and instrumental in bringing the group together. Through their knowledge of Grange work, the idea of Grange work spread through the community. It took hold and the organization was formed, 52 charter members were signed. The first master was elected. He was Arthur Barthel who served for seven years followed by Orville Koerber for two years, John Weigand for one year, Lavern Lang for two years, Theodore Klein for one year, and again Orville Koerber for two years and again Arthur Barthel in his third term. On October 23, 1952 the Grange held its first meeting in its new hall.

Will, Kayla, Ava, and Blake, I think the Floraville population today is still about 200 people. There hasn't been a lot of growth. Several commercial buildings like the general store and telephone exchange were repurposed and the old one-room school is now a private home. I remember the Modern Woodman Hall where the local Grange first met. I was age six or seven when I tumbled all the way down the Grange Hall stairs from the second floor to the first. A lot of adults came over to see if I was okay. My only injury was embarrassment.

That Grange used to be the Flora Hotel mentioned at the bottom of page 2. Its operator, Mr. Hartmann, was also the founder of the area Grand Army of the Republic club in Millstadt where your great great great grandfather Frank Reiss was a charter member. This photo is probably a GAR function at the Flora Hotel attended by Civil War veterans and their sons. Maybe Grandpa Frank is in this picture. I wrote about the GAR in a Granddad's Mondays story on 11/11/2013. The Grange eventually upgraded the Woodman Hall by removing the second floor and then five years later demolished that building when their new hall was completed on the east edge of the village about 1955.

Love, Granddad

St. Michael's Church
Paderborn, Illinois

Dear Will, Kayla, Ava, and Blake,   September 21, 2015

We could see this church from the upstairs of my Reiss grandparent's home on the family farm. There was a café tavern next door to the church which had red neon lights at night time which made it easy to see the church and village of Paderborn. The distance was about 1.5 miles.

Dominic Reinhardt spent 25 years writing a history of St. Michael's before publishing it in 1962. Parts of it appear below with my yellow highlights which identify our family connections to that church.

FOREWARD

It was the year nineteen hundred thirty-three. One hundred years since the early settlers came to Prairie du Long had passed. The late Father Fredrick Beuckman, Pastor at St. Mary's in Belleville, and Diocesan historian, asked me if I could obtain more historical data concerning the origin and the early church history of Paderborn.

At first this assignment seemed a simple one, but all too soon I found myself groping in darkness and running up against blank walls. Only one year later my friend and pastor, the historian, passed on to his reward. Yet, as time went on, those words of his would not leave my mind. As if driven by an unseen force, I kept stumbling along over a trail as it were that had long been abandoned and covered over.

Then began the pouring over old church records, old newspapers of long long ago, and checking of tombstones of older people I knew when they came to this country. Traditions of families would have it that grandmother was five years old when she came to this country. Then checking the date of death and age gave the exact year of their arrival here. Thus the years of the earliest settlers were determined. Checking records at the public library, old history books, and old St. Clair County Atlas . . . . all in the hope for a morsel of information.

Twenty-five years have passed. Indeed it was trying at times and yet as I look back it was a pleasure. I was delighted to meet so many kind people who so eagerly lent a helping hand. Now that I feel my job is done, I am grateful to all, especially to God and His Blessed Mother for the health and strength, for the will to carry on. It was not I, it was the Hand from above that led me through. . . . . . Dominic Reinhardt

CHAPTER 1 – HOW IT ALL STARTED
GERMAN SETTLEMENT OF PRAIRIE DU LONG

History records that a great portion of Europe suffered extremely from the aftermath of the Napoleonic War during the early years of 1800. The spiritual life of the people to a great degree was at a low and deplorable ebb. So much so that Our Blessed Mother appeared several times during the first half of that century pleading with mankind to return to more Christian living. It was at LaSalle, France, where she appeared and warned that famine would strike, and crop failure after crop failure would come if people would not cease offending God especially by violating the Sunday. The famine came. A million or more people died from starvation in Europe.

Hunger, therefore, was perhaps the main reason for migrating into a strange land where certainly hardships would have to be endured. An old German jingle tells the story very well. "Die weise reiben, haben mich aus Deutschland vertreiben. Hate due Mutter fleish gekocht, So were ich langer geblieben." (By the turnips out of Germany I was chased, Had Mother served meat, I would not have left is so much haste.) Therefore the migration that took place in the 1830's was not so much a wanderlust or perhaps the idea of get rich quick, but rather, an avenue of escape.

We will briefly review the history starting with the eventful years of 1830-31. The revolution in France rekindled the smoldering fires of German patriotism and freedom. A movement of rebellion against oppression was gaining momentum. In 1832 the Bavarian government became alarmed and started to suppress or forbid the movement. However, the populace disregarded the order. Enthusiasm for reform was unbound. This was answered by military surveillance. All movements were suppressed by the government.

Disappointed, the German populace despaired and was ready to leave the fatherland for a land where one could live in freedom. Thus began the so-called Latin immigration of the 1830's.

Prior to this time, the German press carried articles discussing the feasibility of creating a German State in Brazil or the United States. About the same time a certain Gottfried Deiden gave a report on his journey to the western states of North America. This report was in book form, and became a top seller in Europe. This book, even though idealistic, gave a rather accurate description of the general conditions of the land, climate, soil conditions and commercial facilities. He favored Missouri rather than Illinois. To him the prairies did not appear productive. His contention was that the prairie land was too poor for even trees to grow. He also pointed out that the stagnant ponds in the prairies, like the swamp land in the bottoms, were mosquito breeders, with resultant typhoid and malaria.

The Germans placed great confidence in Deiden's writings. Therefore, the early settlers did not settle in the prairies, but rather on the hilly and rolling timber lands. Those who came later took the fertile prairie land where no clearing of timber was required, but simply some drainage to get rid of the water "in the ponds" as Deiden called them.

At the same time, as we mentioned before, there was hunger in Germany. There was one crop failure after another. To this was added the overcrowded population. All of this gave cause for rebellion. It seems at Giesen, there was a college. This became a sort of melting pot for ideas. At any rate, it was there that the so called "Geisener Geselschaft" originated (Geisen Organization). However, as good as their plans may have been, they only served to get the ball rolling. For soon after their departure, the organization more or less lost itself due to several reasons: (1) not all could leave at the same time, (2) many stopped at various points after arriving in this country and thus lost contact with each other or (3) many died on the journey.

Another migration group was the Hesse group, made up of mostly Bavarian residents. Both migration groups existed about 1833-34. Reference <u>Latin Immigration in Illinois</u> by G. H. Beinlich.

By 1834 active operations were in full swing. There was no more postponing. Migration was definitely planned and nothing would stop it. There were instances where mothers with newborn infants only a few weeks old were in these immigration groups.

There were two divisions as to the port of immigration. One group decided to go by way of New Orleans, the other by way of Baltimore. All started from Havre, France. Many of those who went by way of New Orleans died from cholera, smallpox, or yellow fever. The departures were not at all smooth since there were so many. There never was enough room on the ships and many had to remain behind to wait for another ship.

CHAPTER II – EXPRESSION OF FAITH
GERMAN SETTLEMENT OF PRAIRIE DU LONG

Indeed, a strong and rugged people they were, quite hardened from all the suffering and hunger endured while still in the Fatherland. Now they were surrounded by manifold dangers and hardships on every side. First of all, the uncertainty of possible attack by the Aborigines. The Kickapoo Indians were definitely hostile after having been driven from their hunting grounds.

Even the climate seemed not too friendly. It is recorded that the winter of 1834 was severe. The month of January registered 20 to 24 below zero for almost a week. One must realize the untold suffering that took place since the housing and cover materials were poor and scarce. There were no stores within twenty to twenty-five miles. Roads or trails were in no shape to travel. Walking was often the only way to and from the points of supply.

Then there were the dangerous outbreaks of disease. The most dreaded of all was cholera which stalked the immigrant wherever he went. When summer came and when planting and harvest was to be done, there again was malaria, typhoid fever, and many disorders of the digestive organs. These were caused by the lack of good drinking water, lack of sanitation, and the mosquito infested swamps in the bottoms and prairies that had not as yet been drained.

CATHOLIC PIONEERS USE SOFT SOAP TO HEAR SUNDAY MASS

Old wood carts were constructed entirely of wood including axle and the hub of the wheel. As a matter of fact, the wheel was a slice cut off the end of a log. There were no rims on these wheels. On the T-shaped frame which was the axle and pole or tongue, was the body of six uprights or stakes. The coach which was simply willow or hazel witches woven in wicker fashion was built around these stakes.

Soft soap served as lubricant. It had to be applied freely. Often a good supply of home-made soap had to be carried on a trip. Quite a soapy trail was left behind when crossing the American Bottoms by wagon or cart. And on these journeys it would also give opportunity to call on the ordinary of this great territory. He was the Rt. Rev. Bishop Rosati who was the first Bishop of St. Louis. It was with Bishop Rosati that arrangements were made for occasional visits by priests. They came on horseback a few times a year. They said mass and took care of spiritual needs of these people. Who these visiting angels may have been has been very difficult to ascertain.

The first masses offered on the soil of Prairie du Long Township was some time in the years 1834 – 42. This occurred on the John Roth farm, presently owned by Gustave Metzger. The foundation of the original log cabin in which mass was said still stands. The Holy Sacrifice was also offered on the Adam Reiss farm, presently owned by George W. Reiss, a grandson of the aforementioned. Until recently, the logs that were in the original dwelling were still preserved and in use.

CHAPTER III – FIRST CHURCH AND MISSION OF ST. THOMAS

It was not until the latter part of 1841 that John Basler (*our Johann Basler*) obtained or purchased a portion of the land which today is the farm owned by Michael Mueth. Mr. Basler, apparently an immediate relative to the aforementioned Adam Reiss' wife *(her father)*, on January 24, 1843, sold two acres of land for one cent for the purpose of building a church thereon. This transaction is recorded in the St. Clair County recorder's office Book N, page 165, and again on page 488. This second entry is a warranty deed to the Rt. Rev. Peter Kenrick, Bishop of St. Louis. This same year, November 1843, it is recorded that Mr. Basler conveyed his farm with exception of two acres upon which a Catholic Church is built. This gives evidence that the first Church was built in the Year of Our Lord Eighteen Hundred and Forty-Three (1843). This church was known as the Church of St. Thomas the Apostle.

It is believed that Father J. F. R. Loisel was the founder of this parish. Father Jean Francis Regis Loisel, a native son born in St. Louis, was a great missionary of his time. Even though he was of poor health, he accomplished much in spreading the blessings of the Church to many people.

In the parish history of Centerville (Millstadt), it is recorded that Fr. Loisel met with the people and arranged the building of a log church in 1836. Then on January 24, 1837, said Mass in the St. Thomas Chapel which was built on a farm owned by Thomas Laughlin, two miles southwest of Millstadt. That both churches were named in honor of St. Thomas the Apostle is a matter of either coincidence or devotion to the Saint on the part of Fr. Loisel. Fr. Loisel was resident pastor of Cahokia from 1836 to 1845.

The log church, which is a proven fact, stood on the original two acres. It was a one-room structure built of logs and clap board roof. The altar most likely was a table. There were no pews or benches. Tradition tells us that the people brought chairs or seats from home. These were also used to sit on while en route to and from church. It was a custom in those days in many places, instead of pew rent, there was a rental for the space on which one placed his chair.

There is a mistaken belief that the Church of St. Thomas stood on the Louis Hagen farm, presently owned by John Mueth south of Paderborn. The fact is that after the present stone church was built, Mr. Hagen bought the log church and moved it to his farm to be used as a farm building. Thus old timers used to refer to the building as the old church, not mentioning that it was no longer on its original site.

ATTENDING CLERGY OF ST. THOMAS AND CHOLERA

The Rev. H. Lierman attended the mission from 1850 to 1859. Rev. F. Carel succeeded from 1859 to 1861. This brings us to the period of the building of the present sandstone church.

However, we shall deviate and insert a part which left a very depressing mark in our history of this parish. A cholera epidemic swept this area somewhere along the year 1849. It is claimed that fifty-two persons died and were buried in the old cemetery. Most of the graves were never marked, but the location was along the extreme west end of the old cemetery. This may be the reason that some family names recorded in the early church records are no longer here. The "Belleville" cholera epidemic claimed 236 lives from May 18 to July 31, 1849. (*One of those was our Adam Reiss who died on May 23, 1849. He is buried in St. Augustine Catholic Cemetery in Hecker.*

Johann Basler's wife Katharina was born in Switzerland on December 27, 1793. She died March 5, 1841 in Prairie du Long Township. We do not know her gravesite but perhaps it is here near the original log church in Paderborn. Their second daughter Sophie Basler married Frantz Stauder in the log church on March 19, 1842. Perhaps these are reasons why Johann Basler formally donated these two acres of land on January 24, 1843. Little did anyone realize that Sophie Basler Stauder would die young at age 42 and be buried here on July 25, 1865. Her sandstone marker is the second one from the northeast corner in the old cemetery.)

CHAPTER IV – BEGINNING OF ST. MICHAEL'S, PADERBORN

After the opening of the baptismal records and parish records by Father Caspar Ostlangenberg in 1846, it is recorded that Rev. H. Liermann attended the mission from 1850 to 1859, and Rev. F. Carel from 1859 to 1861. During this latter's administration the present stone church was being built. The cornerstone which is still here (however, it was removed from its original place when the tower and sanctuary were added) reveals the date. Inscription reads as follows: "Floria In Escelsis Deo. Erbaut In Dem Yahre Des Heren 1859" (Build in the Year of our Lord 1859).

Also, a brief entry in the old church record book reads as follows: "This designated church was erected in the year 1859 and was under roof December 11 .... Door and window sills ...."Also recorded on the same date .... A total of $1,700 had been contributed by the parishioners and $40.75 by others. Resolutions and by-laws governing the administration of the parish were drawn up and ordered in force. Given at Prairie du Long, December 11th. (Signed by) Bernhard Wolf.

It has been a well established fact that the church was not built by a contractor, but mostly by the volunteer help of the parish. Most likely this was under the supervision of the pastor and the men of the parish.

When the first resident pastor, Father William Busch, arrived in 1861, he found a partly finished church and no priest house. The old log church still was used for worship. The people, still the original settlers, were German immigrants with the exception of three families. The number of families or households recorded was 45. The amount of contributions varied from $100 down. There were six $100 contributors. Compared to the present day dollar value, this was a large sum of money.

Father Busch apparently was a man of action. He found himself surrounded with many problems. He found himself out in nowhere without residence, and a parish divided into two factions, and an unfinished church. Since the entire settlement was known as the German Settlement of Prairie du Long, he named the village Paderborn.

St. Clair County History records that Paderborn was laid out by a Valentine Berg on August 18, 1862. Church records, and Father Ferber's notes, reveal that Father Busch built an eight-room rectory of brick construction in 1862. The school was built in 1863.

The division of the parish was this. The northern or rather northwestern portion of the settlement wanted the church built at Flora (Floraville). They were out-voted, so they independently started building a brick church at Floraville in the same year, 1859, when the Paderborn Church was started. Just before the arrival of Father Busch in 1861, an agreement was reached. This agreement was entered upon the records by a Peter Herbert and five members of both factions. It stated that both parties would build a rectory at Paderborn, but the pastor was to say mass at Floraville once a month. Within a year Father Busch had affected a reconciliation of both factions and the brick church at Floraville was sold for a district school building. This building, being a public school, was often a mystery to strangers. On the façade a large cross was imposed in the brickwork. The windows were Roman arched. The building was razed about 1920.

The stone church at Paderborn was completed and dedicated on May 8, 1862 by the Rt. Rev. H. D. Junker, Bishop of Alton, in the presence of nine priests. This was on the feast of the Apparition of St. Michael the Archangel. The church was named in his honor. This is officially recorded in the second baptismal record book on page 1.

It may also be noted that the same day, perhaps for the first time, the Sacrament of Confirmation was administered here in St. Michael's.

Along with all the building program carried on by Father Busch, there was a large expenditure of furnishing the church and rectory. All of this is carefully itemized and recorded in the parish records. However it is almost illegible from age. The only information about Father William Busch personally is a small insert in the records which translates to "Rev. Wilhelm Busch from Furstenburg, Westfalien."

BELFRY

The original wood bell tower stood somewhere in the vicinity of the old cemetery. In 1884 under the Rev. Bernard Claus, the arrangement of the church was reversed. The altar had stood at the east end of the church and the entrance on the west end. The addition of a sanctuary and sacristy on the west end and the bell tower steeple on the east end with a main entrance gave the church edifice a more church-like appearance as well as more interior room.

There are claims as to where the stone was quarried for the church. One claim is that it was taken from the Joseph Buss farm on the far west of the parish. Another claim is that it was taken from the Reinhardt farm near Paderborn along the creek bank.

It is further claimed that stone on the Reinhardt farm was a natural sandstone cave used by the Indians in this vicinity. Thus the same stone walls that once echoed the chant and prayer ceremonies to the "Great Spirit" by the Indians, today are giving sanctuary and abode to Our Lord and Savior, recognized by our Christian civilization. It may well be that the stone for the church came from both sources of supply since, by careful examination, one will note that the stone in the tower in particular is of a different strata. May these stones give a foundation for greater things to come in honor and glory of God.

INTERIOR OF CHURCH BEFORE 1962

In 1960 the renovation of the church program began. The windows were all reset in steel frames. In September 1961 a resolution was adopted to install a new LP gas boiler, to replace the present roof, to install copper gutter and downspouts, to sandblast, tuck-point, and waterproof the exterior of the church. This exterior work on the church was completed in May of 1962. On May 7, 1962 the trustees together with the pastor adopted a resolution to renovate the interior of the church. With the permission of the Bishop, the Blessed Sacrament was transferred to the multi-purpose room of the school. Devine services were celebrated there during the period of reconstruction.

The people of St. Michael's cooperated in 1962 in as grand a fashion as their forefathers had in 1862. The entire interior of the church was gutted. The ceiling was removed, the plaster was chipped off, and the floor was completely removed. Then the reconstruction started. New footings were poured. A foundation of concrete blocks was built inside the old foundation. Pre-cast concrete slabs with reinforced steel rods were put in place to form the floor. Then the entire floor was covered with terrazzo. The walls and ceiling were then finished with new plaster. New windowsills were installed of pink Tennessee marble. The sanctuary was adorned with a black imperial marble altar and communion rail. The statues were repainted. The balcony was remodeled. The electrical system was completely rewired. The pews will be placed in the church as soon as delivery can be made. Today in 1962, just as in 1862, the people of St. Michael's have a new church.

The people of St. Michael's can be justly proud of their church because they made so many sacrifices and personally performed much of the labor in the renovation of the church. Every group of parishioners – the men, the ladies, the high school students, the grade school students – worked for the improvement of the church. The general contractors in charge of the renovation were Joseph Schaefer and Frank Klein. Both are faithful members of St. Michael's Parish.

CEMETERY

The first cemetery is part of the church grounds. One of the ancient tombstones in this old cemetery marks the burial place of an individual born in 1777. During the course of years, many of the stones have deteriorated. Today only fifty-five monuments are left to mark the graves of the early settlers of the area.

In 1876 a new cemetery was laid out a short distance to the west of the parish grounds. Two former pastors have been buried in the priest's section of this cemetery in front of the crucifix. They are Father John T. Sonnen who died in 1932 and Father Francis Wiskamp who died in 1943. May they, and all who are buried in these cemeteries, rest in peace.

Will, Kayla, Ava, and Blake, had we been raised as Catholic instead of Protestant, we would have attended St. Michael's Church during our quarterly visits to the Reiss family farm. Consequently, we attended St. Paul United Church of Christ in Floraville which you learned about in my Granddad's Mondays story last month.

Love, Granddad

1980 – 1989

1980 Population of St. Clair County is 267,531.

1980 States total 50, national population is 227.22 million.

1980 President is Jimmy Carter. Ronald Reagan is inaugurated in 1981 and George Bush in 1989.

1980 Mount St. Helens erupted killing 57 people.

1981 First launch of a US space shuttle.

1981 IBM introduced the personal computer.

1982 The Vietnam Veterans Memorial dedicated in Washington, DC, holding the names of the more than 58,000 killed or missing.

1989 The Berlin Wall came down.

Reiss Sesquicentennial Reunion 1984

Dear Will, Kayla, Ava, and Blake,

August 3, 2015

Can you recognize your dads holding the Reiss sign in the front row? This is the group of relatives that gathered in mid-1984 to celebrate 150 years of Adam Reiss buying his first 40-acre farm on April 1, 1834. Grand DD is in red in the third row and I'm in red in the fourth row. All the names appear below but there are 21 unknowns in the last grouping. The reunion was held at the Smithton Sportsmen's Club on our home farm.

Front row from left – Tammy McBrayer, ??? Reiss, Cindy Reiss, Will Freeman, Richard George, Meg George, Kim Bald, Grant Reiss, Adam Reiss, Stephanie Parnell, Melissa Parnell, Abe Soule, Katy Standley, ???, ???, ???, Terry DeLeeuw, ???, ???, ???, ???, ???, ???, Lisa DeLeeuw, ???

Second row from left – Lucille Lang, Linda Freeman, Eugenia Teel, Berta Reiss, Dot Reiss, Viola Bald, Sandy Bald, ???, ???, Jo Ellen Standley, Lillian Standley, Syvilla McCall, Nancy Stepp, ???, ???, Ruth Reiss, Jessie Shau, Lela Shau, Gerry Reiss, Judith Peters, Beulah Dintelmann, Delores Walker, Patty Walker, Roya Singleton, Colleen Kelley Singleton, Judy Dietz, Dixie Reiss, Lisa Bright

Third row from left – ???, Ralph Bald, Shelly Karten, Ed Dintelmann, Irene Quirin, Lavern Lang, Helen Reiss, Maggie Young, Mary Kay Parnell, Don Bald, Diane Reiss, Mary Reiss, Doug Peters, June McBrayer, Jim McBrayer, Betsy Reiss, George Reiss, Sally Reiss, Steven Reiss, Wendy George, Kate Freeman, Dwight Teel, Steve Singleton, Bill Reiss, James Knight, Earl Frey, Ruby Frey, Bob Stepp III

Fourth row from left – Jack McCall, Joe Pat Knight, Earl Reiss, Slade Young, Royal Reiss, ???, Irv Reiss, Ken Reiss, ???, Phil Reiss, Ron Parnell, George Freeman, Franklin Reiss, Lonnie

Standley, Steve Reiss, David Freeman, Keith George, ???, ???, ???, Ken Frey, Leslie Shau, Phil Knight, Robert Stepp II.

The 21 unknowns in the picture could be: – Mike Bald, Joan Bohnenstiehl and Mark Denger, Daniel R. Dietz and son Thomas D. Walker, Wayne and Pat and Morgan Freed, Richard and Debbie Knoth Jane Knight, Patricia and Tim and Barbara Meehling, Cindy Meehling and Bill Buckley, William and Roger and David and John Reiss, Amy Roth, Hilda Schanherr, Rob Sneehley, Marilyn Young.

There were lots of outstanding desserts made by the Sportsmen's wives. They were outstanding hosts that worked well with our committee. Here's my cousin June Ann McBrayer and husband Jim. She was animated about something. Who's that over her shoulder?

My dad was master of ceremonies for the reunion program. His vest had buttons from my great grandfather Frank Reiss' membership in the Grand Army of the Republic. Maybe you remember my story on the GAR from 11/11/2013 about the veterans of the Civil War. The names in the background are Adam Reiss' children. His first son John is off to the left. Representatives from each of the five branches made short presentations.

Here are my dad's remarks – One hundred and fifty years is a long time and it is hard for me to imagine how things were then. So if you will join with me, we will turn back the clock 150

years and see first what was going on in Germany at the time Adam Reiss must have decided to leave his native land and then what were the circumstances in the new world and specifically the state of Illinois where he decided to make his future home. Bear in mind that Adam Reiss was born in 1804.

In 1834 there was only one state, Missouri, west of the Mississippi River. Illinois became a state in 1818 with 75% of the people working as farmers. Adam Reiss was one of them. Now Illinois is only 3.5% farmers. Why did he settle in the hills of southern Illinois? Remember that Illinois is one of the prime agriculture states with 84% of its land farmable. There was plenty of timber for houses, fuel, and fences plus many streams for year round water.

229

John Deere had not yet invented the steel moldboard plow to tame the prairies. Cyrus McCormick had not yet invented his reaper, so Adam did a lot of work by hand. For many years it was the day of horse and buggy, butchering days, barn raisings, home preserves, the blacksmith shop and no computers. The Treaty of Chicago, the last Indian treaty in Illinois, was signed on September 26, 1833.

What was it like in central Europe when Adam Reiss was growing up? The early 1800s were impacted by the Napoleonic Wars. For the generation that lived between the final defeat of the French in 1815 and the second major French Revolution of 1848, it was in Germany, as in most of Europe, a period of retrenchment and indeed reaction.

It is probably a fair assumption that for the young man Adam Reiss there was considerable political and economic instability.

How much these circumstances influenced Adam Reiss' decision to leave a presumably reasonably stable family situation in northern Bavaria and emigrate to a foreign land about which at best he must have known very little, again is a matter of considerable conjecture. But come he did and I for one am glad that he did for I wouldn't be here if he hadn't. I have traveled the world over many times so that I can say with real conviction, I'm glad to be an American.

We are gathered here to commemorate the 150 anniversary of the founding of the Adam Reiss farm in St. Clair County, Illinois. We share a common heritage in our roots. But from there the Reiss family tree has grown. Its branches now spread far and wide in many directions. And shortly we want to find out among those present the extent of that dispersion. Before we get into that, I have a few housekeeping chores to attend to.

The real reason for doing this is to establish and re-establish the fellowship and kinship that our common heritage makes so dear to us all. To facilitate this you have all been labeled by your branch of the family tree, the generation to which you belong and whether your lineage is direct or via a spouse.

My friend, the illustrious Will Hayes, was credited with the saying "things don't just happen, they are brought about." And so it was with this reunion – it didn't just happen. You all contributed by coming here and in other ways. But there are a few shakers and movers that contributed much of their time and talents to get this affair organized and I feel it proper that they be recognized. First, the idea and the continuous pressure came from my wife, Mary. She and I presented the idea at a cousins meeting a couple of years ago and we found an enthusiastic response from Lillian Reiss Standley.

When you registered when you arrived, you were color coded – that was for identity, not segregation. There were five original surviving branches in the Adam Reiss family tree – four sons John, Frank, Charles, Martin, and one daughter Kathryn.

I haven't yet read the minutes of the last reunion but while we are at it, why don't we get some data for this meeting. Will all the descendants of the John Reiss family please stand, then the

Frank Reiss family, then the Charles Reiss family, then the Martin Reiss family, and then the Kate Reiss Wittig family.

It might be interesting to find out how far the family has scattered. Forget about branches now. Everybody from Illinois please stand, now Missouri, now Indiana, and so on. Judging by the young people I see here, the sap is still flowing, the tree is still growing. Let's check for age brackets.

Prayer before lunch – To the god that gave life to Adam Reiss and to the rest of us in turn, we give thee thanks. We ask thy blessing. The Reiss family has grown and prospered and enjoyed thy many blessings in many ways and in many places for this we are grateful. Thank you for the privilege of meeting here today so that we can enjoy the kinship and fellowship.

Will, Kayla, Ava, and Blake, you missed a great party. **You four and your parents are in charge of the next one which celebrates 200 years in 2034.** Here's my brother Ken photographing Adam Reiss' tombstone about five miles south of our home farm.

Love, Granddad

Irv Reiss Reflects on One Sunday Down on the Farm

Dear Will, Kayla, Ava, and Blake,   October 19, 2015

This is a story my dad wrote on May 21, 1987 for the "Sullivan Daily Times" in our Indiana hometown. The rest is his except for my final paragraph.

We had an established routine that characterized our regular Sunday activities. Specifically, Sunday was a day for church going, rest, recreation, and visiting relatives. Mom has six sisters and four brothers and Pop had four brothers and two sisters. So there were lots of aunts, uncles, and cousins to visit. Even though we did no field work on Sunday, the horses were turned out to pasture for their day of rest, the chores still had to be done – the cows milked, the pigs slopped and the chickens fed and watered. I must confess chores were delayed a little on Sunday mornings. We didn't get up as early, but chores had to be done before it was time for church.

We followed a self-imposed ritual on Sunday mornings. With no bathroom and only one wash basin, I found out early in life what it meant to take turns, and I assure you with two older brothers, mine wasn't first. When it got down to my turn, washing was a lick and a promise and I usually skipped my ears. Part of the ritual was while Mom did my ears and whatever else I missed, Pop would wind the eight-day mantel clock on his handmade walnut desk.

One Sunday the decision was made that today we would go on a trip – we would visit "Falling Springs" along the bluffs of the Mississippi River. Because of the travel involved in a Model T Ford, we would have to start early, skip going to church so we would be back for evening chores before dark. Some of the preparation involved Mom frying two spring chickens and baking an angel food cake (among Mom's many virtues those two things were outstanding). But it was Pop this day that made the delightfully startling announcement, "since we will be going through Waterloo, I'm going to stop at the Creamery and buy a gallon of ice cream." One whole gallon of ice cream – oh boy, gee whiz – if I worked it right, there were five of us, I could probably get close to a quart of "store-boughtt" ice cream for myself. I didn't know there was that much ice cream.

Let the record show we did get to Falling Springs in our Model T Ford touring car. And, Pop, being a man of his word, stopped at the Creamery in Waterloo and bought one gallon of vanilla ice cream. The Falling Springs area is what geologists call a karst limestone formation. Water under pressure forms carbonic acid which dissolves the limestone causing sink holes. The water through underground aquifers finds its way to the Mississippi River bluffs where it is discharged in a beautiful falling spring. It's a lovely place for a picnic, for climbing and for dashing into the falling water and other things that boys can innovate. It was a great day – friend chicken, angel food cake and store-bot ice cream – what more could anybody possibly want.

It is now Monday noon – we are sitting around the kitchen table having dinner – when one of us said, "Listen, the clock has stopped, it didn't strike 12." All of a sudden we all knew why … Pop did not wind it when we were getting ready to go to church because we missed going to church yesterday. We sat in silence for a moment. The silence was broken by the following comments

232

"I wonder what else we missed? – we didn't even repeat the Lord's Prayer – and we didn't thank God for our lives and our daily bread."

As I reflect on this incident that happened some 50 years ago, the details are still vivid in my mind because I think there is a message there for me and maybe others. Maybe like that old clock on Pop's desk, some of us run down during the week and need to be wound up again on Sunday. Or maybe some of us get so embroiled in the passions of the everyday world, that we lose our perspectives and need to be brought back to reality by some simple words like – not my will, but Thine be done.

Will, Kayla, Ava, and Blake, isn't that an interesting story. I really like Dad's writing style where he starts out with a broad picture, narrows it down to a one-day trip, further narrows it to a gallon of ice cream, and then uses a missed 30-second clock winding as his bull's eye. There are lots of lessons for us.

Love, Granddad

PS: That creamery in Waterloo was the Fountain Creamery. It's no longer there. Here is Falling Springs in Dupo, IL. It's still there.

233

Golden Weddings

Dear Will, Kayla, Ava, and Blake,   September 15, 2014

I recently did a mental exercise of naming the descendants of Adam and Margaret Basler Reiss who had celebrated golden wedding anniversaries by being married 50 years or longer. I came up with half a dozen names. Thinking I had missed a few and wondering what couple was the longest married, I consulted our family tree and put together the list below. I was missing a few wedding and death dates so my list may be short or long by one or two couples. The colors identify generations with grey as first, green as second, blue as third, and none as fourth.

John Reiss branch – 76 adults born before 1990 with 4% making gold

John R. Reiss (12/11/1838 – 6/18/1919) married Maria Josephine Gass (2/6/1844 – 12/2/1920) on 10/22/1861 in Paderborn. Married for 57 years, 7 months, 27 days.

Margaret Jane Meehling (10/9/1927 – 10/27/1995) married Arthur R. Engquist (10/1/1924 – 4/22/2002) on 5/5/?? Married over 50 years.

Mary Reiss (12/23/1863 – 8/9/1945) married Jacob Ferkel (7/1/1862 – 4/17/1938) on 12/23/1887. Married 50 years, 3 months, 25 days.

Frank Reiss branch – 127 adults born before 1990 with 10% making gold

Frank Joseph Reiss (9/27/1841 – 11/21/1921) married Anna Antonia Syvilla Feder (9/26/1844 – 5/14/1930) on 4/9/1866 in a double ceremony with his sister Kate and Max Wittig. Married 55 years, 7 months, 12 days.

George William Reiss (4/22/1873 – 8/19/1964) married Catharine Charlotte Luetzelschwab (3/25/1890 – 10/17/1986) on 4/16/1911 at St. Paul's Church in Floraville. Married 53 years, 4 months, 3 days.

June Ann Reiss (12/2/1936 --) married James McBrayer (7/7/1936 --) on 8/2/1958 in Belleville, Illinois. Married 56 years, 1 month, 13 days and counting.

Franklin Jacob Reiss (10/31/1915 – 7/8/2002) married Geraldine Hulet (6/1/1916 – 9/10/2008) on 8/22/1940. Married 61 years, 10 months, 16 days.

Irwin Reiss (9/18/1917 – 4/11/2007) married Mary Leone Stephenson (3/15/1921 – 5/16/2010) on 11/8/1942 in Atascadero, California. Married 64 years, 5 months, 3 days.

Lillian Zola Reiss (11/25/1911 – 5/30/2002) married Lonnie Maurice Standley (12/16/1907 – 7/31/2007) on 5/13/1934 in Sikeston, Missouri. Married 68 years, 17 days.

Linda Lee Reiss (6/19/1935 --) married David Freeman (6/24/1931 --) on 6/17/1956 in Darien, Connecticut. Married 58 years, 2 months, 29 days and counting.

Lewis Philip Reiss (1/28/1937 --) married Sally Strangman Quicke (10/23/1936 --) on 8/9/1958 in Darien, Connecticut. Married 56 years, 1 month, 6 days and counting.

Roya Ann Reiss (11/27/1936 --) married Edward Earl Singleton (5/13/1931 --) on 3/24/1956 in Newport, Rhode Island. Married 58 years, 5 months, 22 days and counting.

Earl L. Quirin (5/9/1934 --) married Carol Lemons (4/3/1936 --) on 1/27/1954. Married 60 years, 7 months, 19 days and counting.

Arthur F. Quirin (10/14/1936 --) married Betty Landleff (7/14/1938 --) on 10/28/1961. Married 52 years, 10 months, 18 days and counting.

Viola Petry (3/11/1916 – 7/26/2008) married Ralph William Bald (9/17/1914 – 3/17/1992) on 11/30/1939 in Smithton. Married 52 years, 3 months, 17 days.

Eugenia Petry (10/3/1917 – 8/21/1993) married Franklin Dwight Teel (8/24/1918 –) on 3/14/1942. Married 51 years, 5 months, 7 days.

Charles Reiss branch – 72 adults born before 1990 with 10% making gold

Rolland Charles Reiss (7/27/1931 – 8/28/2004) married Selda Brendel (2/28/1934 --) on 10/17/1953. Married 50 years, 10 months, 11 days.

Lucille Reiss (7/21/1908 – 4/13/1982) married Henry Dietz (2/29/1904 – 1/??/1985) on 10/12/1931. Married 50 years, 6 months, 1 day.

Barbara Ann Dietz (2/23/1935 --) married Dr. Richard Paul Peters (10/12/1931 --) on 5/30/1962. Married 52 years, 3 months, 16 days.

Charles Frederick "Tinker" Reiss Jr. (7/26/1873 – 10/28/1958) married Rose Schilling (5/10/1884 – 1/18/1972) on 6/3/1903 in St. Louis. Married 55 years 4 months, 25 days.

Jessie M. Reiss (1/5/1904 – 12/14/1996) married John Delbert Schau (10/25/1890 – 11/18/1973) on 5/5/1920. Married 53 years, 6 months, 13 days.

Earl William Reiss (7/3/1901 – 6/29/1990) married Helen Hughes (8/1/1913 – 6/9/2006) on 4/12/1930. Married 60 years, 2 months, 17 days.

Eva (Evelyn) Julia Reiss (6/18/1918 – 3/21/2008) married Kenneth C. Bevirt (2/27/1915 – 9/30/2000) on 6/4/1938. Married 62 years, 3 months, 26 days.

Martin Reiss branch – 10 adults born before 1990 with 10% making gold

Nancy Louise Rice (12/27/1919 – 3/8/2005) married Robert Earl Stepp Jr. (5/28/1918 – 5/24/2005) in 1936. Married over 61 years.

Kate Reiss Wittig branch – 29 adults born before 1990 with 24% making gold

Catharine (Kate) Reiss (3/23/1847 – 4/2/1916) married Charles Max Wittig (1/16/1838 – 1/30/1918) on 4/9/1866 in a double ceremony with her brother Frank and Anna Feder. She actually died one week short of their 50th anniversary but I included them anyway.

Georgia Elizabeth Keener (8/25/1910 --) married Kenneth Stolp (3/2/1907 – 12/26/1992) on 3/29/1942 in Chico, California. Married 50 years, 8 months, 27 days.

Frida Catherine Wittig (9/28/1878 – 1961) married Ernest Fred Colville (3/1/1876 – 4/??/1964) on 8/19/1903 in Davenport, Iowa. Married over 57 years.

Jean Catherine Colville (7/22/1908 – 9/26/1997) married Caldwell Buck (12/7/1903 – 5/24/1985) on 2/20/1932 in New York City. Married 53 years, 3 months, 4 days.

Roger Colville Buck (4/13/1936 --) married Adale Elias Tannous (3/8/1940 --) on 7/13/1963. Married 51 years, 2 months, 2 days and counting.

Fred Charles Buck (8/28/1939 --) married Betty Darlene Owen (12/5/1938 --) on 6/22/1964 in Covina, California. Married 50 years 2 months, 24 days and counting.

Patricia Louise Colville (11/1/1920 --) married Gerald Waldsmith Giard (9/11/1914 – 5/19/1995) on 2/22/1941 in Yakama, Washington. Married 54 years, 2 months, 27 days.

Instead of half a dozen golden weddings, I found 31. The yellow highlights identify 7 couples who were married 60 years or more, one of which is still counting. Lillian and Lonnie Standley hold the record at 68 years. Must be something about decades of drinking Reiss Dairy milk!!!

These weddings were celebrated every month of the year except September. April, May, June, August, and October were the most popular with four weddings each.

Here is a very faint invitation to our first golden wedding celebration, that of John and Maria Reiss held on 11/3/1911 in Belleville. The stationery belongs to their unmarried daughter Barbara Reiss who lived with them at 322 South Church Street.

Here is a certificate of record dated 4/15/1915 confirming that Frank Reiss and Anna Sevilla Feder were married on 4/9/1866.

Will, Kayla, Ava, and Blake you four come from a long line of relatives who celebrated 50 and more years of marriage. Grand DD and I are at 43 years, my parents had 64 years, and Dad's parents had 53 years. Your parents are on track for long marriages of their own.

Love, Granddad

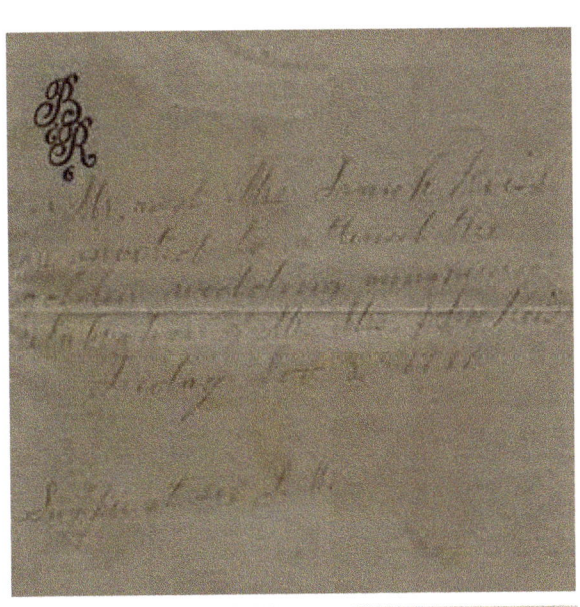

Reiss Family Farm History by Franklin Reiss

Dear Will, Kayla, Ava, and Blake,   August 24, 2015

What follows is a history written by Frank Reiss in June 1985 for the <u>St. Clair County History</u> book published by the St. Clair County Genealogical Society in 1988. He had included a family tree and farm layout which appear in that book but not below. The rest of this story is by Frank Reiss except my closing paragraph. He had an amazing gift for writing and public speaking.

People have long been prone to identify themselves through family and land. Ownership and control of land have been among the most coveted and highly-prized of man's possessions, whether the owners be kings, knaves, or commoners. Pride in lineage and familial antecedents is often a concomitant of land ownership. We offer this brief history not out of a sense of pride, but rather a source of information for those, mainly our children, who seek to know and thus to identify and understand themselves through that knowledge.

For obvious reasons, our effort shall be bounded in time, space, and family dimensions. The time frame begins with the date of November 14, 1756, and ends with the time of this writing, June of 1985, a span of over 200 years. The spatial bounds shall be the 160 acres we shall call the home 160 acres of the George Reiss Farm. The family bounds shall be the line of descent embodied in the person and descendants of one Johann Adam Reiss who was born on May 7, 1804 in Obernau, Aschaffenburg, Bavaria, Germany, and who emigrated from there to America and established the initial Reiss family ownership in the home 160 acres of the George Reiss Farm. The family setting for this Johann Adam Reiss is shown below.

Since 1984 was the sesquicentennial year (the 150th) of the founding of the Reiss Farm in 1834, a family reunion was held on June 23, 1984 on the George Reiss Farm which includes the home 160 acres. Some 115 family members attended the celebration. A similar reunion had been held on October 14, 1934 to celebrate the 100th anniversary of the Reiss Farm. About 140 people attended that event.

The family antecedents in Germany have already been identified in the family tree below. The second and third charts below portray the principal owners of the home 160 acres from the founder, John Adam Reiss, down to the present owners Mrs. George W. Reiss (Catherine Charlotte Luetzelschwab Reiss).

The original owner, John Adam Reiss, died from an attack of cholera in 1849 at the age of 45 years. The farm was left in the hands of his widow, Margaret Basler Reiss, and five small children, the oldest of which was her step-son, John R. Reiss, just eleven years old. Being only 31 years old herself, she married Conrad Ebert, an adjoining property owner and owner of the fourth 40 acres that we have included as part of the home 160 acres.

Franz Joseph Reiss, eldest son of John Adam and Margaret Basler Reiss was only eight years old when his father died. It is not known how the farm operation was carried on, but it is well known that Frank J. Reiss (Franz) emerged as the ultimate owner of the 160 acre farm. In between his father's death and that achievement, Frank grew up, served in the American Civil

War (Co. G, 31st Illinois Infantry), and married Anna Antonia Syvilla Feder, a native of Popendorf, Bordenstein, Bavaria, Germany then living on a farm north of Belleville, Illinois.

The transfer of the land ownership was achieved through gradual purchase of partial interests by Frank from his brothers and sister, and finally, in 1906, the purchase of the Ebert 40 acres in Section 7 from his mother's heirs. Exactly when Frank and Anna took possession and operation of the farm is not known, but it probably was shortly after their marriage in April of 1866.

The second transfer was, by contrast, a simple affair. George W. Reiss, the eldest living son of Frank J. Reiss and Anna A. S. Feder Reiss, had stayed on the farm, working it with his father. His younger brothers left the limited opportunities of the home farm and became professional in various fields including pharmacy, photography, refrigeration and farming. John J. Reiss, the second oldest, settled on a farm near Sikeston, Missouri, and eventually established a commercial dairy operation. George and Catherine Reiss residing on the home farm, produced a family of three sons, William, Franklin, and Irwin, and so in 1917 they purchased the Schaefer farm and an additional 40 acres ostensibly to move there and achieve an independent farm operation.

As the land purchase by George and Catherine left no one to carry on the home farm, Frank and Anna in 1920, asked George and Catherine to purchase the home 160 acres to assure the continuity of the Reiss family on the farm. The timing and the price of this transaction was such as to coincide with the post-World War I farmland inflation. Coming on top of their existing debt obligations on the Schaefer farm, this purchase of the home farm by George and Catherine entailed years of economic struggle. They agonized for several weeks over the request, but finally agreed to the transfer. It was Catherine who scrimped and saved and came up with the cash to meet all of the mortgage payments. Even so, it was 1940 before all of those debts were fully retired.

George W. Reiss died in 1964 at age 91. He left a simple will. All of the land was to go to his children, William, Franklin, and Irwin but the income was to go to Catherine, his wife, for her life. This request was duly carried out. However, the purchase of the home 160 acres was accomplished by means of joint tenancy deed with right of survivorship. Catherine became full and sole owner of the Reiss home 160 acres, and she remains as such at this writing at age 95.

The Larger Farm – The original owner and operator of the Reiss Farm, Johann Adam (or John Adam or J. Adam) Reiss accumulated a total of 160 acres of land, 120 that is still a part of the home farm, and a 40-acre tract a few miles away in Monroe County. The Monroe County 40 acres were sold following the untimely death of J. Adam Reiss.

The loss of this 40 acres was restored, in a sense, by the purchase of the 40-acre Ebert tract to complete the home 160 acres by Frank J. Reiss in 1906. It was, however, George W. Reiss, son of Frank and grandson of the original John Adam Reiss, who not only carried on the family ownership of the original Reiss farm but who substantially enlarged the total holding. His first purchase was a 20-acre tract purchased from the Ebert family at the same time that his father purchased the Ebert 40 acres. His next acquisition came in 1914, a detached 30 acres situated about 5 miles from the home farm. But his major addition was the purchase of the adjoining 120 acres from the Schaefer family plus 20 additional acres one quarter mile east. About the same time, he purchased the 40 acres now (1985) rented to the Smithton Sportsmen's Club on a long term lease.

The attachment gives an overall picture of the Reiss farm as it grew to its peak under the ownership of my father and mother, Mr. and Mrs. George William Reiss. Of this total acreage, the Schaefer 140 acres and the 30-acre tract partly in Monroe County, have already been transferred by gift and inheritance to the fourth generation of Reisses, consisting of William, Franklin, and Irwin, sons of George William and Catherine C. Reiss.

The Larger Family – We have already noted the succession on the home farm, largely through Frank J. Reiss and his son, George W. Reiss. Stepping outside the bounds of the land ownership one finds a fairly large number of individuals who are or were direct descendants of Johann Adam Reiss, our initial immigrant from Germany. John Adam, himself, was the father of five children. His oldest son, John R., by his first wife, produced 5 children, 4 girls, and 1 son who died childless, thus halting the perpetuation of the Reiss name from that source.

The 4 children of John Adam by his second wife had a total of 18 children, or less than 5 per family. In total to date, June 1984, there were 286 direct descendants from John Adam Reiss. Of his 5 children, Frank J. Reiss accounted for 114 of the 286, John R. was second with 70, Charles was third with 65, Catherine was fourth with 25, and Martin was last with only 12. The family has not been prolific in perpetuating the Reiss name. As of June 1984, there were only 25 direct descendants of John Adam Reiss who carried the surname Reiss, and only 18 of these are males, many of whom are beyond reproduction age.

At this point one might recall Shakespeare's words of wisdom: "What's in a name? A rose by any other name would smell as sweet." And so, perhaps, with the Reiss family. Beginning with John Adam Reiss's two wives, and on down to June 1984, there were 140 spouses, both male and female, that married a direct Reiss Descendent. That is both a rich and welcome contribution to the family gene pool to create and support the rich and varied contributions of the family to human progress.

Will, Kayla, Ava, and Blake, we are blessed that those who have gone before us have written their stories and saved their photographs. We're also blessed by the Internet which has made billions and billions of additional records available to the general public. Then the challenge is how to organize all that and consolidate it into a practical and fun summary to explore for years to come. I've chosen to record it as over 200 stand-alone stories for the four of you. I've also learned how much fun it is for me to learn more family history by putting these stories together. Thanks for being my audience.

Love, Granddad

1990 – 1999

1990 Population of St. Clair County is 262,628.

1990 States total 50, national population is 249.44 million.

1990 President is George Bush. Bill Clinton is inaugurated in 1993.

1996 At the Roslin Institute in Scotland, Dolly, the sheep, becomes the first mammal to be cloned.

1999 The Euro currency is introduced.

1999 The Dow Jones Industrial Average closes above 10,000 for the first time.

Reiss Family Bible

Dear Will, Kayla, Ava, and Blake,   June 8, 2015

There is or was a Reiss family bible, but we don't know what happened to it. The notes below were copied from that bible by <mark>Mildred Tatum Reiss</mark> at this Reiss family reunion on the Reiss home farm on May 26, 1940. Mildred and her husband Royal are near the right end of the back row. Their daughter Roya is front row left end. It is Roya who transcribed these notes of her mother's into what appears below in March 2003 and then made copies available to relatives.

Middle row – George Reiss, Ferdinand Reiss, George Dintelmann, Jeanette Reiss, Evelyn Reiss Bivert & son, Syvilla Reiss McCall, Lillian Reiss Standley, Helen Reiss, Etta Reiss, Emily Reiss, Katie Reiss

Back Row – John Reiss, Robert McCall, Edwin Dintelmann, Henry Reiss, Kenneth Bivert, Anita Reiss, Marjorie Pivoda Dintelmann (6 months pregnant with baby Dale), <mark>Mildred Reiss</mark>, Royal Reiss, Bill Reiss, Earl Reiss – Children – Roya Ann Reiss, Francis Jane Reiss, June Ann Reiss, Jo Ellen Standley

Notes from the Reiss Family Bible appear on the next page.

JOHN ADAM REISS – Born 1804 – He came to this country in the yr 1833 & settled in St. Clair County in 1834 – married Miss Schuesseler from the same place where he was from in the yr 1838. In Dec. 1838 his son John Reiss was born & his wife died the same day. He married again in August 1840 a Miss Margaretha Basler. She was born Oct 23, 1818 in Niterglin Canton Aran Swiss. Their first son Franz Joseph Reiss was born Sept 27, 1841. Second Charles Joseph Reiss born Feb. 17, 1843 – 3rd Martin Reiss born June 19, 1845. 1st daughter Catherine Reiss born March 23, 1847. 2nd daughter Barbara born & died 1849. Said John Adam Reiss died of collera [sic] May 23, 1849.

Civil War Co, G – 31 Ill Inf.

Said Franz J. Reiss – son of Jno Adam Reiss married the 9th of April 1866 a Miss Anna Antonia Sibylla Feder dau. of Geo Feder & his wife Anna S. Feder (a born Rau) Said Anna A.S. Feder born Sept 26, 1844 at Popbendorf Landgericht, Borderstein, Kaenigreig, Baiern. Came to U.S. in 1845 with her parents & in 1846 they came to St. Clair Co. Ill & settled down 2 mi north of Belleville.

Children of Franz J. Reiss & Anna Sibylla Reiss

Charles Martin	born Oct 17, 1867 died Nov. 18, 1874
Adam Joseph	Sept 25, 1869 Nov 5, 1874
1st daughter Catherine	Nov 11, 1871 June 16, 1872
Geo. William	April 22, 1873
Anna Margeretha	Sept 20, 1875
John Jacob	Nov 4, 1877
Henry William	March 30, 1880
Louis Phillip	Sept 7, 1882
Louisa Kate	Sept 22, 1884
Lizzie A	July 4, 1888 March 2, 1889
William Martin	Sept 17, 1890

Above children of the said John Adam Reiss & his son Franz J are all born in the old residence of the said John Adam Reiss – situated on the SE quarter of the N.W quarter of section 7 Town 2S, 8W in the county of St. Clair State of Ill. USA

Franz J. Reiss died Nov 1921   Anna Sibylla Reiss died May 1930

(The above was copied by Mildred Tatum Reiss during a visit to Belleville for a reunion on 26 May 1940. My assumption was that it was from a family bible. Transcribed by Roya Reiss Singleton March 2003.)

Will, Kayla, Ava, and Blake, we need to find that family bible. It's safe to assume that the bible belonged to Frank and Anna Sybilla Reiss because it listed only their children and because that transcribing by Mildred happened in their home. We do have a few years to find that bible since none of you is old enough yet to be sworn in as President of the United States by the Chief Justice.

Love, Granddad

WASHINGTON (AP) — President Barack Obama is putting a symbolic twist on a time-honored tradition, taking the oath of office for his second term with his hand placed not on a single Bible, but two — one owned by Martin Luther King Jr. and one by Abraham Lincoln.

Family Streets and Roads

Dear Will, Kayla, Ava, and Blake,   June 8, 2015

You have several ancestors who were farm owners or important people in other ways such that city streets or county roads were named after them. Here's the list:

Basler Street in Sacramento, California – Martin and Anna Maria Basler took a covered wagon from St. Joseph, Missouri to Sacramento in the summer of 1852. They eventually did quite well financially and at one point owned over 1,000 acres several miles north of the city. Today it's all part of the city near the Sacramento River. They have 76 letters from 1852 to 1886 in our book, It Takes A Matriarch. They mention the river flooding their farm at times.

Dintelmann Church Road per plat book – Here is what my cousin Dale Dintelmann learned. This is a 2.4-mile long east-west road south of St. Libory, Illinois or 19 miles south-southeast of Smithton. Before 1874, a catholic church was built on 80 acres on the west part of the road almost at the county boarder. St. Liborius Church now owns that land. As rural routes were being updated to named roads, the Fayetteville Township Road Commissioner renamed the road to Dintelmann Road. As this was confused with Dintelmann Lane (below), the road was renamed to Dintelmann Church Road.

Dintelmann Lane in Freeburg, Illinois – This is where Ron Dintelmann and his father Eugene live in two houses and small farm. Ron is the Public Works Director of Freeburg and as such may also assign names to new roads.

Luetzelschwab Road per plat book – This road borders the west side of the historic Luetzelschwab farm south of Millstadt. It's called Luetzelschwab Road on the plat book but on Google Earth it's called Algonquin Forrest Road.

Reiss Avenue in Belleville, Illinois – This street is northwest of downtown Belleville. We had several Reiss family relatives in Belleville but I don't know the history behind this particular street.

Reiss Road in O'Fallon, Illinois – This part of the city is the former Charles Reiss farm.

Reiss Road on our home farm – This is the farm lane leading to the Reiss family farm from both the west and north entrances.

Reiss Road per plat book – This is the east west road at the Reiss farm mailbox but on the satellite photo it's called Klein Road after the next farm west. You can see the George Reiss Road between Sections 6 and 7 in the map below.

Steve Street and Diane Drive – You'll recognize this as the driveway crossing in our yard in Dunlap, Illinois. **Reiss Lane** is the name of our front walkway. I'm ordering another sign for our driveway that says Reißstraße.

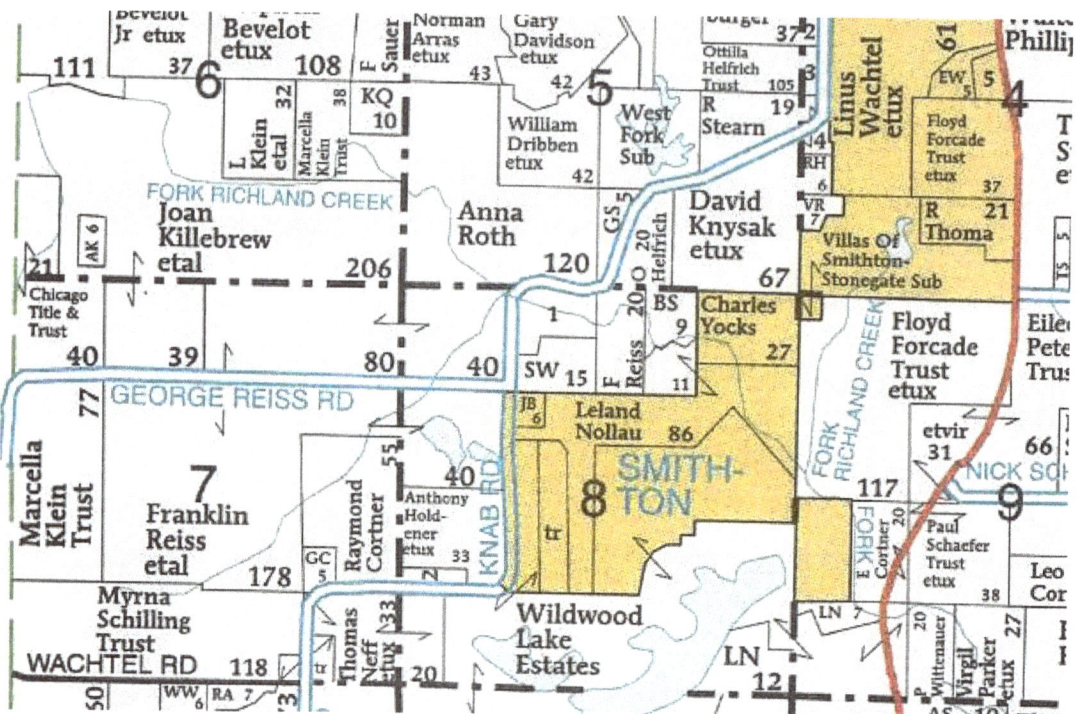

Knab Road runs from Highway 159 to the Smithton Sportsmen's Club and beyond. Here's an old sign from the Sportsmen's corner before the George Reiss Road was changed to Klein Road. Without that name change, signs at our mailbox would have shown the intersection of George Reiss Road and George Reiss Road. Cool!!!

Will, Kayla, Ava, and Blake, maybe you remember three road signs from our yard that appear on the next two pages. We could add similar signs for some of the wildlife game trails and brick pathways that need names. How about Will Way, Kayla Krossing, Ava Avenue, and Blake Boulevard. Whaduyasay?

Love, Granddad

Belleville, Illinois

Dear Will, Kayla, Ava, and Blake,   September 28, 2015

Belleville is the County Seat of St. Clair County which was the first county in the State of Illinois. It's where my dad and his brothers went to high school. It's where dozens of our relatives in the John Reiss branch lived and are buried. It's where our family went for the county fair and various festivals in the 1950s and 1960s. It's where we went for German meats at Streck and Weyhaupt Packing Companies. It's where we took Grandma and Pop to shop for furniture, clothes, and supplies. It's where we always looked to see if the fountain in the middle of the downtown circle was shooting into the air. It's were Dad's brother Bill lived with his family. Belleville was on the route from Sullivan, from Peoria, and from Urbana for our quarterly visits to the home farm.

One of the unique items given to me from the estate of Frank and Gerry Reiss is The New International Encyclopedia published in 1912. The next paragraph is what it mentioned about Belleville, Illinois over 100 years ago. That's followed by several paragraphs from Wikipedia.

A city and county-seat of Saint Clair County, Illinois, 17 miles east by south of Saint Louis, Missouri, on the Illinois Central, the Louisville and Nashville, and the Southern Railroads. It is the seat of a Roman Catholic bishop, and contains the Belleville Fairgrounds, a public library, founded in 1836, Saint Elizabeth Hospital, Saint Vincent Hospital, and Saint John's Orphan Asylum. The city is in a productive agricultural and coal-mining region, and is noted for its manufacturers, including stove-works, foundries and machine-shops, nail-mill, tack-works, glass-works, shoe factories, brickyards, ice plant, distillery, breweries, and flour mills. Settled in 1814, Belleville was incorporated first in 1846. The government is vested in a mayor, elected biennially, who appoints all the important administrative officers, and a council. Population in 1906 was 18,756.

The city of Belleville was named by George Blair in 1814. Blair was born in 1760 and his father was born in Scotland. Blair donated an acre of his land for the Town Square and an additional 25 acres that adjoined the Square for the new County Seat, causing the county seat to be transferred from the village of Cahokia. Belleville was incorporated as a village in 1819, and became a city in 1850. It is said that Blair named the city Belleville (French for beautiful city) because he believed that a French name would attract new residents. Since major immigration in the mid-19th century occurred following revolutions in Germany, most of the population is of German heritage.

Many of the educated people fled their homeland after the failure of the German Revolution in 1848. Belleville was the center of the first important German settlement in Illinois. By 1870, an estimated 90% of the city's population was either German born or of German descent.

After the Civil War, Belleville became a manufacturing center producing nails, printing presses, gray iron castings, agricultural equipment, and stoves. Belleville became known as "The Stove Capital of the World." The first brewery in Illinois was established in Belleville and in 1868, Gustav Goelitz founded the candy company that is known today as "Jelly Belly."

An immense deposit (400,000 acres) of bituminous coal was found in St. Clair County. By 1874, some farmers had become coal miners. One hundred shaft mines were in operation in and around Belleville. The coal brought the steam railroad to town, which allowed for the transport of many tons of coal to be shipped daily from Belleville to St. Louis. Later, Belleville would have the first electric trolley in the state.

The first style of homes in Belleville was simple brick cottages, known locally as "German street houses" or "row houses." Over or 700 properties are listed on the Belleville National Register District. The "Old Belleville Historic District," was formed in 1974 and is the city's first historic district. The city also had two more historic districts: "Hexenbukel" (est. in 1991) and "Oakland" (est. in 1995).

Belleville's early German immigrants were scholarly, with most of them having graduated from German universities. They were nicknamed "Latin Farmers" because of this. After 1836 Gustav Koerner contributed to establish the city's public library. The Belleville Public Library is the state's oldest, predating the Illinois State Library by three years. The German settlers also founded choral and dramatic groups as well as literary societies. Belleville was also home to one of the first kindergartens in the country.

The city celebrated its Bicentennial in 2014.

Will, Kayla, Ava, and Blake, we need to spend several weekends in Belleville and St. Clair County. We can visit our family farm, catch fish in the Sportsmen's lakes, eat fish at the Legion in Smithton, go to church in Floraville, go to a baseball game in St. Louis, and check out the many unique sites in Belleville.

Love, Granddad

Frank Reiss – My Story
A Scrapbook for Jesse Reiss in 1999

Dear Will, Kayla, Ava, and Blake,   November 23, 2015

Here's a fascinating and very informative story written by your great great uncle Franklin Reiss. He was my dad's next older brother, college roommate, fellow agrarian, good buddy, and frequent sounding board. What follows is Frank writing to his first grandchild Jesse.

I am Franklin Jacob Reiss. I was born on October 31st, 1915. I am the middle son of George William Reiss and Catherine Charlotte Luetzelschwab. I was christened Frank Jacob but was called Franklin (little Frank in the German language) by my grandfather, Frank Joseph Reiss. Our home was a farm in Southern Illinois, St. Clair County, Prairie du Long Township – about 20 miles east of St. Louis or 12 miles south of Belleville, IL – County Seat.

My family spoke German at home. My father, George William Reiss, was one of five boys and two girls.

I spoke German until I went to school in a village one-room school house, about 2 miles from our home. The village was Floraville. The school was taught by a man, Oscar Probst. He refused to allow German to be spoken in or on the school grounds. So my brothers and I grew up speaking English without an "accent."

Our mother let us play after school, but once a week, Saturday night, we had to have baths. We went to church on Sunday in our best clothes. Our Uncle Will came to Sunday dinner and took our pictures.

When I got into high school, my dad let me buy a rifle and I had a trap line, skinned small animals, and sold the fur skins to earn money. I remember catching a skunk one time. My uncles and older brother had told me that if I held the skunk by the tail, it could not "squirt" its protective scent. Ha! Ha! – not true! The skunk had crawled down under some tree roots until the trap caught and I pulled it out by the tail. As it cleared the hole, it let go that scent – in my face! I nearly smothered! Thank the Lord, there was snow on the ground and I rolled over and over in the snow. When I got home, my mother made me strip outdoors, my father had to bury my clothes, and I had a hot bath on the porch and it wasn't Saturday!

After I completed the eight grades at Floraville, I went to a small town about seven miles west of Floraville, it was called Millstadt – in German – Milltown. They had a flour mill and a two-year high school. I stayed with my mother's brother, Uncle John Luetzelschwab and his wife, Aunt Katy – they had two boys, Edgar and Rolly. We had good times – Aunt Katy was a good cook.

Millstadt had only a two-year high school, so with a neighbor, I went to Belleville High School for my last two years. I graduated in 1932 – in the upper 2% of my class – but it was the bottom of the Depression! No jobs to be had.

I worked on the farm, with my father, planting corn, raising hogs, for nearly four years. This was during the Depression. I also had other jobs working part time as a part of a surveying crew, measuring land for the AAA programs in the 1930s. I measured farms with sinkholes for some of St. Clair County has the karst limestone areas where the ground subsides into deep holes. Many underground caves and streams are here.

I traveled to Champaign-Urbana a couple of times to attend farm programs and exhibits. Our county farm advisor took me and other farm boys. He encouraged me to write the county exam for tuition to attend the University of Illinois. Also I decided to write the Civil Service exam about the same time. I was pleased to learn that I passed both exams. I was offered the County Scholarship to the University of Illinois and also a job with the Postal Service. This was decision-making time. My brother Bill did not get to go to college – he later took night classes in Belleville. I decided on the U of I but my family had little money. I got a job waiting tables in the fraternity for my meals. I worked in an office in the Agricultural Department to earn money for my room. I studied hard, and was able to complete the four years of classes in 3.5 years. I started on a Master's Degree before I graduated from the University in 1940. I was in the top group of my class – graduating with Highest Honors – my name is on a Bronze Tablet, on the wall of the University Library.

I was brought up by my family to attend church and Sunday School – in German "Samstag Schjule" – really Saturday School where we learned our catechism in German. Our church in Floraville was the Evangelical Church, and while I was young, the services were in German. My mother said that when I was four years old, I spoke a verse, in German at a Christmas program.

"Ich bin nu rein kleinest kind
Aber Ich kannst sage: "Die Christ Kind heute geborn ist."
(I'm only a small child but I can say: The Christ Child is born today.)"

In college, I went to the McKinley Presbyterian Church – nearby where I worked in a fraternity. Here I noticed a pretty girl who sang in the choir. Later I met her at the Foundation where we were in a War play together. This was in 1938.

One Sunday evening, we had a supper in the McKinley Foundation, then we performed. I took the part of an American General. This was before the US was involved in World War II. The pretty girl, Miss Geraldine Louise Hulet, played the part of a German spy – ala Mati Hari. I'm sorry to say, that during the play, I had to have Miss Hulet shot at sunrise! – yes! Off stage!!

Later, nearly a year or more, we were married – in McKinley Foundation Chapel, on August 22, 1940. I had graduated from the University of Illinois in May of 1940 and accepted a position in the Agricultural Economics Department as a teaching assistant. I taught classes in Ag Econ. I worked in the Farm Record Office. Later as a special interest, I developed and taught upper class students (juniors and seniors) in Farm Appraisal classes. Also I did research in the Farm Records, wrote farm leases and many farm reports.

I traveled throughout the State of Illinois, talking to farm groups, mainly on keeping records of crop production and use of written farm leases. Many Illinois farms are worked by tenants, not farm owners.

In my family, Gerry (Geraldine liked the nickname) and I were blessed to have a son. George Henry Irwin Reiss was born on February 26, 1942. He was a big and healthy boy. He weighed 10 lb, 2 oz at birth. My father was delighted to have a grandson named for him. He wrote me a letter, I kept it for years, he said he "knew" the evening before George was born, that he had a grandson who would be named George. Gerry and I hadn't really firmly settled on the name beforehand, so we were quite surprised at Poop's comments. He seemed truly delighted. We later remembered that my older brother, Bill and wife Anita, lost a son shortly after birth. So Pop was indeed pleased!

In the meantime, the US declared war on Japan – Pearl Harbor in the Hawaii Islands was bombed on December 7, 1941. My brother, Irwin, was in the Army stationed first in California. Ironically Irv, as all of us spoke good German, the US also declared war on Germany, so the Army – typically – sent Irwin to Yale, taught him Chinese, then sent him to India and he directed Chinese workers along the Burma Road. I was declared in a position of importance – helping to provide food for the soldiers and civilians. Being married and having a child also kept me out of the draft. In one way I was glad, but in another way, a bit sad.

Irwin and I learned that one of our buddies from the home area of Floraville and Millstadt had been killed in the Battle of the Bulge – Delbert Seibert. Another friend, he even roomed with us on Oregon Street while going to the U of I – Eugene Rank, was a prisoner of war in Germany. I wrote to him, mid-July 1944 but my letter was returned in May 1945 – it had been censored. He never got this least letter – I saved it as a souvenir of the times.

Irv came home on leave and here he and I posed by our 1938 Chevy. We didn't have much gas coupons. I remember travel by train to the farm, Bill met us in St. Louis. Also I often went by Greyhound bus to farm meetings.

Mary Stephenson Reiss came to the farm to meet her new family. Irwin and Mary were married on November 8, 1942. They Army sent Irv to India to assist in building the Burma-Ledo Road. Stephen William was born to Mary and Irwin on June 12, 1944.

Two years and nine months after George was born, our second son, Richard Franklin Reiss, was born on November 21, 1944. He too was a big healthy baby who weighed 9 lbs., 15.5 oz. The nurse said, "If I put my thumb on the scales, you would have another 10 pounder!" The next summer, my father was equally pleased to have another grandson. Gerry and I were indeed blessed with our two fine healthy and intelligent children. George was very good and watched out for Richard. As they grew older, they had different interests. George enjoyed sports and Richard liked music and played piano for years.

We spent many summers on the farm in St. Clair County with Pop and Grandma. The Reiss family thought of the farm as "Home" – always the relatives were welcomed and fed. From about 1952 until 1979 Gerry taught in the Urbana Public Schools. Her mother, Mrs. Linna Irene Massey Hulet, lived with us and helped Gerry keep house.

Gerry's brother, Richard E. Hulet, was in the US Army Quartermaster Corps. He was scheduled to go overseas, home on leave at Christmas, he contracted appendicitis, his appendix actually broke open before the doctors at Chanute Field operated, so they shook penicillin in the wound and said "Well, he'll live or die – we'll know in a few days!" What a Christmas present for his mother and family. Fortunately, he lived! We were relieved!

At last the war was over, Richard and Irwin came home safely, married and raised their families. Gerry and I welcomed them often in our home. We celebrated Pop and Mom's 50th Wedding Anniversary in April of 1961. George Reiss, aged 88 years, Catherine aged 70 – had a large family gathering in the Sportsmen's Club on the 40 acres I helped Pop & Mom lease to the Smithton Sportsmen Club. The ladies of the club served a fine dinner for our family and guests.

In 1946 we lived in a downstairs apartment of a two story house near the corner of Oregon and Lincoln Streets. I took my boys riding in their red wagon. Richard, two years, still quite blond and George, 4.5 years, dark hair and brown eyes. I bought a National Homes "pre-fab" at 601 E. Washington Street and, since it had only two bedrooms, we built on a dining room and big bedroom for the two boys. I planted redbud trees that I brought up from the farm.

In June of 1952, I completed my thesis and was awarded a Doctor's degree. My whole family came to the graduation ceremony, I was the first one in our family to earn an Academic Doctor's Degree.

I was busy these years in the 1950s and 1960s with seminars, classes, and workshops. I set up locations away from campus to collect and check the Farm Records that selected farmers kept each year. Then I wrote the data and the department published the final form in the annual Farm Bureau Farm Management Report. I traveled many miles speaking to farm groups for the U of I Farm Extension Department. Actually I had an unusual appointment of 50% Extension, 25% time teaching, and 25% time research. Gerry used to say: Frank spends 50% of his time traveling (Extension), 50% teaching, and 50% researching farm records. I guess I hadn't been spending enough time at home!

Will, Kayla, Ava, and Blake, isn't that a wonderful story by a wonderful man. Frank passed away on July 8, 2002 so you never had a chance to meet him. I remember him taking lots of pictures and then showing his slides to family and business associates in well-organized presentations. I remember taking lots of walks in the Reiss farm woods with Frank and his family. He always wore bib overalls plus a white shirt and tie as his walk uniform. I often thought that was overkill until I realized that was also his work uniform from conducting hundreds of ag extension meetings with farmers. Below is a letter congratulating Frank on being elected to *The American Society of Farm Managers and Rural Appraisers'* Hall of Fame.

Love, Granddad

**The American Society of Farm Managers
and Rural Appraisers, Inc.**
950 S. Cherry Street, Suite G-16
Denver, Colorado 80222
(303) 758-3513

February 6, 1984

Dr. Franklin Reiss
2003 South Anderson Street
Urbana, Illinois 61801

Dear Frank:

Congratulations on receiving the Illinois Chapter of the American
Society of Farm Managers and Rural Appraisers "Hall of Fame"
award.   You are certainly very deserving of this award because of
your many years of service to the Illinois Chapter and the
American Society. We are very happy for you and I could not think
of a better person to recieve it.

Again congratulations!

Sincerely,

Eldon Greenwood, A.F.M.
President Elect

2000 – 2009

2000 Population of St. Clair County is 256,208.

2000 States total 50, national population is 282.17 million.

2000 President is Bill Clinton. George W. Bush is inaugurated in 2001.

2001 Islamic fundamentalist terrorists hijack four U.S. airliners and crash them into the Pentagon and the World Trade Center in New York City.

Hunting on the Reiss Family Farm

Dear Will, Kayla, Ava, and Blake,   March 24, 2014

In 2004 our owners signed on with Farmers National Company and their area manager, Bret Cude, to manage the 360 acres of our family farm in St. Clair County. We had several meetings with Bret in the early years and have been very pleased with his communication skills and overall management. One of the things he pushed for was using FNC's subsidiary, Hunting Lease Network, to professionally manage our farm for hunting wildlife during various official seasons. That's normally just deer and turkey but it could include squirrels, pheasants, quail, etc. Bret explained how HLN qualifies their hunters, insists on adequate insurance, posts "no trespassing" signs allowing just the approved hunters, and complies with all hunting and environmental laws and regulations.

I created the map below as an Excel spreadsheet. The hunting area appears in green. The yellow areas are part of the family farm but are not open to hunters. You can see the 40 acres leased to the Smithton Sportsmen's Club which has built three lakes. The 20 acres west of them does not have many trees and is kept as a buffer for the Sportsmen's Club. The other 20 acres at the far right abuts a housing subdivision and is open only to trespassers looking for mushrooms!

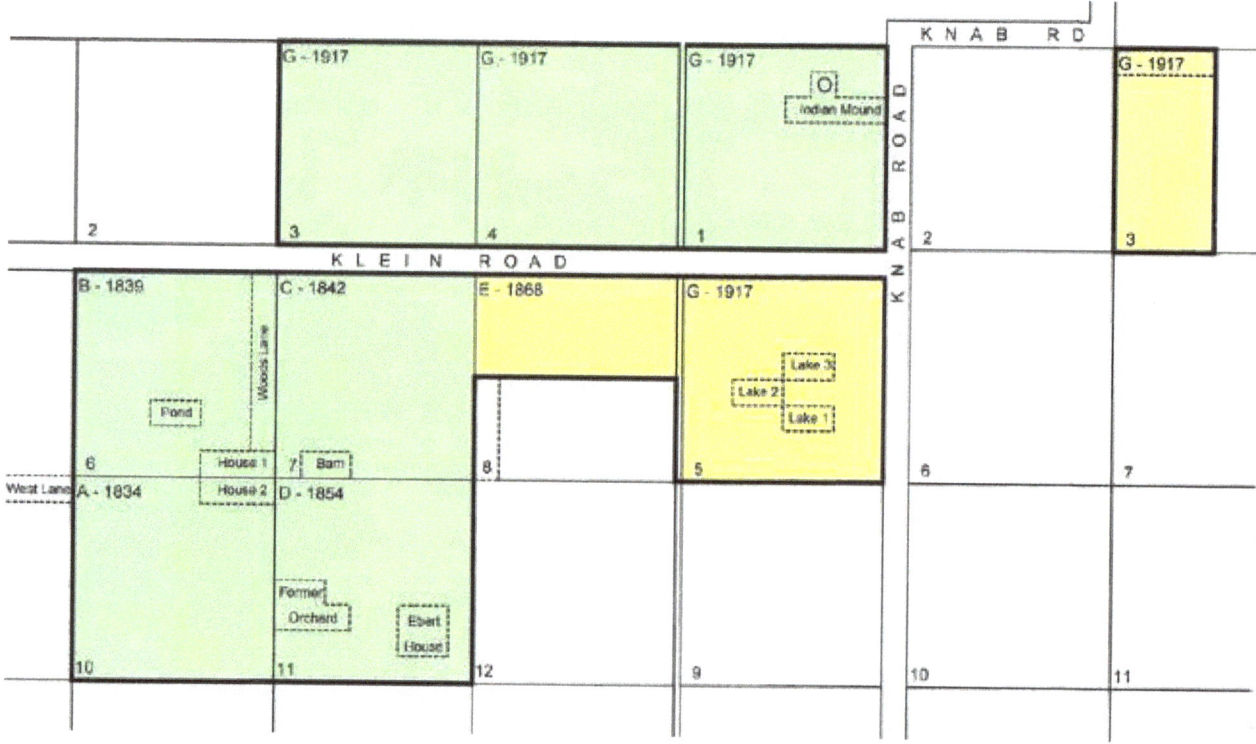

Hunting Lease Network created the two maps on the next page, one from a satellite photo and one from a topographical map. Between the two of them, potential hunters can identify potential deer stand and game trail camera locations before actually walking the property.

HLN   ILSO-0052   St. Clair County, IL
278 Acres +/-
Boundaries Are Approximate

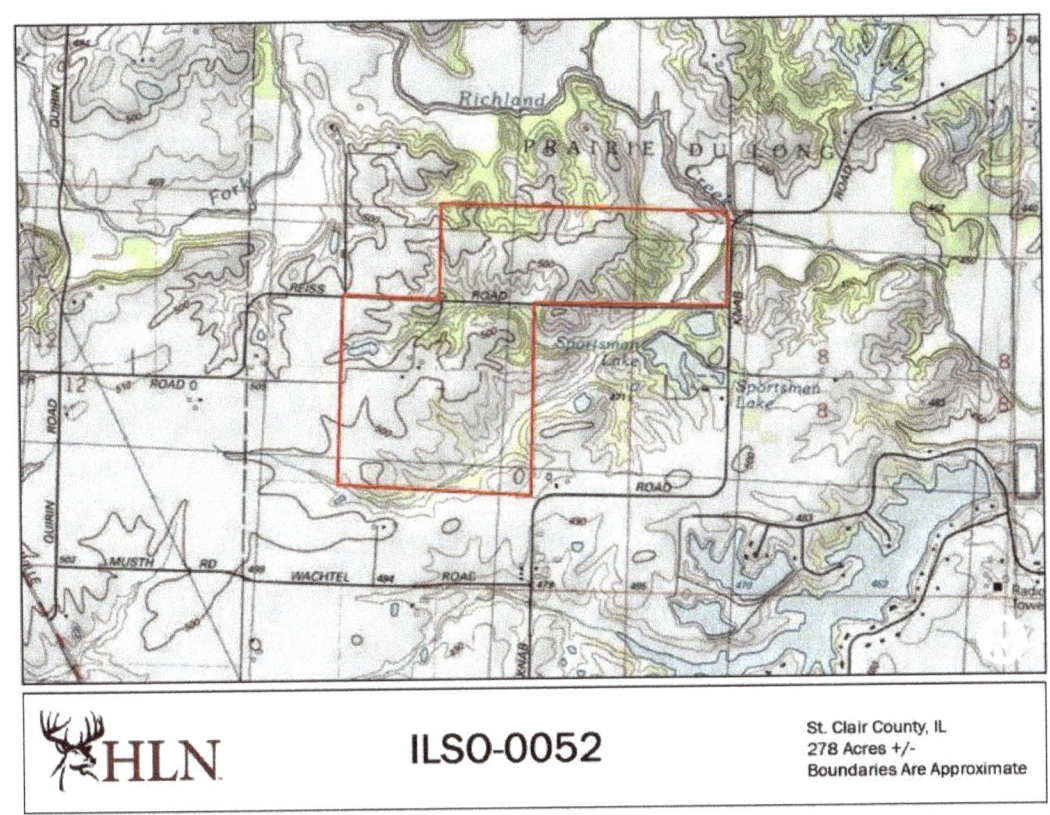

HLN   ILSO-0052   St. Clair County, IL
278 Acres +/-
Boundaries Are Approximate

In the satellite photo you can see the homestead in the left center with various buildings. Hunters are supposed to check in with the tenants to say they are on the property and may even leave their vehicles and campers nearby. You can see four major areas of trees. One of our hunters from Vermont bagged this 14-point buck on our farm in 2010. I met him a month before the season opened when he was setting up game trail cameras. He had seen this big buck on the cameras and became obsessed. I don't remember his name but he impressed me as a guy who could take charge in a woods full of armed men in illegal tree stands. He was a supervisor with Blackwater Security in Iraq and was a really tough dude. His arms were as big as my legs.

Will, Kayla, Ava, and Blake, the year shown in the upper left corner of each box in my first map is the year that particular 40 or 20 acres was added to the family farm. However the 1834 year shown in the lower left box is wrong. It should be 1838. My Granddad's Mondays story to you four next month on April 28 will explain how our family farm dates from 1838, not 1834. All the reunions, etc. we've had over the last 180 years got it wrong!!!

Love, Granddad

Reiss Dodransbicentennial Reunion on June 5/6, 2009

Dear Will, Kayla, Ava, and Blake,   August 3, 2015

I don't see any of you in this family picture from mid-2009. Don't you guys like a good party? Well, your absence is because none of you were born yet. Our Springfield family was married on 4/26/2008 and our Chicago family was married after the reunion on 8/29/2009. That's your great grandmother Mary Reiss on the far left. She was age 88 at the reunion. By the way dodransbicentennial means we're celebrating 175 years since Adam Reiss purchased his first farm in St. Clair County, Illinois in 1834.

We had 114 relatives attend including Rosie Reiss-Palmer on the left and her daughter Constance on the right. Rosie was born in Obernau, Bavaria, Germany and has lived in Atlanta, Georgia since the early 1980s.

Below is a proclamation by the Illinois House of Representatives recognizing our 175-year Reiss Reunion. There are six "whereas" statements and then the following "resolutions" statements: **Resolved, by the House of Representatives of the Ninety Sixth General Assembly of the**

State of Illinois, that we recognize the Reiss Family Farm for its 175th Anniversary in St. Clair County, and commend the vision, dedication, and hard work by the Reiss Family through the years, and **Be It Further Resolved**, that a suitable copy of the Proclamation be presented to the Reiss Family as an expression of our esteem.

Signed: **State Senator Dale Risinger** and **State Representative David R. Leitch**

Will, Kayla, Ava, and Blake, there is a second congratulatory message on the next page. Only problem is that it came seven months after our party was over. I can't quite make out the sender's signature.

Love, Granddad

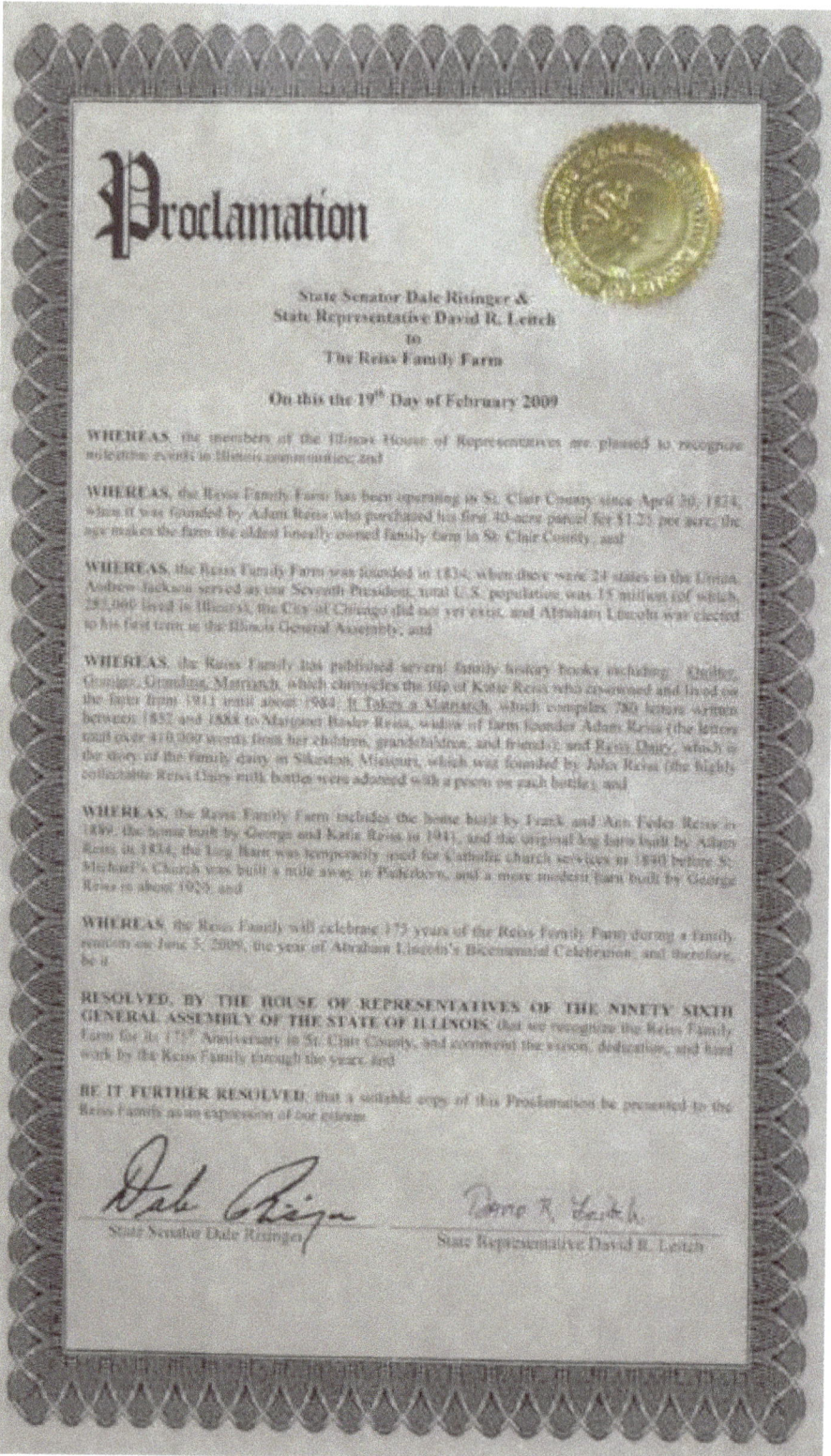

THE WHITE HOUSE

WASHINGTON

January 12, 2010

The Reiss Family
c/o Stephen W. Reiss
700 West Savanna Court
Dunlap, Illinois 61525

Dear Friends:

I am pleased to offer my warmest greetings as you gather to celebrate your family reunion.

Families are central to the American identity. They are our strongest connections to the past and clearest lens into our future. They offer us support, guidance, and unconditional love.

As you reflect upon your family's heritage, I hope you enjoy your time together and create many wonderful new memories. I wish you all health and happiness in the years ahead.

Sincerely,

[signature]

Illinois Farm Provides a Good Beginning to Life

Dear Will, Kayla, Ava, and Blake,   October 19, 2015

This is a story my dad wrote for the "Sullivan Daily Times" in our Indiana home town on April 30, 2003. Everything which follows is Dad's except for my last paragraph.

Even though my wife, Mary, and I have lived in Sullivan for over 50 years, neither of us was born here. Mary was born in Canada, and I first saw the light of day on a farm in St. Clair County, Ill. about 25 miles southeast of St. Louis. The farm has been in the Reiss name since 1834. I was born in the room over the summer kitchen on the farm 2 miles east of Floraville. That is where I went to Sunday school – speaking only German.

In 1833, a man named Adam Reiss left Bavaria in eastern Germany on an empty cotton boat headed for New Orleans. During the next year, he worked his way up the Mississippi River Valley to the St. Louis area with a lot of other Germans. He was a farmer, so he looked for land. At that time, the flat prairie land had not been broken for farming and access to water was necessary – so he took to the hills and creek bottoms. Little did he realize that someday his great-grandson would have to hoe corn on those hills.

My father, George W. Reiss, was born on this farm in 1873. He was the first of seven children that survived under the primitive and difficult circumstances. And it was he that stayed on this farm and added many more acres to the original land purchase. I have gone back to visit the house and relive the memories.

Of all the rooms in the house, I liked the summer kitchen best. It was here that Mom baked our daily break, molasses cookies, and prizewinning angel food cakes. The heat to do the cooking and baking came from burning wood. We had no electricity. We did have a coal oil stove for quick heat. The house had a basement where we stored our homegrown potatoes and fruit from our orchard. This was our haven when bad storms blew up – we went into the basement and prayed until they were over. It was also where we made our homemade ice cream when our cousins from Millstadt brought the ice.

Pop kept his horses in the barn. We didn't have a tractor. Everything had to be done by "horse power," the plowing, disking, and drilling. Horses ate hay, which had to be grown, harvested, and put in the barn loft. That was a dirty, sweaty job. We raised chickens and swine. We had over 500 laying hens. Gathering eggs from the nests every evening was fun until late one night when I grabbed a live snake in the nest instead of eggs. The chickens had to be fed and watered every morning. Pumping water from the well into buckets and carrying those to the chicken house was my daily chore in addition to gathering eggs in the evening.

My two brothers had to work in the fields – so it was the kid brother who worked at the home. I learned my responsibilities early in life. We stored wheat and oats in the granary. Part of the granary was built with logs. This historic building survived the modernization of the farmstead.

Cedar Tree Lane was the road to Floraville. My church and school were both in Floraville, a town with 104 inhabitants. I went to German Saturday and Sunday school. One teacher taught in the public one-room school that held all eight grades. My father was clerk of the school board of directors for 24 years. Did that help my grades? I don't think so, but I studied hard. When I took the county examination that was required of all about to be graduated from eighth grade, I made the highest marks in the county. I was, thus, awarded a scholarship to what is now Southern Illinois University.

I walked to and from school for a total of four miles a day. Today, the thought of walking four miles just makes me tired!

Will, Kayla, Ava, and Blake, can you imagine growing up without electricity and no indoor water, not even a bathroom with a toilet and shower? There was also no refrigerator, no telephone, no television, and no iPad. Can you imagine? Well, somehow Dad survived it and remembered it, and believed it worthwhile enough to write this story for the newspaper. We are so blessed.

Love, Granddad

Irv Reiss' Last Story

Dear Will, Kayla, Ava, and Blake,   November 9, 2015

This is the last story my dad wrote for the "Sullivan Daily Times" in our Indiana hometown. It was dated November 10, 2004 which will be eleven years ago tomorrow. A lot of major family events have happened in the last decade.

Trip to Hometown Brings Back Memories

Three weeks ago I got an invitation to attend the 145th anniversary of St. Paul's United Church of Christ, Floraville, IL. I could not turn down an opportunity to go back to the church where I had been confirmed, joined the church, and attended Sunday school for over 20 years. I attended Sunday school from the time that I was 4 years old.

Floraville is a small town in southwest Illinois about 30 miles from St. Louis. When I was there 75 or 80 years ago, Floraville had a population of about 100 people. It had two grocery stores that were well-patronized by the farmers in the area.

I was born and raised on a farm about two miles east of Floraville. My hometown had a grade school that provided the first eight grades. I took all of them with one teacher. My father was secretary of the school board for more than 20 years. I walked the two miles to school each morning and home after school. We had no paved roads. Rain and snow in the winter were real problems. When it was too muddy to walk, my Pop took me in the horse-drawn buggy.

After I took my final exams, I was awarded a Southern Illinois College scholarship. I could not go from the eighth grade to college, so I attended a county seat high school for four years. I had no money for college, so after I finished high school I worked in the government farm program and saved my money for college.

My wife, Mary, and I got to the church homecoming an hour early by mistake, but this provided me with an opportunity to do some reminiscing. The minister came early and I was able to talk with him about my church. We were standing in the same spot where our Christmas programs took place when I was a 4-year-old boy. Ours was a German community and everybody spoke that language during Sunday school and church services. So when I got to the stage that Christmas Eve to say my first piece, it was in German. In English, my piece was: "I am a small fellow. I can't say much, but I'll say it anyway so that you will all know that Jesus Christ was born today."

Will, Kayla, Ava, and Blake, isn't that a nice story? Floraville still has about the same population that it did 80 years ago. Here's the church my dad mentioned. It dates from 1857.

Love, Granddad

Reiss Family Farm Residents

Dear Will, Kayla, Ava, and Blake,   September 29, 2014

Who do you think lived the longest on the Reiss family farm? I could guess the top two or three relatives but did not know how many there were altogether or how long each had stayed, so I went to our family tree and put the following list together. Yellow is the first generation, then grey, then green, then blue, and then no highlight for the Lang children. Purple is the top five.

For those born and dying on the farm, overall tenure was easy to calculate accurately. But for those born on the farm who moved elsewhere, I used birth date and wedding date. For those born elsewhere and marrying into the farm, I used wedding date and death date. Exceptions were Katie Luetzelschwab Reiss who worked as a domestic on the farm a year before she married George Reiss and Martin Reiss who left home at age 17 to work 22 years in various locations before marrying.

Johann Adam Reiss (5/7/1804 – 5/23/1849) married Mary Schuessler (?? – 12/11/1838) on 5/15/1838 but she was already expecting so we assume an earlier common law wedding. Mary died in childbirth and Adam then married Margaritha Basler (10/22/1818 – 6/23/1902) on 9/10/1840. Adam was 10 years, 8 months, 22 days from date of land purchase. Mary was 1 year. Margaret was 61 years, 9 months, 13 days with two husbands.

John R. Reiss (12/11/1838 – 6/18/1919) married Maria Josephine Gass (2/6/1844 – 12/2/1920) on 10/22/1861 in Paderborn. John was 22 years, 10 months, 11 days.

Frank Joseph Reiss (9/27/1841 – 11/21/1921) married Anna Antonia Syvilla Feder (9/26/1844 – 5/14/1930) on 4/9/1866, the same day as his sister Kate married Max Wittig. Frank was 80 years, 1 month, 25 days. Anna was 64 years, 1 month, 5 days.

Charles Martin Reiss (10/17/1867 – 11/18/1874) is buried in St. Augustine Catholic Cemetery in Row 2. Charles was 7 years, 1 month 1 day.

Adam Joseph Reiss (9/25/1869 – 11/5/1874) is buried in St. Augustine Catholic Cemetery in Row 2. Adam was 5 years, 1 month, 11 days.

Catherine Reiss (11/11/1871 – 6/16/1872) is buried in St. Augustine Catholic Cemetery in Row 2. Catherine was 7 months, 15 days.

George William Reiss (4/22/1873 – 8/19/1964) married Catharine Charlotte Luetzelschwab (3/25/1890 – 10/17/1986) on 4/16/1911 at St. Paul's Church in Floraville. George was 91 years, 3 months, 28 days. Katie was 71 years, 6 months before moving to Urbana.

William George Reiss (5/6/1912 – 8/29/1989) married Anita Theresa Hesse (8/12/1917 – 12/17/1960) on 6/9/1935. Bill was 23 years, 1 month, 3 days.

Franklin Jacob Reiss (10/31/1915 – 7/8/2002) married Geraldine Hulet (6/1/1916 – 9/10/2008) on 8/22/1940. Frank was 24 years, 9 months, 22 days.

Irwin Reiss (9/18/1917 – 4/11/2007) married Mary Leone Stephenson (3/15/1921 – 5/16/2010) on 11/8/1942 in Atascadero, California. Irv was 25 years, 1 month, 21 days.

Anna Margaretta Reiss (9/20/1875 – 8/31/1940) married George Dintelmann, Sr. (2/1/1867 – 2/27/1945) on 4/22/1908 as his second wife. Margaret was 32 years, 7 months, 2 days.

John Jacob Reiss (11/4/1877 – 8/28/1957) married Mary Etta Sellards (11/11/1884 - 09/20/1947) on 1/24/1910. John was 32 years, 2 months, 20 days.

Henry William Reiss (3/30/1880 – 10/4/1953) married Emma Eberlein (1878 – 6/17/1930) in 1906. Henry was 26 years 2 months.

Louis Phillip Reiss (9/7/1882 – 4/25/1968) married Harriet "Hattie" F. Wright (1879 – 6/8/1963) before 1905. Louis was 22 years, 9 months.

Louisa Kathryn Reiss (9/22/1884 – 10/22/1969) married Philip Heinrich Petry (3/5/1879 – 11/10/1942) on 6/2/1909. Katie was 24 years, 8 months, 11 days.

Elizabetha (Lizza) A. Reiss (7/1/1888 – 3/2/1889) is buried in St. Augustine Catholic Cemetery in Row 2. Lizza was 8 months, 1 day.

William Martin Reiss (9/17/1890 – 7/??/1975) married Mabel J. Golden (8/??/1885 – 7/2/1962) in 1913. Will was 22 years, 8 months.

Charles Joseph Reiss (2/17/1843 - 5/13/1931) married Eva Dintelmann (6/25/1844 – 11/29/1910) on 11/15/1866. Charles was 23 years, 8 months, 29 days.

Martin Charles Reiss (Rice after 1867) (6/19/1845 – 1898) married Margaret Williams (3/23/1862 – 8/5/1891) in 1883. Before marrying at age 38, he worked as a harness maker in 17 towns and villages in Indiana, Illinois, Missouri, and Kansas. Martin was 17 years.

Catharine (Kate) Reiss (3/23/1847 – 4/2/1916) married Charles Max Wittig (1/16/1838 – 1/30/1918) on 4/9/1866 in a double ceremony with her brother Frank and Anna Feder. Kate was 19 years, 17 days.

Barbara Reiss (1849 – 1849) is mentioned in Latin records at St. Michael's Catholic Church in Paderborn dated 1856. Barbara was 1 day.

Later Margaret Basler Reiss (10/22/1818 – 6/23/1902) married Conrad Ebert (5/11/1811 – 7/23/1880) on 4/2/1850. Conrad was 30 years, 3 months, 21 days.

Anna Maria Ebert (9/14/1851 -- ??) was baptized at St. Michael's Catholic Church in Paderborn on 9/20/1851. Anna was 1 year.

Louisa Ebert (12/??/1853 – 5/21/1875) married George W. Neff (11/16/1849 – 11/1/1903) on 11/6/1873 at St. Michael's Catholic Church in Paderborn. Louisa was 19 years, 11 months.

Margaret Ebert (10/29/1856 – 4/19/1926) married Conrad Charles Neff (12/26/1853 – 4/1/1917) on 9/7/1877 in St. Michael's Catholic Church in Paderborn. Margaret was 20 years, 10 months, 9 days.

Lavern and Lucille Lang lived on the Reiss farm from April 1954 to November 1998 as crop share tenants. Lavern is the nephew of Katie Luetzelschwab Reiss and first cousin to the other blue highlights above. Lavern and Lucille were 44 years 7 months.

Lynette Lang (5/18/1955 --) married Donald Schaeffer (3/18/1953 --) on 4/26/1975. Lynette was 19 years, 11 months, 8 days.

Lana Lang (8/17/1957 --) married Jerry Korte (11/15/1953 --) on 9/12/1980. Lana was 23 years, 26 days.

Leon Lang (9/9/1958 --) married Pam Onana (4/15/1957 – 12/9/1992) on 6/26/1981. Later he married Joan Meyer (5/10/1966 --) on 7/12/1989. Leon was 22 years, 9 months, 17 days.

Will, Kayla, Ava, and Blake, the top five longevities are in purple. George Reiss is the winner with 91 years, then his dad Frank with 80 years, then his wife Katie with 71 years, then his mom Anna Sybilla with 64 years, and then his grandmother Margaret with 61 years. Everyone else is less than 33 years except the Langs with 44. I think it's significant that three of our top five longevities married into the Reiss family. That says a lot about those matriarchs as well as the hardworking Reiss farmers they married.

Love, Granddad

Lang Family Tenant History

Dear Will, Kayla, Ava, and Blake,   August 17, 2015

On October 22, 2013 I had a two-hour interview meeting with Lavern and Lucille Lang in their rural Smithton home. I also asked Lavern to send letters about any ongoing thoughts on his four decades of farming the Reiss family farm. Here are interview notes and parts of four letters.

On December 10, 1948, Dewey Hirsch told Mom if I wanted to be a substitute rural mail carrier, I should be at Millstadt Post Office at 6:00 p.m. at which time I learned to sort Rural Route #2. After three days learning and helping carry, I would carry west of town on Rural Route #1 and Roachtown. If it was bad weather, we went together.

September 27, 1950 I had to go to St. Louis for my Army exam. November 8, 1950 was my last day on the mail route. November 9 was my first day in the Army. My two years of Army counted toward my mail route time so by 1952 I had four years.

February 15, 1953 I married Lucille Ries at the Zoar United Church of Christ in New Hanover. April 1954 we moved to George and Katie Reiss' 1889 house which needed kitchen cabinets and a bathroom. We bought cabinets and found a cast iron sink top and put them in place. Built bathroom in north end of the kitchen, put in septic tank and drain line west to the 1940 house drains. Installed water pump and pipe to cistern west of summer kitchen. I installed an old furnace in basement.

July 1954 when three days were 114 and 115 degrees, very hot and dry all summer. In 1955 we dug a 12-foot diameter by 13-foot deep cistern near the old shop to drain barn and shed roofs into it. *I remember watching this cistern-digging as an eleven-year old boy.*

Put up 1,000-bushel metal grain bin. Built three-door concrete block garage with 700-bushel storage upstairs. Built 7-foot wide by 30-foot long by 14-foot high ear corn crib. Built 12-foot wide, 30-foot high metal silo, put in concrete floor and feeding bunk. Built 56-foot by 26-foot deep loafing shed, north of feeding floor. *A loafing shed is typically a one-story, three-sided metal building where livestock can get out of the weather. They would open to the south. It's where cows go to "loaf."*

Installed water line from back of pond to well east of pond to add water to well, controlled by a float valve. Installed water line and electric line from north side of shed and waterline on to hog pens and into loafing shed. Always had water for hogs and cattle. Added 28 feet to north shed of corn crib, sometime later added 28-foot shed to west for equipment storage.

Remodeled shed near 1889 house, then years later when a tornado messed up the big chicken house west of house, I used siding and roof material to add 30-foot by 30-foot shop next to east of shed. I bought and put up 3500-bushel bin, a 2000-bushel bin, and then moved the 1000-bushel bin too. Franklin bought a 2000-bushel bin altogether north by the woods. Then I added grinding shed to grind feed for hogs.

Here are the Lang children in 1962, from left are Leon, Lynette, Lana. Everyone has the same LL initials.

Below are Lucille and Lavern on October 22, 2013 when I visited in their home for a rambling interview. They look rightfully proud of what they've accomplished in 60.5 years of married life. Here are their comments on my miscellaneous questions:

- No field corn fed to chickens.

- Feed grinder man visits and grinds corn for pigs. Cows got ground corn, cob, and seed. Pigs got ground corn, no cobs, and seed.

- Langs were married 2/15/1953. Moved to the Reiss farm in April 1954 and stayed until November 1998 when they bought their own home. That's 44.5 years.

- They butchered pigs only, no cows. Shot in the head with a rifle and then quickly cut near throat and heart for blood to be collected for blood sausage. Also made head cheese from the skull but not on the same animals as blood sausage. Also made liver sausage.

Small intestines turned inside out for pork sausage. Large intestines used for larger sausage. Rendered lard used to seal fried-in sausage in crocks. No refrigeration.

- Three sheep pastures – north of barn, east of barn, west of mailbox.

- Lavern's dad, Henry Lang, rented 28 acres by the mail box, by the pine forest, and in the sheep pasture east of the barn from about 1942 to 1947. Lavern helped with wheat in Schaeffer fields in 1942. Louis Stumpf helped with combining corn for two years in the 1940s. He married Lavern's sister, Vera Lang.

- Lavern born in 1928. One year of high school in Millstadt.

- Lavern built wire mesh corn crib north of old house. He had a two-row corn picker attachment mounted on his tractor and towed a wagon. Only minor use of old wooden corn crib south of the barn. It measured about 8 feet square.

- Old building in northwest corner of old house yard was used for hogs and later for confinement chickens. He built another chicken house 32 by 44 between that one and the old house but removed it in later years.

- 50 years of cattle. Lived there 45 years from 1954 to 1998. Before him was Edwin Joseph and son Raymond.

- Blew loose hay into barn mow rather than used hay carrier for loose or baled hay.

- Never used log granary.

- Leon and Pam lived there 2 years. Brandon and Tina lived there 2 years.

- Grange used to be Modern Woodmen of America Hall (insurance). Dance hall upstairs. Sold that building for $30,000 to build new grange. Grange now has 83 members with 73 paid. Langs have been members for 44 years. Their daughter Lynette Schaeffer became state president on 9/20/2013.

- The 1838 log cabin had a wood burning stove, no fireplace. There was one room and no loft. Dirt floor. Used later for butchering.

- Whose hogs are visible in the 1942 aerial photo? Joseph and George Reiss. Westerheides were before Lavern and Lucille. Josephs were before Westerheides.

- Private telephone line south to Shillings and west to Kleins.

- Had three or four chicken yards.

- Lavern dug the cistern on the north side of the 1940 house, about 8 feet in diameter and 10 feet deep.

- Water pump near old 1889 house gate was for a well, not a cistern. Cistern was near summer kitchen. Also pumped water from the pond for toilets, hogs, and cattle.

- Peacocks – #1 and #2 for 10 years in the pecan tree. No food offered.

- Just one collie dog named Fritz. Ripped Oscar Koerber's pants.

- Farm lease was crop share with 2/3 to operator and 1/3 to owners. House rent was $100 per month for first five years and then zero.

- Dairy business in 1957 – Registered Jersey cows owned by George Zeibold. Quit in 1962 when he got a job as a rural mail carrier which continued to 7/30/1989. Had previously carried mail in 1948/1950. DHI testing for 20 dairy cows and calves.

- Was the Cedar Row Farm name significant to the mail carrier? No, we just used Box 98 or 99. There are 40 trees in the south cedar row.

- Concentrated on beef cow business and pigs from farrow to finish of mixed breeds, mostly whites. Grew about half of the corn we fed.

- Chickens – Egg route in south county several years. Delivered eggs. Had confinement chickens of 8 cages with about 100 chickens per cage. Cages were double stacked.

- Schaeffer house – never saw house but well is still there yet. It's covered by a concrete slab about a foot underground. It's near the crest of the hill.

Marcella Klein interview comments from 10/22/2013

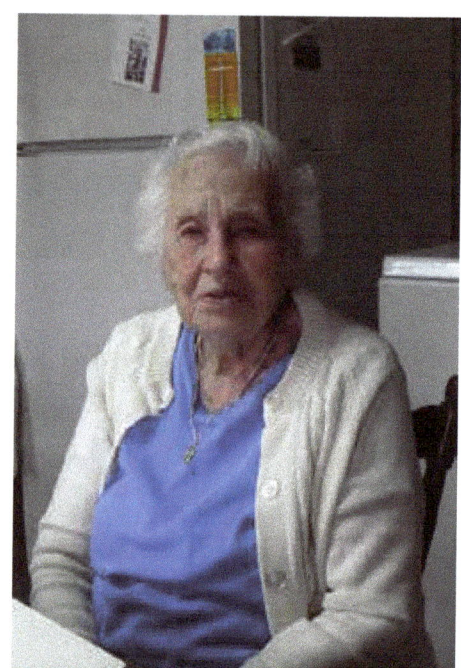

- Kleins got electricity from Illinois Power in 1939, Shillings in 1942. Cost was $5.00 per month.

- Look at north window of Reiss summer kitchen in the 1942 aerial photo and notice box where Katie stored milk and butter since it was slightly cooler.

- Marcella married Bube in 1940. All went to St. Michael's School. She was born on 2/20/1920.

- They raised and sold 240 dozen eggs per week. Leave lights on at night in chicken houses so they would eat more.

- Apron – keeps everything clean. Common farm wife practice.

- Gladys Wittenauer married Ray William Thiele of Waterloo on September 14, 2013. Ardell Roider was matron of honor. Both are from high school class of 1948.

- Played Figmill board game with our children.

- Used cistern water for washing because it was soft water.

Will, Kayla, Ava, and Blake, maybe you know that Lavern Lang and your great grandfather Irv Reiss were first cousins because their mothers were sisters. That makes me second cousins with the three Lang children. Below is another Lang family picture from the Smithton Centennial in 1961. Lavern was quite proud of his beard.

Love, Granddad

Dedication of the World War II Memorial in Washington, DC

Dear Will, Kayla, Ava, and Blake,   May 25, 2015

Today is Memorial Day. This is a story Uncle Ken and I wrote which appeared in the June 16, 2004 *Sullivan Daily Times* newspaper in our home town of Sullivan, Indiana.

Sons Acknowledge Dad, Military Service

Over the years you've seen lots of articles in this newspaper written by our father, Irv Reiss. Here's one written by his sons, Ken Reiss of Houston, Texas and Steve Reiss of Peoria, Illinois who just returned from taking their dad to the Dedication Ceremony for the World War II Memorial in Washington, D.C. on May 29.

The day was magnificent in every way, with clear skies and a temperature close to 70 degrees. We walked the mile from our hotel to the seating area near the new memorial just west of the Washington Monument. Dad wore his uniform jacket from 1942 and a ball cap which said "WW II Veteran." He was conspicuous!

The streets were full of other veterans with some in uniforms, some in wheelchairs, and all looking rightfully proud. Dozens and dozens of strangers came up to these veterans all day long to shake hands, give a hug or a salute, and to say "thanks for serving, we appreciate what you did," or "we're proud of you." Sometimes there were tears, gifts of Bibles, and once even a bouquet of flowers.

We tried to enter the Memorial but found it closed for several hours to accommodate Congressional Medal of Honor winners, their families, and other dignitaries. But the three of us were photographed by the Smithsonian Institute who was documenting the day. They are also inviting veterans to submit their "stories" for eventual publication. We bought the new "first day issue" stamps of the Memorial, stuck them on our programs, and had them canceled. Dad shook hands with former Senator Bob Dole, who chaired the $180 million fundraising campaign which paid for the Memorial. Even though Bob is close to age 80, he doesn't have that first gray hair on his head.

We did toured the Memorial the next day along with thousands of others. The individual state columns had all been further decorated by visitors who left flowers, letters, photographs, ribbons, medals, and teddy bears to further honor their veterans. It was a very moving visit. Lots of people were taking pictures, but Dad said he was getting flashbacks from the war and found it difficult to smile.

Several veterans recognized Dad's CBI shoulder patch for the China-Burma-India Theater where he was a personnel officer on the Ledo Burma Road. Others recognized his first lieutenant's bar and length of service stripes, which totaled 4.5 years from before Pearl Harbor until after the Japanese surrender. It was a great four-day weekend and an absolutely wonderful memory for the Reiss family. Once again – we appreciate you for serving, Dad. . . . Ken and Steve Reiss

Will, Kayla, Ava, and Blake, on New Year's Eve or 12/31/2003, Grand DD and I were at the home of Dave and Connie Sinn along with another couple Steve and Patti Bash. Those guys asked me if my dad was a World War II veteran at which point I said "yes, why." They explained they were taking their dads who were veterans to Washington, DC for the Memorial Day 2004 dedication of the World War II Memorial. Dave had even lined up a tour of the Capitol building through Congressman Ray LaHood's office. They asked Dad and me to join them on that trip. I called my brother Ken to join as well and he quickly agreed. It was an incredible experience and a memory we'll never forget.

Love, Granddad

Irv Reiss Funeral, Eulogy, and Obituary

Dear Will, Kayla, Ava, and Blake,   August 20, 2012

Dad died on April 11, 2007. Here are pictures from his funeral at Center Ridge Cemetery in Sullivan, Indiana. That's Mom holding the American flag that had draped Dad's casket before the American Legion did their 21-gun salute. I still have two rifle shells from that part of the ceremony.

To the left of Mom is Taha Aswad, my brother's geology friend who drove all the way from Houston for this funeral. Further left is Grand DD. Right of Mom is my cousin June Ann McBrayer, then me, then Ken, and then his daughter Ellie Davidson.

Notice the bolo ties that Adam and I are wearing. My dad had bought those over the years and had about 110 of them in his collection. Mom gave each of us several to keep as mementoes. Looks like Adam's is a silver and turquoise Indian design and mine is an arrowhead with an Indian head penny. The rest went to other relatives and friends.

Mom died three years later on May 16, 2010. See her Granddad's Monday story on 3/10/2014. Here's their tombstone. You can see the dates on their stone and figure out that both lived to age 89, Dad by 5 months more than Mom. Dad had significant Alzheimer's and eventually died of a broken hip and pneumonia. Mom was alert to the end, working two crossword puzzles every day, and died of a heart attack.

On the back corner of their burial plot is this bronze plaque recognizing Dad's 4.5 years of service in the US Army during World War II which includes 1.3 years in India and Burma. All of Dad's military records plus about 1000 letters my parents exchanged while Dad was overseas are in a book we published called From Burma With Love.

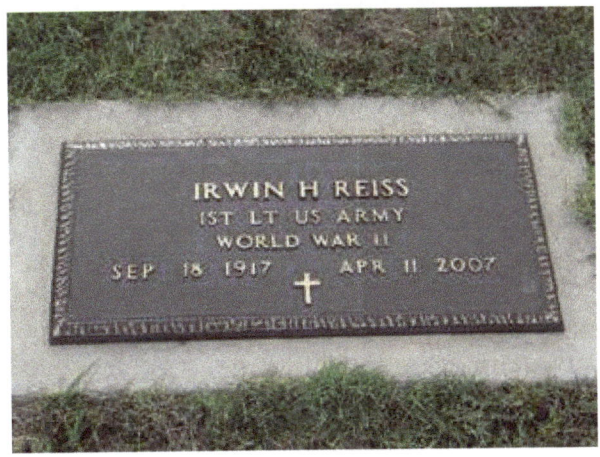

Dad's funeral included a 21-gun salute by the American Legion. That honor guard was commanded by Lt. Col. Louis Ladislas who was in my brother's high school class which was a nice connection. They gave each of the family members two spent cartridges as a memory.

Will, Kayla, Ava, and Blake, your great grandparent's graves are in a nice setting in the newer part of Center Ridge Cemetery and close to several of their friends. It's unfortunate that none of you were able to meet Dad and only you, Will, were born in time to meet Mom. They would have really enjoyed you four and you four would have really enjoyed them. You'll have to settle for pictures and stories and family history books. Dad's eulogy and obituary follow. Mom's are in her story on 3/10/2014. Best of all, some of the grandparenting skills you see in Grand DD and me came from our parents and grandparents. So that part of our family histories lives on.

Love, Granddad

Eulogy for Irv Reiss

We are gathered here today to celebrate the life of Irv Reiss and to honor his memory. His was a life filled to overflowing with an abundance of blessings. He lived in a remarkable time of human history and he shared actively in every facet of the world around him. He leaves behind cherished memories to all who knew him.

Irwin H. Reiss was born September 18, 1917 on the Reiss Family Farm near Floraville, Illinois. His family spoke German at home, Irv would remain fluent in German the rest of his life, telling his own children on an occasional basis, "lass die finger davon" which means "keep your hands off." Irv came of age at the height of the Depression. The farm had no electricity, no phone, and no running water. Irv never wore a new pair of pants, by the time he put them on, they had already gone through his two brothers. For food they ate vegetables they raised in their garden. Irv attended a one-room schoolhouse, the oldest in Illinois. He would boast that he graduated first in his class in eight grade, of course there were only two students. His son-in-law Ron would point out that meant Irv was also second from the last. Irv never lost his deep enjoyment of returning to the family farm and near the end of his life insisted that his picture be taken in several of his favorite childhood spots.

After graduating with honors from Belleville Township High School, Irv attended the University of Illinois in Champaign where he received his Bachelors Degree in Agricultural Economics. He letters in wrestling and waited tables to earn money. He was on his way to a Masters Degree when Pearl Harbor interrupted his life like it did for so many others. Irv was activated into the U.S. Army as a second lieutenant. He met Mary Stephenson at Camp Roberts in California and they were married in November 1942. Theirs was a lifelong companionship of undying mutual devotion and affection.

Because of his superb linguistic skills, Irv was sent by the Army to Yale University to learn Mandarin Chinese. He was scheduled to ship out from New York City to the China-Burma-India Theater in the Second World War. He made one last phone call to Mary the night before he left for war. It was the most intimate, tender, and loving phone call ever made; at least that is what the other 17 people thought who listened in on the party line. Irv took a ship from New York to Brazil, then to Capetown, and then Karachi where he helped to build the Ledo-Burma Road.

One writer calls this famous undertaking the most astonishing engineering feat ever accomplished in a time of war. It is hard to imagine the range of skills required by Irv and his fellow soldiers; it is even more amazing to realize that Irv was in his early twenties at the time from a small farm in Illinois. Tropical fever brought him back home after several hospital stays along the way, back home to his beloved Mary.

Together Mary and Irv raised three wonderful children: Steve, Ken, and Mary Kay. His family was the joy and pride of Irv's life. Irv loved his family. They drove around in a station wagon with "fi-va-vus" emblazoned on the side for all to see. Irv spent countless hours on the floor with his children playing pick-up sticks, marbles, dominoes, and pinochle. He would give Steve a nickel for polishing his shoes, by the time Mary Kay took her turn, the economy had shifted and she earned a dime.

Over the years Irv and his family undertook countless fabulous camping trips, later these included in-laws and grandchildren as well. In 1990 the Reiss's and the Parnells undertook a 33-day 10,000-mile camping trip to Alaska. Irv was always an avid reader and took along on this trip a book about St. Thomas Acquinas which he promptly lost over and over again. "Where is St. Thomas, where is St. Thomas?" he would ask. On another camping trip, a bear got into their campsite and was up on its hind legs outside the test foraging for food. Irv started to put on his shoes so he could go out and get a picture but Mary held him back.

After the war, Mary and Irv started out earning a living on an avocado and lemon farm in California. Irv would pick, Mary would drag the net. But not long after, an opportunity came that changed their lives. A new subsidiary of the Ayrshire Collieries Corporation was being started in Indiana called Meadowlark Farm which would try something never before tried. That was reclaiming land that had been strip-mined coal land for profitable use in farming and recreation. Land reclamation was a cutting edge idea, there were no college courses to attend and there were no textbooks to consult. Irv was asked not only to be the first President of Meadowlark Farms, but to be the first in the nation to practice land reclamation on a large scale. Clearly his youthful instincts as a farmer settled in and he loved the challenge. Irv and Mary settled in the small town of Sullivan, as Irv once said, it was just far enough away from company headquarters in Indianapolis to remain some measure of independence.

Irv and Mary shared a magnificent life together in Sullivan. Many of their friendships centered around their active membership in First Presbyterian Church where Irv would become a Deacon, an Elder, and a Trustee. On Sunday afternoons in the wintertime after church, young couples would come to their home with one important theological question: "Where are we going ice skating today?" Hot dogs and hot chocolate would be brought along for a day's fun and enjoyment. Irv passionately loved ice skating and knew all the best spots in the county. He taught his children to skate when they were very young, using a chair as a prop. Even after dark, they would put kerosene lanterns around the outer rim of the ice and skate they night away.

Three characteristics stand out most clearly about the life of Irv Reiss. The first was the sheer power of his intellect. Irv was a very intelligent man. The range of his vocabulary was phenomenal, his daughter-in-law was forced to study the dictionary to prepare for their visits. Irv was very much at home in the realm of ideas but he strength of his intellect was most evident in his boundless curiosity about the world. Irv never treated knowledge as an end to be achieved and then left alone, the more he learned, the more he wanted to learn about the world around him. His sheer love for learning was surely a prime reason for his great enjoyment of traveling. Mary and Irv visited every part of the world many time over: Australia, South America, India, Sri Lanka, Afghanistan, Egypt, Africa, Tibet, Korea, the Galapagos Islands, and on and on. Wherever they traveled, Irv insisted on reading his favorite newspaper every day. Can you imagine the difficulty of finding a copy of the Wall Street Journal in Skagway, Alaska? Everywhere he went, Irv purchased bolo ties. His family and I are wearing a small sample of his large collection in his honor.

The second characteristic was his cheerful and exuberant love for his beautiful family. He was intensely proud of his children and the fine adult human beings they grew to be. He was equally proud of his children and would nearly burst with pleasure to introduce them in church on a Sunday morning. And at the heart of it all was Mary, the one great love of his life. He simply adored her and never stopped until his last breath.

The third characteristic of his life was his single-minded devotion to the cause of freedom. Through his involvement in the Liberty Fund, Irv was a student of freedom. He spent countless hours reading, discussing, and reflecting on the irreplaceable value of freedom for the human community. But nothing speaks more clearly of his love for freedom than his own actions. Irv's first child, Steve, was born while Irv was serving in Burma during the Second World War. Irv did not lay eyes on his own son until Steve was already nine months old. Mary put a picture of Irv in the crib until the time came, when the young child could reach out to his father when they finally met for the first time.

Jesus said, "You will know the truth and the truth will make your free." Irv Reiss has now reached the end of a fantastic journey through life. He has now found the true beginning of what he treasured most which is freedom.

Rev. Paul McGlasson

Obituary – Irwin H. Reiss

Irwin H. Reiss, 89 of Sullivan, died at 12:10 AM, Wednesday, April 11, 2007, at Miller's Healthcare Facility in Sullivan, Indiana. He was preceded in death by his parents, George and Catherine Reiss, and two older brothers, William and Franklin Reiss.

Surviving are his wife Mary of 64.5 years and three children, Stephen Reiss (and Diane) of Peoria, Kenneth Reiss (and Coral) of Houston, and Mary Kay Parnell (and Ron) of Sullivan. Also surviving are six grandchildren, Adam Reiss of Springfield, IL; Grant Reiss of Chicago, IL; Melissa (Parnell) McCloud (and Sean) of Bolingbrook, IL; Stephanie Parnell of Chicago, IL; Mandy Reiss of Houston, TX; and Ellen Reiss of Galveston, TX.

Irv was born September 18, 1917 on the family farm near Floraville, St. Clair County, Illinois. His upbringing was Spartan with no electricity, no phone, double hand-me-down shoes, walked a mile to a one-room school for 8 years, big garden, summer kitchen, trapped furs, raised chickens,

1925 Model T Ford, and family language of German. That farm was established by Irv's great grandfather, Adam Reiss, in 1834 upon his arrival in this country from Bavaria. That farm is still a family treasure after 173 years.

He graduated with honors from the Belleville Township High School and from the University of Illinois in Champaign where he received a Bachelor's Degree in Agricultural Economics. He took advanced ROTC, lettered in wrestling, and waited tables for pocket money. He was halfway through a Master's Degree also in Ag Econ when he was activated into the US Army as a Second Lieutenant about six months before Pearl Harbor.

He married Mary Leone Stephenson on 11/8/1942 in California in his Army uniform. Because he spoke German, the Army didn't think he belonged in the European Theater, so he was sent to Yale University to learn Mandarin Chinese. He ended up in Burma as a personnel officer helping to build the Ledo-Burma Road as a backdoor supply route to China. This was the China-Burma-India Theater. Irv served a total of 4.5 years in the Army in World War II. The photo above is from 2004 when he attended the dedication of the World War II Memorial in Washington, DC with his two sons.

Irv was President of Meadowlark Farms, having moved to Sullivan for that job in 1948. Meadowlark was the farming subsidiary of Ayrshire Collieries (later Amax Coal) of Indianapolis. His company farmed 100,000 acres of surface lands in Indiana, Illinois, and Kentucky before and after the coal was removed. Irv was an early proponent of coal strip mine reclamation and became one of the coal industry's reclamation spokesmen.

He was active in the Rotary Club for over 50 years and received the Paul Harris Award, the Club's highest honor, for his service. He was also a 50+ year member of the First Presbyterian Church of Sullivan, the Masonic Lodge, the Veterans of Foreign Wars, the American Legion, the Sullivan Elks Club, the Zorah Shrine in Terre Haute, and the American Association of Farm Economists and Rural Appraisers. He served on the Sullivan School Board for 6 years and the Sullivan County Park & Lake Board for 12 years. He was a judge at many Sullivan elections. He also wrote 150 articles for the Sullivan Daily Times over 20 years.

His most prideful accomplishment was being a Founder Member since 1960 of the Liberty Fund, an Indianapolis Foundation. It has grown significantly over the years and now sponsors 165 four-day seminars annually on liberty and freedom at centers in Europe and the Western Hemisphere. This connection fed Irv's travel interests but it also allowed him to walk the talk regarding his strong personal convictions on liberty, individual freedoms, and attached responsibilities.

Irv passed up corporate advancement that would have meant moving to Ayrshire headquarters in Indianapolis in order to raise his family in small town Sullivan. He and Mary were committed parents and saw real value in ice skating in the winter after church with the family and friends, hunting for morel mushrooms in the spring, swimming in the strip pits in the summer, and gathering pecans in the Wabash bottoms in the fall.

Irv and Mary loved to travel. He made 19 trips around the world, crossed the Equator 56 times, and visited over 85 countries on 6 continents. They took up snow skiing in their 50's and made annual winter trips to Colorado well into their 70's. Lots of those memories and adventures were fodder for his many newspaper articles.

Private burial services will be at Center Ridge Cemetery in Sullivan on Friday, April 13, 2007 with Rev. Paul McGlasson officiating. Family and friends are invited to a celebration memorial service at the First Presbyterian Church in Sullivan at 2:00 PM on Saturday, April 14, 2007. In lieu of flowers memorial contributions may be made to the Alzheimer's Association, the Presbyterian Church Community Kitchen, or the donor's favorite charity.

2010 – Present

2010 Population of St. Clair County is 270,420.

2010 States total 50, national population is 310.23 million.

2010 President is George W. Bush. Barack Obama is inaugurated in 2009.

2011 The final shuttle flight landed at the Kennedy Space Center signifying the end of the NASA space shuttle program after 135 missions.

2014 Obamacare, the Affordable Care Act, went into effect for millions of Americans, the largest expansion of the social welfare state in decades.

Serendipities from It Takes A Matriarch

Dear Will, Kayla, Ava, and Blake,   December 29, 2014

Our second family history book was 780 letters which your great great great great grandmother, Margaret Basler Reiss Ebert, saved from 1852 to 1888. It was called It Takes A Matriarch and was published in 2009 just before our 175th reunion celebration of the Reiss Family Farm.

In the five years that the book has been available to the general public, I've heard from several interested readers. Here's a summary:

Mike Sacksteder manages a retirement center in Linton, Indiana about 20 miles east of my home town of Sullivan. He is a descendant of Johan and Johanna Sacksteder who have four letters in our book. Mike and I arranged to meet at the Sullivan County Historical Society museum.

Annie Shimp is another descendant of the Sacksteders. Her email mentions that she plans to visit the Louisville (Kentucky) Free Public Library to research area relatives who are mentioned in our book.

Jerry Prouhet wrote from Foristell, Missouri that he was a descendant of Joseph Stein who has 49 letters in our book. Joseph used the title of "aunt" when mentioning Margaret Basler Reiss Ebert. Joseph was a close friend of Margaret's son, Martin Reiss, but not a Reiss relative. Jerry is researching to see if Joseph is a descendant of Margaret's second husband Conrad Ebert.

Yvonne Juhl wrote from St. Louis asking more about Jeanette Krone who was the daughter of Charles and Kate Basler Krone. There are 97 letters from the Krones in our book. Charles Krone's autobiography of his life in the theater is a complete chapter in our book. Anyway, Jeanette Krone was the piano teacher for Yvonne Juhl's mother. Yvonne wants to write an article for the St. Louis Genealogical Society and asked permission to site various passages from our book.

Ruth Craft wrote – "I am a volunteer at the Center for Sacramento History, and I processed the Jerome R. and Helen Basler Fletcher Collection. After searching on the internet to gain more information on the Basler family, I found your book It Takes A Matriarch and found that the letters from Sacramento were from members of this family. The collection contains many unidentified photographs, and I hoped that you might be able to identify some of the people. . . ." Well, I was able to identify Martin and Anna Maria Basler and two of their children.

Sandi Owen Livingston is my fifth cousin on my mom's side and probably my seventh cousin on my dad's side. She lives in Tulsa, Oklahoma where we had lunch together on 2/14/2007. We talked family genealogy for two hours. She has 130,000 names in her database of relatives including 11 different US presidents. Maybe I should send Sandi a copy of <u>It Takes A Matriarch</u> because I haven't heard from her recently.

Will, Kayla, Ava, and Blake, isn't it great to have so much information about your roots and know that it has been preserved in books which are available on the Internet. It's even greater when friends and relatives find those books, appreciate their content, and make contact with the author for more information. We are so blessed to descend from four generations of packrats who saved all their old papers and photos so we can now make family history come alive for the present and future. I hope I make it to heaven some day so I can connect with 200 years of relatives that we know about from their letters and photographs.

Love, Granddad

Two Reiss Weddings – April 16, 1911 and August 29, 2009

Dear Will, Kayla, Ava, and Blake,   April 15, 2015

Can you see similarities between these two pictures? The black and white photo was taken <mark>104 years ago this Thursday</mark> on April 16, 1911 when your great great grandparents, George William Reiss and Catherine "Katie" Charlotte Luetzelschwab, were married at St. Paul United Church of Christ in Floraville, Illinois. The color photo was taken on August 29, 2009 when your parents/aunt/uncle, Hany Sober and Grant Andrew Reiss, were married at the First United Methodist Church in Peoria, Illinois.

Here's my list of similarities and differences in these two photos. See what else you can find.

- Two beautiful brides looking slightly away from the camera

- Both brides are dressed in white gowns, standing, and holding flowers on their left arms

- Both brides have their right hand resting on their husband's left arm

- Two handsome grooms looking straight ahead

- Both grooms are seated and have corsages on their left lapels

- No one is smiling, nevertheless these were very joyful occasions

- Only wedding ring visible is George's which is a monster size 13, now in my possession

- In the older photo are white gloves for George and a veil for Katie

- On Katie's necklace is a gift from George, a gold watch now in my sister's possession

- Between these two wedding dates are 98.369 years

Fast forward 25 years to April 16, 1936 when George and Katie celebrated their silver wedding anniversary at a party in their honor at the Broad Hollow Grange midway between Smithton and New Athens in St. Clair County, Illinois. Here's a newspaper article from that occasion.

BROAD HOLLOW GRANGE IS SCENE OF SILVER WEDDING CELEBRATION

Broad Hollow Grange was the scene of a merry gathering Thursday night, April 16, when the silver wedding celebration of Mr. and Mrs. George Reiss, prominent members of Broad Hollow Grange took place.

At an appropriate time when all the guests had gathered, the Master, Amiel Werner, announced the commencement of the exercises, after which Miss Inez Carr, the pianist, played a march, while the assistant and lady assistant stewards conducted the celebrants to their seats of honor. Mrs. Harry Favre, the lecturer, then took charge of the program and complimented Mr. and Mrs. Reiss on their active work in the grange.

Mrs. Reiss is chairman of the Home Economics committee.

The songs, "When You and I Were Young Maggie," and "Love's Old Sweet Song," were sung and Miss Harriet Stallman sang "Sweetest Story Ever Told," accompanied at the piano by Miss Inez Carr. The celebrants were addressed in a most appropriate manner by Dr. G. G. Bock. Franklin Reiss was called upon for a talk and responded with a few remarks. The chaplain, Miss Elenora Eberhardt offered a prayer and the songs "Smile, Smile, Smile" "Where There's a Will There's a Way" and "Home Sweet Home" were sung. The master made the closing remarks.

As Miss Carr played the congratulatory march, all filed past the couple and extended congratulations, after which the orchestra played for dancing. As Mr. Reiss does not indulge in dancing, Mrs. Reiss danced her first waltz with her son Franklin. The table centerpiece was a large three-tiered wedding cake, baked by Mrs. Henry Vogler and decorated by Mrs. Vogler and Miss Ellen Werner and another pretty cake decorated with the words "Best Wishes' presented by Mrs. Gus Metzger. Several bouquets also adorned the table.

Mrs. Harry Favre, the lecturer, read a poem, composed in honor of the occasion.

Did you see this sentence about dancing? I wonder if Pop had known this would appear in the newspaper article, whether he would have tried to fake a few waltz steps?

dancing. As Mr. Reiss does not indulge in dancing, Mrs. Reiss danced her first waltz with her son Franklin. The table centerpiece was a

One of the gifts my grandparents received in 1911 was two bottles of red wine. They opened one of them at this silver wedding anniversary celebration in April 1936 and the other one at their golden wedding anniversary celebration in April 1961 which was held at the Sportsmen's Club. A lot of us tasted a small sample. It was terrible and tasted like vinegar.

On the next page is the head table at their 50th anniversary. Pop looks a little apprehensive. Maybe it was that 50-year old wine or maybe he was afraid he would have to dance!!!

Will, Kayla, Ava, and Blake, you may need to take a day off work to celebrate Hany and Grant's milestone anniversaries. Their 25th is on a Tuesday and their 50th is on a Friday. Strangely enough Adam and Heather's 25th is also a Tuesday and their 50th is also a Friday.

When you four eventually find those special persons and plan to marry, we'll add four more similar photos to our collection. No rush – just make sure you search for the right person. Your parents can be a big help.

Love, Granddad

In addition to the many Grange members present, the following relatives and friends attended the celebration: Mr. and Mrs. Henry Reiss, Miss Grace Schroaf, of St. Louis; Mr. and Mrs. William Reiss, of Alton; George Dintelman, of Wood River; Mr. and Mrs. Ferd Reiss, Mrs. Earl Reiss, Miss Jennie Reiss, Miss Evelyn Reiss, Kenneth Bevirt, all of O'Fallon; Mr. and Mrs. Anden Feder, Mr. and Mrs. William Feder, Mr. and Mrs. Ed. Feder, Miss Willette Feder, Miss Doris Feder, Miss Norine Feder, Milton and Paul Feder, Mr. Knobeloch, Mr. and Mrs. Cyrus Holcomb, Mr. and Mrs. Emmet Klein and Mr. and Mrs. Wersching, all of Belleville; Mr. and Mrs. Joseph Beuchle, Miss Helen Beuchle, Orville Young, Irwin Beuchle and friend, all of Mascoutah; Mrs. John Luetzelschwab, Roland Luetzelschwab, Miss Pearl Luetzelschwab, Miss M. Diesel, Miss Delores Diesel, Miss Edna and Miss Helen Rodemich, all of Millstadt; Miss Ethel Deucker, of East St. Louis; Mr. and Mrs. Philip Petri, daughters Misses Viola and Eugenia, Mr. and Mrs. Gus Metzger, Mr. and Mrs. Dominic Klein, Miss Gertrude Kreher, Dominick Kreher, William and Ignatius Klein, Mr. and Mrs. John Rapp, Mr. and Mrs. Philip Etling, daughters Misses Helen and Dorothy and sons Norman and Edmund, all of near Floraville; Mr. and Mrs. Henry Reiss, Mrs. Wiemer, son Billy and friend, Charlie Carr, Wiemer Carr and Susie Carr, all of St. Louis; Mr. and Mrs. George Dintelmann, sons George, Jr., and Edwin, of Broad Hollow, and Mr. and Mrs. William Reiss.

My Best Birthday Gift Ever

Dear Will, Kayla, Ava, and Grant Jr.,   June 23, 2014

We don't know your formal name yet, so let's call you Grant Jr. Here is the first sonogram of you taken on June 12, 2014 which by wonderful coincidence was my 70th birthday. That's what makes you the best birthday gift I've ever received. The sonogram says you are 7.7 centimeters long which is about 3 inches. You are about 6 weeks old based on the due date of January 26, 2015 that your doctor calculated.

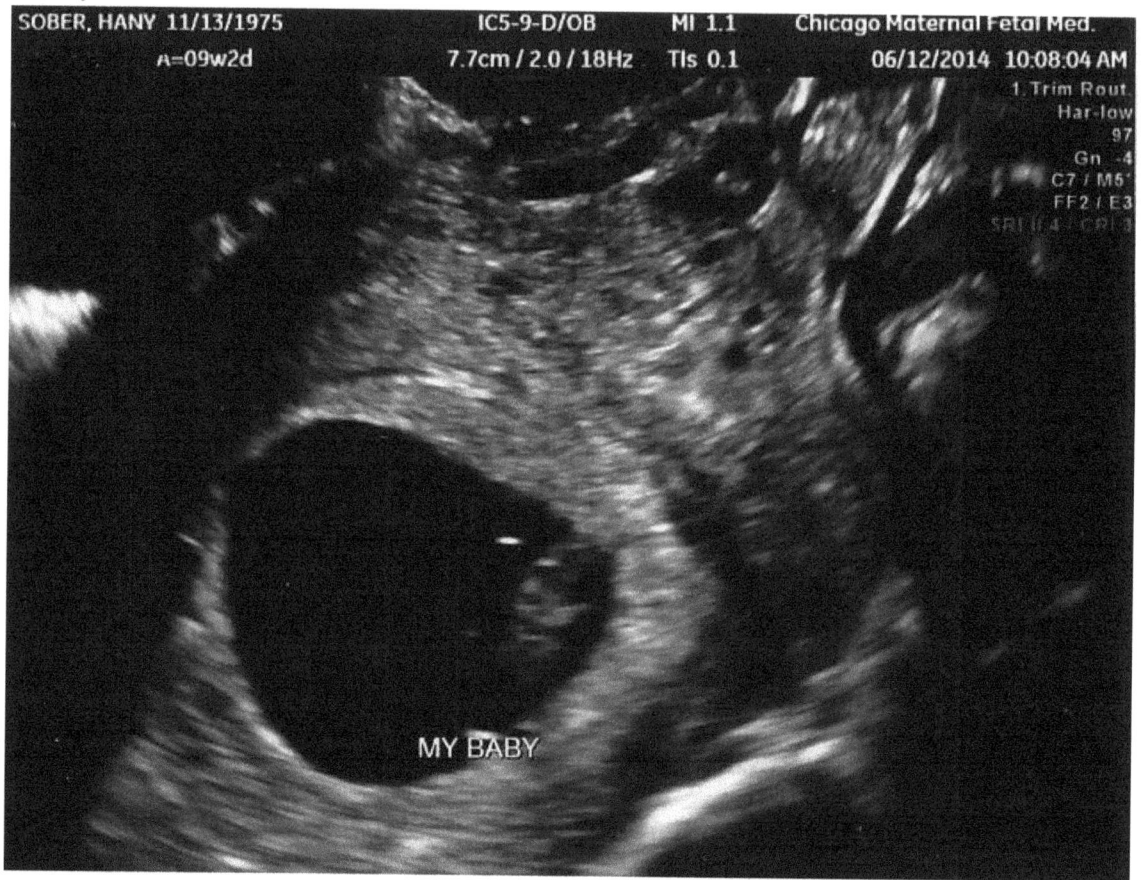

Grant Jr., that's you on the right side of the black circle. Pretty handsome dude don't ya think? You look a lot like your sister did at this point and she turned out to be a real beauty. I expect you will have her skin color and dark brown or black hair. You'll be tall like your dad and a good athlete. You will be intelligent, curious, and kind like both of your parents.

Will, Kayla, Ava, and Grant Jr., this is the first retro Granddad's Mondays story I've written. Your mom gave me this sonogram as a gift two weeks after my birthday when we were visiting in Chicago a day before we flew to South Africa. That's how she announced her pregnancy. There was no chance to write this story for the date shown above which was the nearest Monday. So now I'm six months late but I wanted to get this story into our 2014 book of stories which will be back from the publishers soon. We now know your name is Blake Saber Reiss.

Love, Granddad

Here you are now, Blake, on your first birthday January 14, 2016. Congratulations!!! Looks like you're getting ready for your first business trip.

Total Solar Eclipse over the Reiss Family Farm on August 21, 2017

Dear Will, Kayla, Ava, and Blake,   June 9, 2014

T total solar eclipse will take place on Monday, August 21, 2017. A solar eclipse occurs when the Moon passes between Earth and the Sun, thereby totally or partly obscuring the image of the Sun for a viewer on Earth. A total solar eclipse occurs when the Moon's apparent diameter is larger than the Sun, blocking all direct sunlight, turning day into darkness. Totality occurs in a narrow path across the surface of the Earth, while a partial solar eclipse will be visible over a region thousands of miles wide.

The eclipse will have a magnitude of 1.0306 and will be visible from a narrow corridor of 70 miles maximum width through the US. The longest duration of totality will be 2 minutes 40 seconds at 36°58.5′N 87°39.3′W in the Bainbridge/Sinking Fork area of Christian County, Kentucky just northwest of Hopkinsville, Kentucky. This is located on a historical farm named Orchard Dale.

A partial solar eclipse will be seen from the much broader path of the moon's penumbra, including all of North America, northern South America, western Europe, and Africa. This eclipse is the 22nd of the 77 members of Saros series 145, the one that also produced the solar eclipse of August 11, 1999. Members of this series are increasing in duration. The longest eclipse in this series will occur on June 25, 2522 and last for 7 minutes and 12 seconds.

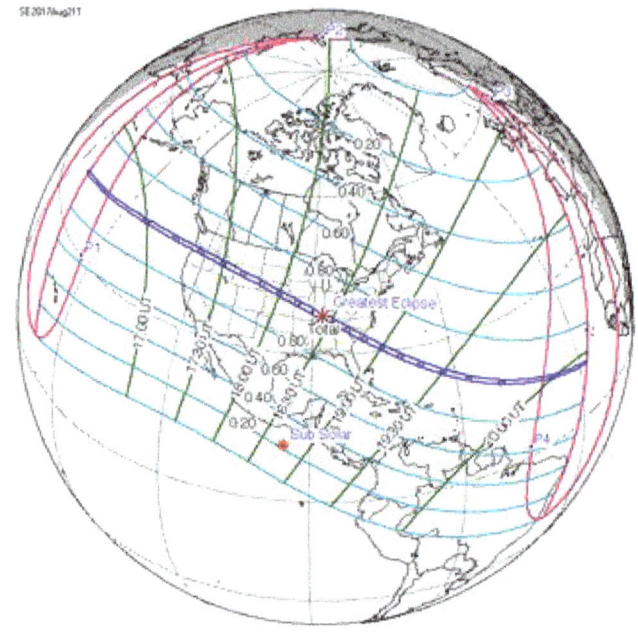

Check out the US map on the next page. The yellow inner band from Oregon to South Carolina shows where the total solar eclipse may be observed. The red curves show the duration of the total solar eclipse in 10 second intervals.

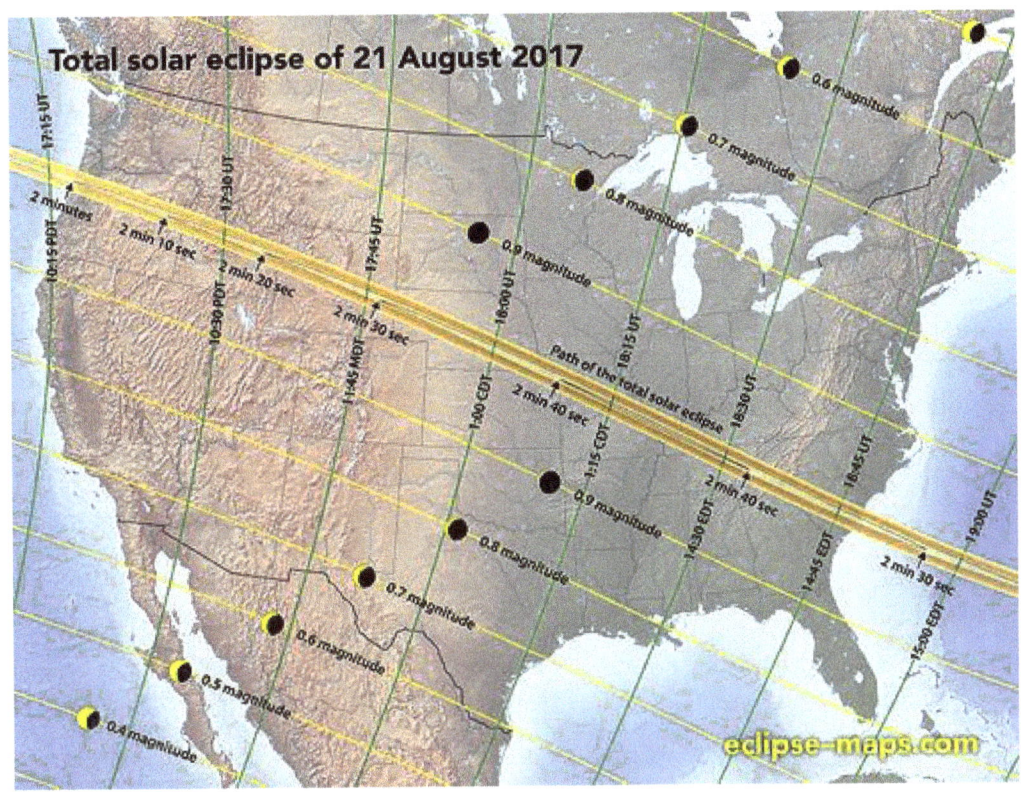

Related eclipses over the United States -- This eclipse will be the first visible from the contiguous United States since 1979 when the path of totality passed only through the states of Washington, Oregon, Idaho, Montana, and North Dakota. Many visitors traveled to the Pacific Northwest to view the eclipse, since it would be the last chance to view a total solar eclipse in the United States for almost four decades.

Some American scientists and interested amateurs seeking to experience a total eclipse Participated in a four-day Atlantic Ocean cruise to view the solar eclipse of July 10, 1972 as it passed near Nova Scotia. That event was mentioned in the pop song "You're So Vain" by Carly Simon.

The August 2017 eclipse will be the first with a path of totality crossing the USA's Pacific coast and Atlantic coast since 1918. The path of this eclipse crosses the upcoming path of the total solar eclipse of April 8, 2014, with the intersection of the two paths being in southern Illinois in Makanda just south of Carbondale. A small land area, including the cities of Carbondale, Cape Giradeau, Missouri, and Paducah, Kentucky, will thus experience two total solar eclipses within a span of fewer than seven years.

Will, Kayla, Ava, and Blake, you can thank cousin Jesse Reiss for discovering that this upcoming total solar eclipse would pass over our home farm. We should all gather at the Smithton Sportsmen's Club on August 21, 2017 and again on April 8, 2024 for two solar eclipse picnics. You three can even write special songs for each occasion!

Love, Granddad

295

Generativity

Dear Will, Kayla, Ava, and Blake,   September 7, 2015

This is a new word for me. I heard it for the first time on 11/3/2014 in a four-week class I took at Bradley University titled "Natural Born Thrillers!" which was about improving your written storytelling skills. I enjoyed the class but it was a lot more philosophical than I expected.

The term "generativity" was coined by the psychoanalyst Erik Erikson in 1950 to denote "a concern for establishing and guiding the next generation." It can be defined as creativity between the generations. Generativity can be expressed in literally hundreds of ways, from raising a child to stopping a tradition of abuse, from writing a family history to starting a new organization. One can try to "make a difference" with one's life, to "give back," to "take care" of one's community and one's planet.

Major Question: "How can I contribute to the world?"

"Generativity versus Stagnation" is the seventh stage Of Erik Erikson's theory of psychosocial development. This stage takes place during middle adulthood between the ages of approximately 40 and 65. During this time, adults strive to create or nurture things that will outlast them; often by having children or contributing to positive changes that benefit other people.

Erikson's theory: Generativity vs. Stagnation

♦ Contributing to the next generation by performing meaningful work, creative activities, and/or raising a family OR become stagnant and inactive (frequently cynical as well)

Contributing to society and doing things to benefit future generations are important needs at the "generativity versus stagnation" stage of development. Generativity refers to "making your mark" on the world, through caring for others, creating things, and accomplishing things that make the world a better place.

Stagnation refers to the failure to find a way to contribute. These individuals may feel disconnected or uninvolved with their community and with society as a whole. Those who are successful during this phase will feel that they are contributing to the world by being active in their home and community. Those who fail to attain this skill will feel unproductive and uninvolved in the world.

Will, Kayla, Ava, and Blake, I don't think of myself as a very psychological or philosophical person. My formal education was left brain like how to make a better bulldozer and why do grey squirrels eat my green apples? But having looked at this new term for a few months, it explains some of my current priorities which include church, Habitat for Humanity, writing family history books, and writing to my precious grandchildren. I'm not saying "it's all your fault" but you four certainly have provided a huge specific opportunity for my remaining life when we're not otherwise together at family events. Now I just have to convince Grand DD that I need to spend so much time on the computer writing stories!!!

Love, Granddad

What Your Heirs Really Want

Dear Will, Kayla, Ava, and Blake,   June 1, 2015

We have several accounts at PNC Bank in Peoria. Here's an interesting article that recently came as an email attachment from them. Let's see what the experts have to say. The yellow highlights are mine where I strongly agree but maybe some of that is just my cherry picking. Look at the first heading below called "Start Talking." We should be doing more of that, so start gathering your thoughts. Here's their article:

Your heirs want this even more than your money. It's never about the money, it's always about the heirlooms.

The economic downturn, steep health-care costs, and longer lives may mean less money being left to baby boomers by their parents – but boomers are unlikely to complain about that. Why? It turns out it's not about the money. Instead, baby boomers say personal keepsakes, family stories, and last wishes are a far more important bequest than money.

Fully 86% of baby boomers and 74% of Americans aged 72 and older said family stories and keeping their family history alive is the most important piece of their legacy, according to a 2012 survey conducted for Allianz Life Insurance Co. of North America.

And 64% of boomers and 58% of elders said family mementos and heirlooms are a key inheritance. Just 9% of boomers said they're eager to inherit money, and 14% of elders said financial assets are an important legacy to leave. The findings closely matched a similar Allianz survey in 2005.

"The things that make your family unique – not money, but stories and personal possessions – those are most important in the legacy discussion," says Katie Libbe, vice president of consumer insights for Allianz Life, in Minneapolis.

But there are two problems: Families often fail to record their histories, so those stories tend to die with aging relatives, and family mementos are among the most common causes of conflict after a relative dies.

"It's never about the money. It's always about the tangible personal property," says Mary Jane Olsavsky, a manager of PNC Wealth Management's Pittsburgh estate settlement group, who for almost 25 years has worked with families to distribute estates.

"Money can be divided pretty evenly, but the teacup that grandma always used? Maybe there's only a $2 value associated with that teacup, but because of the sentimental value and the emotions around it, that causes the controversy."

To avoid problems, consider the following steps.

1. Start talking

As you develop your estate plan, find out who among your family members might like specific keepsakes. If you have an aging parent, consider broaching the topic: What items would your parents like to give to whom?

Parents who create a mechanism for disposing of keepsakes go a long way to prevent conflict later, says Malcolm Greenhill, a certified financial planner and president of Sterling Futures in San Francisco.

"The parent has to take responsibility and realize there's a very high likelihood of arguments and disputes. There's something about death that polarizes – it either brings families together or splits them apart," he says.

He described a situation where parents left a treasured vacation home to their children to share. One sibling, in need of cash, wanted to sell the property; the others wanted to keep it. The dispute resulted in professional mediation.

To avoid that situation, the parents should have talked with their children individually and as a group, Greenhill says. "You sort this all out beforehand and then you make it public. 'This is what we're going to do and here are the reasons for it.'"

Also, take time to tell – and record – family stories. Olsavsky says she often encounters people who regret not finding out more about family photos. Write on the backs of photos who it is and how they are related, she suggests.

2. Create a memorandum

To ensure your financial wishes are carried out, your estate plan should include a will, possibly a trust, a power of attorney in case you're incapacitated a health-care power of attorney and a living will that clarifies your wishes with regard to end-of-life care.

But given that family heirlooms can spark fiery conflicts, create a memorandum that details how you want to divvy up your personal property.

"Most people's wills, the language is very general," says Kate Byrne, a Pittsburgh-based senior wealth planner at PNC Wealth Management. "'I give my tangible personal property to my wife and kids.' The best thing to do is to have a memorandum with your will."

The memorandum describes who shall receive specific items. The will then references the memorandum; for example, "I direct my executor to distribute my tangible personal property in accordance with a signed and dated memorandum to be found with this will."

Relatives may be unhappy with your decisions, but they're less likely to be angry at each other. Make sure your executor knows where to find the memorandum, and be specific about items. In one example, a woman said her diamond ring should go to a daughter, but she didn't clarify which diamond ring, says Olsavsky. Attaching photos of the item and referencing each photo in your memorandum can help. Another way to prevent arguments after you're gone: Give items away before you die. But be wary of gift taxes, warns Byrne.

In the memorandum, you aren't likely to list all of your possessions. A common approach to deal with the remaining items is that each relative, starting with the oldest child, gets to pick one item, and then they go around the room again.

In family disputes, Olsavsky says, one option is to have all the items be put up for auction. Family members can bid on what they want. The money goes back to the estate to be divided equally.

3. Avoid fomenting discord

Got a favorite niece or grandson? Consider demonstrating that affection before you die – and make your post-death division of property more equitable.

"If your legacy is that you'd like your family to remain a harmonious unit, then plan to treat them equally, so you don't cause that discord that can occur if one of the children thinks they've been slighted by a parent," Olsavsky says.

4. Consider hiring a professional executor

Choosing your estate's executor is tricky business. You're giving power to one family member – that can lead to arguments.

To keep things fair, some people name co-executors, but that gets complicated, too. For example, they may all need to appear in court or show up to sign documents, Byrne says. Remarriages are another source of complications: a stepsibling's actions may not be viewed as fair by family from a previous or later marriage.

In such cases, hiring a corporate fiduciary as executor through your bank or trust company may make sense. You can name a professional executor in your will, or your chosen executors may opt to hire a professional after your death.

5. Share your values

Sharing family values can be among the most treasured of bequests. An ethical will, which might be a one-page document or a bound book and is not legally binding, lets you pass along your life story and values.

For Greenhill, his ethical will – that is, the document detailing his values – is his online blog, where he writes about wide-ranging subjects. Referring to his now-teenage daughter, he says, "There is nothing else I want to her to do one day than refer to that."

While an ethical will can take many forms, often it's a letter tucked in with the will. These can be tough to write. The frequently-asked-questions page at PersonalLegacyAdvisors.com, a website that sells related products and services, can help you figure out how to create an ethical will.

Another idea: A journal that prompts you to write down information such as the location of important financial documents and your wishes for your family. Check out the "When I'm Gone" journals sold at JournalsUnlimited.com.

Andrea Coombes is a personal-finance writer and editor in San Francisco. She's on Twitter @andreacoombes.

Will, Kayla, Ava, and Blake, I have a major problem with this article. That Allianz Insurance survey is for and by baby boomers (born 1946 to 1964) and anyone older. Of course they are going to say that passing along their stories and their stuff is their first priority. That's only natural for that age. That survey says nothing about what the next one or two generations have as interests and priorities. What are their needs? What do they have space for? What do they have free time for? What can they store for a few years and where, rather than decline to accept? What will they be doing and what will their interests be in another ten or twenty years? How do you best store stories and pictures? A possible reference is the following codicil to your great great grandmother Katie Reiss' will. She died at age 96 in 1986. Otherwise, dear grandchildren, your homework assignment is to start thinking so that then we can all start talking.

Love, Granddad

CODICIL TO LAST WILL & TESTAMENT OF
KATIE C. REISS   (Same to George W. Reiss

This Codicil being intended to re-affirm, clarify, and
amplifly the original will of Katie C.Reiss, RR #1,Freeburg, Ill.

It is my wish and intention that the real property
be held in Tenancy in Common, under the management and
mutual consent of my three children, namely:

The Home to stay as it is at my death, including the
furniture for one year. After the one year period, the
three children to agree as to what is to be done with the
furnishings.

It is my desire that the grandchildren shall all
receive the following cash awards.
$5.00 upon graduation from the 8th grade of School.
$50.00 upon the graduation of 4 years of High school.
$100.00 upon the graduation from College.
$200.00 upon being married.
However, if some one of the grandchildren are not married at the
age of 25 years, then they shall receive the $200.00 at that age.
Also if some one of the grandchildren cannot go thrugh high school,
or college for some reason or disability, then they shall receive
the $50.00 at the age of 18 and the $100.00 at the age of 21.
At the present time the grandchildren are as follows:
George Henry Irwin Reiss
Stephen William Reiss
Richard Franklin Reiss
Kenneth Irwin Reiss
Mary Kay Reiss
June Ann Reiss McBrayer.
June Ann Reiss McBrayer has already received her awards.

Also should there by any other grandchildren besides the
ones named herein, they are also to receive the above listed awards.

*George Henry Irwin Reiss
has already recived his awards.*

301

Reiss and Basler Family Graves
in St. Clair County, Illinois

Dear Will, Kayla, Ava, and Blake,   September 14, 2015

Here's a summary of where our various Reiss and Basler relatives are buried in St. Clair County. The indentations denote the next or second next generations. Most families buried their relatives in respective cemeteries usually because they had family plots. All 27 graves in Walnut Hill Cemetery in Belleville, for example, are from the John Reiss family except the last one.

Belleville, Illinois 62223
Valhalla Gardens of Memory

Earl William Reiss (7/3/1901 – 6/29/1990) and **Helen Hughes Reiss** (8/1/1913 – 6/9/2006)

William George Reiss (5/6/1912 – 8/29/1989) and **Anita Theresa Hesse Reiss** (8/12/1917 – 12/17/1960). His third wife Dorothy Hadley Reiss (5/23/1918 – 2/13/2003) is buried in Walnut Hill Cemetery in Belleville.

Irene Ida Petry Quirin (9/27/1912 – 2/9/1999) and **Leroy Quirin** (8/1/1907 – 2/??/1981)

George A. Reiss (9/??/1871 – 7/25/1957) and **Bertha Pfeifer Reiss** (2/2/1886 – 9/??/1970)

    Ruth J. Reiss (8/3/1909 – 2/12/1999)

Belleville, Illinois 62220
Walnut Hill Cemetery

John R. Reiss (12/11/1838 – 6/18/1919) and **Maria Josepha (Josephine) Gass Reiss** (2/6/1844 – 12/2/1920) both in Lot **167 in the Fifth Addition in the west half of the block bounded by streets called Monument, Carnation, Cypress, and Rose.**

    Louisa Elizabeth Reiss Muehling (7/31/1862 – 2/9/1920) and **George Muehling** (3/7/1859 – 12/24/1921) both in Lot **167.**

        John Meehling (4/14/1889 – 5/14/1935) and **Celestine Lehr Meehling** (3/??/1890 – 5/18/1959) both in Lot 809 in the original section next to their son Xavier below.

            Xavier Meehling (6/5/1910 – 4/14/1951) and **Hilda Schobert Meehling** (6/7/1913 – 2000). He is in Lot 809 in the original section next to his parents. She remarried to ??? Schanherr (?? -- ??) and is buried in Shiloh Valley Township Cemetery.

Margaret Meehling Hippard (5/31/1894 – 2/28/1975) and **Clemence Hippard** (11/2/1892 – 5/18/1933) both in Lot 974 in the original section a block west of the chapel.

Mary Reiss Ferkel (12/23/1863 – 8/9/1945) and **Jacob Ferkel** (7/1/1862 – 4/17/1938) **Lot 18, Block 12 near southwest corner.**

William J. Ferkel (9/10/1887 – 9/18/1915) **Lot 18, Block 12**

Mary Josephine Ferkel Wolfort (1/13/1891 – 9/17/1965) and **Lee W. Wolfort** (3/13/1887 – 11/14/1960) **Lot 18, Block 12**

John W. Ferkel (4/12/1893 – 9/22/1944) and Ruth Boushey Ferkel (1902 – 1980) **Only him in Lot 18, Block 12**

Henry A. Frekel (2/3/1900 – 8/18/1977) and **Lorene ? Ferkel** (1901 – 1981) and later **Frances E. Arth Ferkel** (7/2/1903 – 1/9/1992) **He and second wife in Lot 18, Block 12**

Emma Reiss Frey (4/30/1867 – 12/23/1960) and **Jacob G. Frey** (3/8/1864 – 4/27/1933) in **Lot 48, Block 12 near the center.**

Joseph George Frey (3/12/1891 – 6/3/1969) and **Angelina Hempe Frey** (1897 – 7/13/1964) in **Lot 12, Block 10 which is third block from the highway and on the south side of Cypress.**

Cathlyn Frey (1/16/1916 – 7/31/1916) in **Lot 12, Block 10**

George Jacob Frey (8/15/1892 – 3/25/1947) I. M. & F. W. U. of N. A. 182, in **Lot 48, Block 12**

Henry Albert Frey (2/20/1894 – 2/5/1953) Pfc. Co. B, 28 Bn US Guards World War I, in **Lot 48, Block 12**

Clara R. Frey (3/19/1896 – 8/23/1898) in **Lot 167.**

Irma B. Frey Kloess (2/3/1898 – 10/11/1885) and **Ervin Louis Kloess** (9/11/1898 – 8/5/1938) I. M. U. of N. A. 182, in **Lot 48, Block 12**

Mary J. Frey (2/3/1898 – 9/19/1923) in **Lot 48, Block 12**

George Reiss (12/31/1868 – 5/13/1888) in **Lot 167 on a tall gravestone shared with three siblings who also died that week.**

Katherine Reiss Eicher (9/30/1871 – 9/7/1953) and **George Eicher** (1/??/1870 – 4/8/1932) in **Lot 71, Block 8 which is the first full block from the highway north of**

Monument Street. Four identical gravestones are to the right of these for **Ernst W. Plegge** (1863 – 1948), his wife **Wilhemina Plegge** (1869 – 1918) and their daughters **Aurelia Plegge** (1886 – 1956) and **Sylvia Plegge** (1894 – 1927).

Eugenia Eicher Hallbauer (1902 – 11/1/1933) and **Fred Hallbauer** (? – 11/1/1933). **She only in Lot 71, Block 8. They died the same day in their early 30's so perhaps they were newlyweds and buried with their respective parents.**

John W. Reiss, Jr. (11/28/1873 – 5/26/1904) in **Lot 167.**

Barbara Reiss (1/31/1875 – 11/22/1957) in **Lot 167**

Charles Reiss (3/?/1877 – 5/17/1888) in **Lot 167 on a tall gravestone shared with three siblings who also died that week.**

Josephine Reiss (6/12/1881 – 5/13/1888) in **Lot 167 on a tall gravestone shared with three siblings who also died that week.**

Anna E. Reiss (11/?/1883 – 5/10/1888) in **Lot 167 on a tall gravestone shared with three siblings who also died that week.**

Sadly, John and Josephine Reiss lost four children in one week in May 1888.

Dorothy Hadley Reiss (5/23/1918 – 2/13/2003), third wife of William George Reiss is buried in Lot 51, Block 13, 4th Addition.

Freeburg, Illinois
Elmwood Cemetery

Conrad Dintelmann (1836 – 1911) and **Margaret Keller Dintelmann** (1841 – 1914). Conrad Dintelmann is the older brother of Eva Dintelmann (6/??/1844 – 11/29/1910) who married Charles Joseph Reiss (2/17/1843 - 5/13/1931) on 11/15/1866. Charles is the son of Adam and Margaret Basler Reiss. He and Eva are the first of three Reiss/Dintelmann marriages. His parents are John and Eva Dintelmann who are buried in Franklin Cemetery in Smithton.

George Dintelmann (2/1/1867 – 2/27/1945) and **Anna Margaret Reiss Dintelmann** (9/20/1875 – 8/31/1940). They are the second of three Reiss/Dintelmann marriages.

Edwin Louis Dintelmann (2/191916 – 10/28/1987) and **Beulah Cox Dintelmann** (2/11/1916 – 5/28/2006)

The third marriage between the Reiss and Dintelmann families is Geraldine A. Taake (3/21/1961 --) who married Dale G. Dintelmann (2/15/1963 --) on 11/9/1991. Her mother is Carol Jean Quirin Taake (5/31/1940 --) whose mother was Irene Ida Petry Quirin (9/27/1912 – 2/9/1999) whose mother was Louisa Kathryn Reiss Petry (9/22/1884 – 10/22/1969) whose father was Frank Joseph Reiss (9/27/1841 – 11/21/1921), the brother of Charles Reiss above.

Hecker, Illinois 62248
St. Augustine Cemetery

Margaret Basler Reiss Ebert (10/23/1818 – 6/23/1902) buried in Row 16. Her first husband **Adam Reiss** (5/7/1804 – 5/23/1849) is buried in **Row 8**. Her second husband Conrad Ebert (?/1812 – 7/23/1880) is buried in **Row 16.**

> Four children of Frank and Anna Syvilla Reiss who are grandchildren of Adam and Margaret Basler Reiss are buried in **Row 2** and share a common obelisk tombstone with information on each of four sides. **Charles Martin Reiss** (10/17/1867 – 11/18/1874), **Adam Joseph Reiss** (9/25/1869 – 11/5/1871), **Catherine Reiss** (11/11/1871 – 6/16/1872), and **Elizabeth A. Reiss** (7/1/1888 – 3/2/1889)
>
> **George Neff, Jr.** ((2/2/1874 – 10/18/1931) married Bertha Anna Staufenbiel Neff (3/28/1878 – 7/29/1901). She died in childbirth and is buried in **Row 6**. He is the son of Louisa Ebert and George Neff. Louisa is the daughter of Margaret Basler Reiss and second husband Conrad Ebert.

Margaret Ebert Neff (10/23/1856 – 4/23/1926) married **Conrad Neff** (12/26/1853 – 4/1/1917). She is the second daughter of Margaret Basler Reiss and second husband Conrad Ebert. Both are buried in **Row 16**

> **Conrad Neff, Jr.** (1877 – 1944) their son buried in **Row 16**
>
> > **Apollonia Neff** (4/21/1883 – 10/15/1964) married **Anselm Kreher** (10/14/1879 – 12/1/1958) are buried in **Row 19**. His parents may be Frances G. Kreher (1858 – 1945) and John A Kreher Sr. (1854 – 1942) who are also buried in **Row 19**.
>
> **August C. Neff** (1/25/1897 – 8/19/1925) buried in **Row 16**

Lebanon, Illinois
College Hill Cemetery

William Henry Reiss (11/15/1867 – 3/14/1957) married **Louisa B. Nies Reiss** (7/10/1866 – 12/24/1943)

> **Edgar Daniel Reiss** (1/25/1895 – 4/16/1960)
>
> **Rolland Charles Reiss** (10/5/1897 – 6/??/1976) and **Edna Townsend Reiss** (5/25/1905 – 8/??/1984)

Marissa, Illinois
St. Peters United Church of Christ Cemetery

Viola Petry Bald (3/11/1916 – 7/2008) and **Ralph William Bald** (9/17/1914 – 3/17/1992)

Mascoutah, Illinois
Mascoutah City Cemetery

Lucille Reiss (7/21/1908 – 4/13/1982) married Henry Dietz (2/29/1904 – 1/??/1985) on 10/12/31. Both plus daughter Marilyn attended the **1934 Reiss Centennial**. The **Social Security Death Index** shows their last residence was Mascoutah. Where are these graves?

O'Fallon, Illinois 62269
O'Fallon City Cemetery

Charles Frederick Reiss Jr. (7/3/1873 – 10/30/1958) and **Rose B. Schilling Reiss** (5/10/1884 – 1/20/1972) in Section A, Lot 187. His parents are Charles and Eva Dintelmann Reiss. Her parents John Schilling and Mary Mersinger are also in Section A, Lot 187, Grave #2.

> **Jessie M. Reiss Schau** (1/5/1904 – 12/14/1996) and **John Delbert Schau** (10/25/1890 – 11/??/1973). Their grave is next to his parents in Section A.

>> **Delores R. Schau** (4/27/1923 – 9/22/1995) and **Thomas D. Walker** (1/12/1923 – 2/24/2000).

>> **Gerald Delbert Schau** (1933 – 4/26/1990)

Louisa Amelia "Lulu" Reiss (12/??/1869 – 8/29/1928) never married, no heirs, and is not mentioned in her father's estate because he survived her. She lived with her parents at 305 E. Washington in O'Fallon. The **1900 Census** shows Lula age 30 living with her parents. The **1910 Census** shows Lula age 39 living with brother Charles below. The **1920 Census** shows Louise age 50 living with her widowed father. Where is her grave?

Paderborn, Illinois
St. Michel's Cemetery

Sophia Basler Stauder (5/13/1822 – 7/25/1865) Her grave is in the northeast corner. She is a sister of Margaret Basler Reiss Ebert who is buried in St. Augustine Cemetery in Hecker.

Shiloh, Illinois
Shiloh Valley Township Cemetery

Charles Joseph Reiss (2/17/1843 - 5/13/1931) married **Eva Dintelmann** (6/??/1844 – 11/29/1910). His parents are Adam and Margaret Basler Reiss who are buried in St. Augustine

Cemetery in Hecker. Her parents are John and Eva Dintelmann who are buried in Franklin Cemetery in Smithton.

Louisa Amelia "Lulu" Reiss (12/??/1869 – 8/29/1928)

Ferdinand Joseph Reiss (6/7/1875 – 11/18/1943) and **Emelia Tillie Koehler Reiss** (1/29/1882 – 12/24/1959)

Eva (Evelyn) Julia Reiss (6/18/1918 – 3/21/2008) and **Kenneth C. Bevirt** (2/27/1915 – 9/30/2000)

Jeanette M. Reiss (9/16/1878 – 5/??/1967)

Meta K. Reiss Young (2/14/1880 – 11/??/1967)

Hilda Schobert Meehling Schanherr (6/7/1913 – 1/19/2000). Her husband is either Paul T. Schanherr (6/27/1912 – 3/11/1997) or John A. Schanherr (8/31/1909 – 10/9/1988).

Smithton, Illinois
Franklin Cemetery

Frank Reiss (9/27/1841 – 11/21/1921) and **Anna Syvilla Feder Reiss** (9/26/1844 – 5/14/1930) in Section 2W3-2. Unmarked and between their graves is **William George Reiss, Jr.** (11/4/1938 – 11/4/1938), their great grandchild.

George Reiss (4/22/1873 – 8/19/1964) and **Catherine Leutzelschwab Reiss** (3/25/1890 – 10/17/1986) in Section SE-70

Louisa Kathryn Reiss (9/22/1884 – 10/22/1969) and **Philip Heinrich Petry** (3/5/1879 – 11/10/1942) in Section 1S-10

Christian Earl Petry (7/31/1910 – 12/28/1910) in Section 1E-108

Johann Dintelmann (5/10/1792 – 4/7/1874) in Section R3-2 and **Eva Mueller Dintelmann** (8/8/1803 – 8/1/1876) in Section R5-6. They are the parents of Eva Dintelmann who married Charles Reiss (son of Adam and Margaret Basler Reiss) and grandparents of George Dintelmann who married Anna Margaret "Gretchen" Reiss (granddaughter of Adam and Margaret Basler Reiss). Charles and Eva Reiss are buried in Shiloh Cemetery and George and Anna Margaret are buried in Elmwood Cemetery in Freeburg.

Will, Kayla, Ava, and Blake, all of these people are your relatives. There are many more graves of other relatives in Indiana, Texas, California, Kentucky, Missouri, Iowa, Ohio, Arkansas, Alabama, and elsewhere.

Love, Granddad

Book Donations

Dear Will, Kayla, Ava, and Blake,   January 25, 2016

One of the serendipities of being an author is doing book signings and autographing books for family and friends. Likewise it's an honor to donate books to unique individuals and non-profit organizations. Here's a summary on such donations of our six public books.

Quilter, Granger, Grandma, Matriarch

Marcella Klein – neighbor to the west who was a close friend of Grandma Katie Reiss
Floraville Grange
Floraville St. Paul United Church of Christ
Smithton Sportsmens Club
St. Clair County (Illinois) Genealogical Society

Granger, Quilter, Grandma, Matriarch

Marcella Klein – neighbor to the west who was a close friend of Grandma Katie Reiss
St. Clair County (Illinois) Genealogical Society

It Takes A Matriarch

Davenport (Iowa) Genealogical Society
Sacramento (California) Genealogical Society
St. Clair County (Illinois) Genealogical Society
St. Louis (Missouri) Genealogical Society
Sullivan County (Indiana) Historical Society
Sullivan (Indiana) Public Library

Reiss Dairy

Merletta Hays Lambert in Nashville, Tennessee – daughter of former employee
Margaret Cline Harmon in Zachary, Louisiana – daughter of former employee
Harry Sharp III in Sikeston – longtime Reiss and Standley family friend
Lucille Hornback of Sikeston who gave me Reiss Dairy cottage cheese and whipping cream jars
Scott Welton of the Sikeston Standard Democrat who wrote newspaper article
Sikeston (Missouri) Depot Museum
Scott County (Missouri) Historical & Genealogy Society
Sikeston (Missouri) Public Library

Family, Farming, and Freedom

Mrs. Don Smith – widow of former Meadowlark employee
Melba McCullaugh – former Meadowlark employee
Gene Fithian – former dragline operator and Ayrshire Collieries executive

Gay Ann Monninger – parents' stock broker
Liberty Fund in Indianapolis
Rev. Paul McGlasson – First Presbyterian Church in Sullivan
Fred and Velma Peterson – farm tenant in Sullivan County
Barry Hardin – farm tenant in Sullivan County
Sullivan (Indiana) Public Library
Sullivan (Indiana) Daily Times – local newspaper
Sullivan County (Indiana) Historical Society

From Burma With Love

Center for American War Letters in Orange, California
The Veterans History Project, Library of Congress in Washington, DC
Camp Roberts (California) Library
Atascadero (California) Public Library
Liberty Fund in Indianapolis
Elaine Coleman – author of From Calcutta with Love which is her parents war letters book, met
    with her in Santa Fe, New Mexico
Betty Jean Elder – author of The Oriole's Song, An American Girlhood in Wartime China,
    Dad met her in 1944 in Burma
Greg Ravatt and Tina Mayer – current owners of Stephenson grandparents' home in Atascadero
St. Clair County (Illinois) Genealogical Society
Sullivan County (Indiana) Historical Society
Sullivan (Indiana) Public Library
Myanmar (formerly Burma) Embassy in Washington, DC

Will, Kayla, Ava, and Blake, I'm very proud of what our various relatives accomplished and endured over the years. The more I research and write, the prouder I get. Putting all that into stories for the four of you every Monday is the heart of my retirement. Thanks for being my audience. Below is my exchange with the Myanmar Embassy in Washington, DC. Two years after that book donation, Grand DD and I spent ten days in that country. Having that book history in front of me made that trip very special.

Love, Granddad

700 Savanna Court
Dunlap, Illinois 61525
December 24, 2011

Embassy of Myanmar
2300 S Street Northwest
Washington, DC 20008-4016

Dear Sir:

I would like to donate the enclosed book to your embassy library. It includes unique history of Burma from 1944 when my dad was a labor officer on the Ledo Road hiring local tribesmen (and a few elephants) to help with construction. Read Dad's letter of October 7, 1944 at the bottom of Page 424. The book title is <u>From Burma With Love</u> and the subtitle is <u>Fifteen months of daily letters between Irwin and Mary Reiss during World War II</u>. They were my parents. I was born six months after my dad went to Asia and we did not meet until I was nine months old.

I've learned so much about my parents and about your country in researching and transcribing nearly 1,000 letters that went into this book. I am extremely proud of what my father accomplished in helping to build the Ledo Road through northern Burma and how the US Army succeeded in expelling the Japanese invaders.

Please accept this gift as a token of my friendship and appreciation for your country. Dad died in 2007 and Mom in 2010. My personal family and I lived in South Korea and Hong Kong from 1987 to 1992 and we've traveled to fourteen countries in the region. Our daughter-in-law was born and raised in Malaysia. My wife and I built houses in Viet Nam, Mongolia, and Nepal with Habitat for Humanity. We even built Habitat houses last year in Washington, DC near Gallaudet University with President Jimmy Carter.

Someday I would like to visit Myanmar and perhaps see parts of your country where my dad served during the war. I wish you all the best in the year to come.

Yours truly,

Stephen W. Reiss
reiss_steve@yahoo.com

EMBASSY OF THE REPUBLIC OF THE UNION OF MYANMAR
2300 S STREET, N.W.
WASHINGTON, D.C. 20008-4089
TEL: (202) 332-3344

Mr. Stephen W. Reiss
700 Savanna Court
Dunlap, Illinois 61525

10 January 2012

Dear Mr. Stephen W. Reiss,

We acknowledge receipt of your letter dated 24 December 2011 and a book namely "From Burma With Love". Thank you so much for your thoughtfulness in donating the said book to our Embassy. We are very impressed your father experience and the historical facts therein. Not only was it the perfect present but it will certainly come in handy for academic studies.

Under these circumstances, we have decided to send your book to His Excellency the Minister for Foreign Affairs in Myanmar who is also very enthusiastic about history.

We hope that one day you could make your trip to Myanmar and visit places where your father served during the war. You are always welcome to our Embassy.

With best regards,

Yours sincerely,

(Soe Paing)
Charge d'Affaires a.i.

311

This Is Not A Box!!!

Dear Will, Kayla, Ava, and Blake,   June 15, 2015

Will, Kayla, Ava, and Blake, remember that "this is not a box." Here we are Googling the last choice of a "Transmogrifier." We learned that it's a Calvin & Hobbs thing. A Transmogrifier is an invention of Calvin's that would turn one thing into another. Like most of his inventions, it was made originally from a cardboard box, though a later model was made using a water gun. Calvin used the transmogrifiers many times, turning himself and Hobbes into quite a wide array of creatures. The transmogrifier

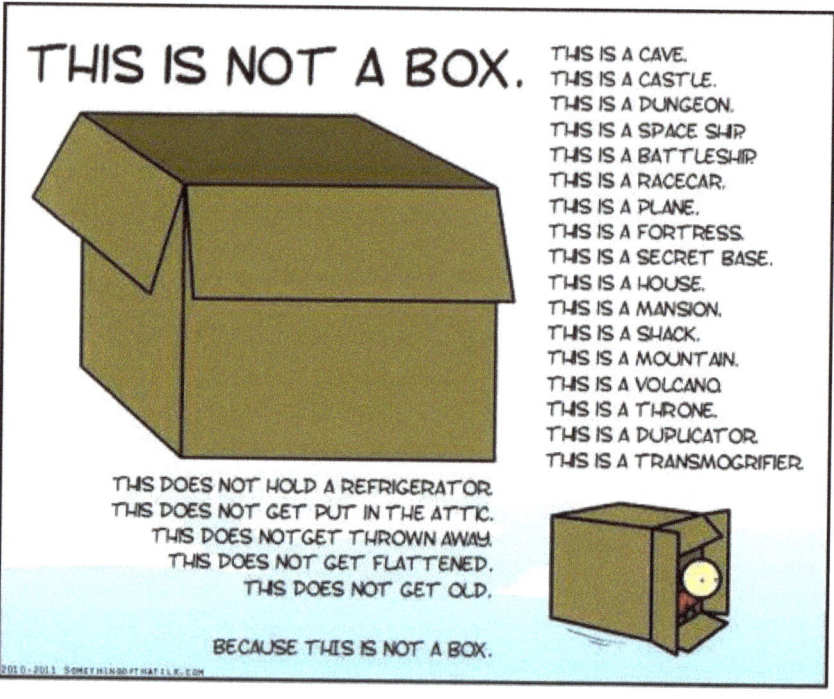

first appeared on March 23, 1987. Now I use them all the time to turn grandchildren into little angels. It works wonderfully well.

Love, Granddad

PS: Check out the last picture. It's your dads in a different box 35 years earlier.

314

Larry Brinker

Dear Will, Kayla, Ava, and Blake,   April 11, 2016

This man sent the following email on 3/31/2016. His email address is brkawy1@sbcglobal.net and his phone number is 618 520 8886.

Hi,

I met you a few years ago at the Reiss Farmstead. My siblings and I came out to see the home where we lived for a while. While going through some of our old photos, I came across some of your great grandparents. I stopped by the old farm recently, but the gentleman there said you have moved, and gave me your e-mail address. If indeed, you are the family I met at the time, if you send me your mailing address, I will mail these photos to you. I have my copies and am the only one that remembers those times. Please take them with my good wishes.

Larry Brinker

I called Larry three times to chat and to say "yes" I'm interested in the photos you have and here is my mailing address. He was talking about our 1889 house and the person he met there several years ago was probably Brandon Lang, grandson of Lavern and Lucille. Larry was born on 2/8/1941, his older brother Robert in 1939, and his younger sister Mary Ann in 1945. Robert has passed and there was an additional brother born in 1953. He said it was the 1946/47 timeframe that his parents, Lester and Marie Brinker, rented that house from my grandparents, George and Katie Reiss. Lester was born in 1914 and Marie in 1912 so they were a generation younger than my Katie who was born in 1890 and George in 1873.

Lester Brinker worked for Touchette Grocery in East St. Louis. They were not involved in farming any of my grandparents' land. Larry and his older brother walked to school at St. Michael's Catholic School in Paderborn. They would cut across farmers' field because it was shorter. Larry remembers being yelled at on several occasions and being chased by a bull.

Larry mentioned that his mom and Grandma Katie remained friends for years after their tenancy ended in late 1947. That's how his mom and her estate ended up with what you see below. Larry was downsizing their collection of family records, found these items, and was kind enough to look for a new home for them. He also said he has written about some of his childhood memories from our farm and will send that along as well. He knows I'm writing this story to you and helped with extra details.

Our book, <u>Granger, Quilter, Grandma, Matriarch, Life on the Reiss Family Farm 1944 - 1948</u>, mentions the Brinkers. That book is Grandma's five year diary and has the following 12 entries:

1946

Sunday July 21 – Fair, warm. We were at Edna's to fish dinner & supper. Bill & Anita & June Ann were there also. Brinkers came in the evening, paid ½ rent.

316

Friday November 22 – Fair, 30 degrees. I painted the screens for the other house. Geo and Mr. Brinker set up the mailbox. Geo also made firewood.

Friday December 6 – Fair, warm. I scrubbed the living room floor in the evening. We were at Marie Brinker's birthday party.

1947

Sunday February 9 – Fair, cold, 7 above. Brinkers were here for dinner. Willie Krehers and Bill & Anita & June Ann came in evening.

Saturday February 22 – Fair, cold, 17 degrees. We baked cookies. Mrs. Brinker brought a birthday cake over for Georgie's birthday.

Thursday February 27 – Fair, warmer, 22 degrees. I washed. Marie hung it out for me. I also ironed in the evening.

Wednesday March 12 – Fair, warm. Had the bed things out to air. Then Marie helped me turn the rug in bedroom. Ed Feders were here.

Tuesday May 20 – Cloudy. Geo disked Brinker's garden. Afternoon it rained, rained very hard by evening.

Wednesday June 25 – Raining. Marie and I picked some dewberries in morning. Early peaches are ripening now. We got our AAA check today, $138.00 and took it to the bank.

Thursday July 10 – Fair, cool all day. I picked beans, so Marie & I canned 14 quarts in her cooker. Schillings finished combining wheat here, 806 bu.

Friday October 17 – Very warm, 82 degrees, thunder and rain by evening. Marie and Mary Ann had dinner with us. Geo finished the roof on the washhouse. Got $18 rent from Mr. Roy F. Howerton.

Sunday October 19 – Fair, cooler. Brinkers moved out today and Howertons moved in today.

Will, Kayla, Ava, and Blake, on the next page is Larry's letter that accompanied the items he mailed. I am very impressed by this man and very much appreciate how he went out of his way to identify and then forward these items. He mentioned having fond memories as a six year old of living in our farm house. Those memories were strong enough that he and his siblings visited our farm about 65 years after they moved out. That's awesome. I'm sending Larry a copy of this story today. . . . . . Thank you again, Larry.

Love, Granddad

Hi Stephen,

The photos I have enclosed were given to my mother by the lady in the photo, whom I believe would be your great grandmother, based on our conversation when we met a few years ago. She and my mom got to be friends during the short time we lived there. I hope they provide you with another peek at the family that you may not have had. If you have any questions about the time we spent there, feel free to call me, although I was only six at that time, I remember my parents talking about our time there.

I enjoyed the visit we had there, and seeing the old house again. I hope all is well with you and your family, and your new home.

All The Best,

Larry Brinker
1015 Alton Ave.
Madison, IL 62060

Phone – (618) 520-8886

Mrs. Reiss Dies at 43

Mrs. Anita T. Reiss, 43, of 437 Clearview Dr., Belleville, died at 6:30 a. m. Saturday in Barnes Hospital, St. Louis, following an illness of 10 months. She had entered the hospital on Friday.

Funeral services will be held at 1:30 p. m. Tuesday at the Union Methodist Church with burial in Valhalla Burial Park. The Rev. Dr. Eugene M. Leckrone, pastor, will officiate and the Albert B. Baldus Funeral Home will have charge. Friends may call at the funeral home after 3 p. m. today until 10:30 a. m. Tuesday, when Mrs. Reiss will be taken to the church.

Mrs. Reiss was a native of Freeburg and a member of Union Methodist Church. She is survived by her parents Mr. and Mrs. Frank E. Hess, Rural Route 2, Freeburg; her husband William G. Reiss; a daughter Mrs. James D. (June Ann) McBrager, St. Louis; a sister Mrs. Elsie Heidenreich, Freeburg; three brothers Siedel Hess, New Athens, Ralph Hess, Rural Route 2 Belleville, and Edgar Hess, Belleville.

319

Thanks, Katy

Dear Will, Kayla, Ava, and Blake,   May 9, 2016

Grand DD and I came home from Menards at noon Thursday and there was a package at our back door. Inside was an old quilt and this card from my second cousin Katy Standley who lives in Maryland. It was indeed a wonderful surprise.

Dear Steve,

I hope you are pleased with this surprise — I think this is a quilt made by Aunt Katie for my grandmother, Mary Etta. I found it in a stack of old quilts. I remember it on Mama's bed. She was a wonderful seamstress but did not quilt. It obviously was much loved and well used. My mother kept it because it was a "family" quilt and because it was on Mama's bed when she died.

So I hope you are pleased. You asked about your grandmother giving a quilt to my grandmother and I think this is it. I have not cleaned it — too fragile.

Love, Katy

My family tree shows that Mary Etta Reiss passed away in Sikeston, Missouri on 9/20/1947. She and her husband John had founded the Reiss Dairy which is another story all by itself. So I looked through the first three years of our book, <u>Granger, Quilter, Grandma, Matriarch,</u> which is my grandma Katie's daily diary for 1944 - 1948. Here are entries from September 1944.

Thurs 7 – Clara came over and helped me set up the quilt for Etta and we quilted till evening. Then I ironed.

Fri 8 – Worked on Etta's quilt and also canned some peaches. Geo ground corn.

Tues 12 – Canned peaches and worked on Etta's quilt. Clara helped me. Geo mixed feed.

Wed 13 – I quilted all day. Geo chopped hedge fence. Got letters from Irwin and Franklin.

Wed 20 – Very hot, 94 degrees. John, Etta, and Audrey were here. John & Katie were here in evening. Got a present from Irwin from India.

320

Here's the center portion of the quilt which measures 6.5 by 7 feet. There are thousands of stitches but no individual pieces stitched together like the other six quits we have from Grandma Katie. This one is far more artsy and intricate. There's a partial letter below which Grandma wrote on this same date to her youngest son Irwin. It's in our book, <u>From Burma With Love</u>, which is 1,000 daily letters my parents and family exchanged during World War II when Dad was in India and Burma and Mom with newborn me was in California.

September 20, 1944

Our Dearest Irwin,

We are going thru such a busy time the last two weeks that we can hardly rest up any more. It's not all work, it's go here and go there and always company in between. Today we had a very nice day here on the farm. Uncle John and Aunt Etta and Audrey were here. Audrey was very much interested in seeing all the pictures from you and Mary and Stevie, also those of your camp life, those many nice pictures from Calif. and Camp Roberts. Audrey said I should say hello to you for her, she wishes so often that she could get to see you all sometime again. She hadn't been here for 10 years. She is 30 years old and is doing office work at some camp in Tenn. She still is very pretty. She liked the pictures of your wife and son. Everybody who sees Stevie's pictures thinks he looks so much like you.

I looked up your record of when you were a baby and saw that you also weighed 15 lbs. at 3 months old, so I guess Stevie is about your size. Irwin, thanks a million for the beautiful flower vases. My, they are pretty, they just came today and Etta and Audrey too think they are beautiful. Now I've got more to show people when they come.

Irwin it's very pretty on the farm now, the woods is turning all colors, wish Mary could see it once at this time of the year. Corn is mostly all ripe, in fact Shillings got one of our fields all picked already. It made 45 bu per acre, our lawn is beautiful. I have a million and one flowers. The people today just stood and looked at all those flowers. But all those things don't mean much to me. Sure I like to work with flowers, but what would be more beautiful than all those flowers, would be if you and Mary and Stevie and Frank & Gerry & Georgie and Bill, Anita and June all could be here and enjoy the farm together. So I hope things will soon take a turn for the better and that you could be with us all real soon.

Audrey brought me three quilts to quilt for her this winter, and Etta has three altho I finished one of Etta's last week and she took it along home today. Etta's are just common patch quilts, but Audrey's are fancy ones and need a lot of careful sewing so you see I'll be busy every day of the year. I love to quilt. I can rest my legs and feet when it's nice outside, then Pop and I are always working together fixing up things and so on. Good luck, dear son.

Love,

Mother & Dad

Will, Kayla, Ava, and Blake, wasn't that nice of my cousin Katy to surprise me with the gift of a quilt my grandmother had made. She will receive this same story that you do as a further thank you from me. Katy made it possible to connect a quilt with a diary and a letter in two of our books. That was very thoughtful and I very much appreciate her generosity.

Did you notice their corn yield was only 45 bushels per acre? Today, four times that would be considered average and with far less labor. In fact, 45 bushels would be a crop failure and trigger an insurance claim!!!

Love, Granddad

Broad Hollow Grange

Dear Will, Kayla, Ava, and Blake,   May 2, 2016

Maybe you remember my Granddad's Mondays story of 1/6/2014 about the Floraville Grange where my grandparents, George and Katie Reiss, were charter members when it was formally established on 3/8/1948. Well, there's an earlier Grange where they were also charter members. It was the Broad Hollow Grange which was formally established on 1/18/1921. It is Grange #1806 with a mailing address of 6733 Robinson School Road, Hecker, Illinois which is a rural location between Freeburg and New Athens.

I learned about Broad Hollow celebrating its 95th anniversary last month from my cousin Lynette Lang Schaefer who is the President of the Illinois State Grange. She was asked to speak at their celebration two weeks ago. Well, Lynette knew I had written lots of stories about our family heritage and history, so she emailed asking what I had on Broad Hollow. My only answer was that I knew Broad Hollow had sponsored the 4H Club where my dad and his brother Franklin were members in the early 1930s. I did not know that my grandparents had helped established the Broad Hollow Grange.

Here's the 2/26/2016 posting from the Broad Hollow Grange Facebook page. What kind of party says "no desserts?" – "Broad Hollow Grange will be celebrating its 95th anniversary on Sunday afternoon April 17 during Grange Month. Event begins with a 1 p.m. potluck (no desserts, please) followed by a program – Broad Hollow Grange history highlights; speaker, Lynette Schaeffer, Illinois State Grange Master; Community Citizen of the Year Award, and Membership Award. Enjoy a special Grange anniversary cake. Music and lots of fellowship." Here's an entry in the *December 13, 1921 Proceedings of the Illinois Grange* – "Broad Hollow Grange was organized on January 17, 1921 by our Worthy State Master E. O. Eckert with thirty-five charter members, and now has a membership of 140."

"Special meetings in order to work in more literary work were held, as so much degree work interfered seriously with lecturer's hour. A new hall has been erected, size 40 x 70, with large stage and auditorium on upper floor, and basement to be used as kitchen and dining room, when thus needed, otherwise as a playroom for children of Grange members. A Grange Choir and Dramatic Club have been organized, and great things are expected from them in the future."

Alex Brandenburger

The *1922 Proceedings of the Illinois Grange* mentions that Broad Hollow Grange held a formal Dedication Ceremony on December 18, 1921.

As you might guess, Broad Hollow is classified on government topographic maps as a valley. That's where the Grange's name comes from. Below are two pictures from Google Earth. I don't see much of a broad hollow or valley.

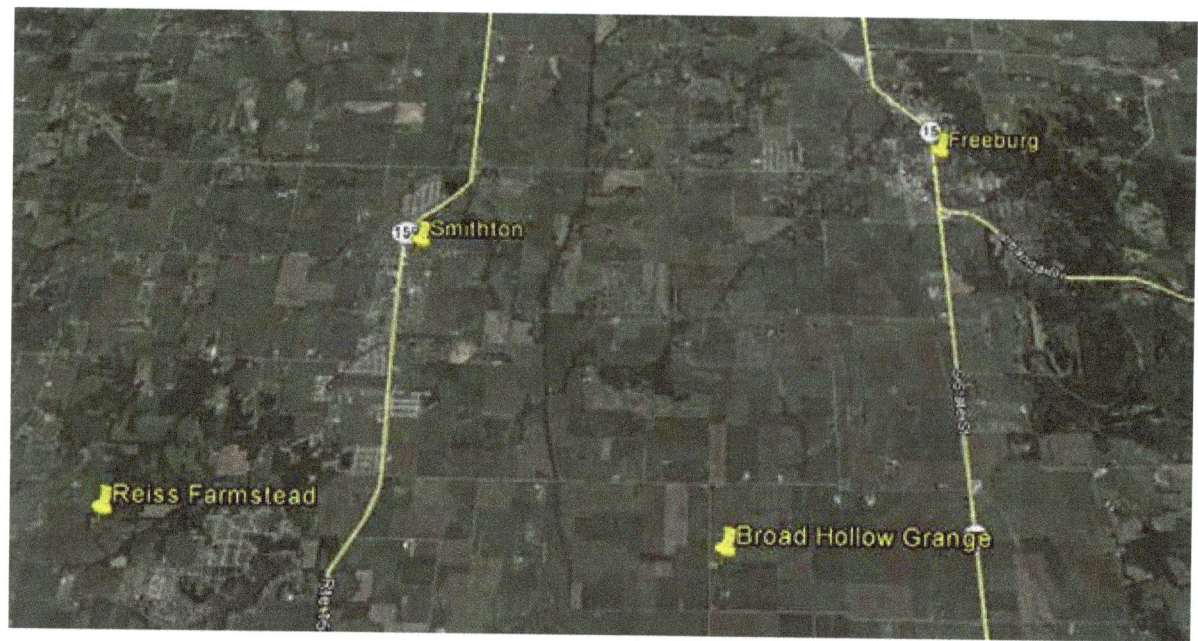

You know that I transcribed about 1,000 letters that my parents wrote to each other during World War II when Dad was in Burma/India and Mom with newborn me was living with her parents in Atascadero, California. Those letters are all in our book, <u>From Burma With Love,</u> which was published in 2011. Here's part of a letter that Dad wrote from Assam, India.

December 20, 1944

My darling Mommie and Irvie, Jr.,

Today I hit the jackpot – eight letters and three packages – isn't that wonderful? Almost all the letters were a month old. They were as follows: 2 from my baby, 2 from Mother, 1 from Frank, a letter and a Christmas card from Toddy, and an official letter from my office. The packages were: 1 from you, 1 from Mom which is obviously a fruitcake, and 1 from **Broad Hollow Grange**. I'll wait to open them until Christmas.

Your own Irvie always,

Will, Kayla, Ava, and Blake, isn't that an interesting history that connects our family with the Broad Hollow Grange? And to think that it all came to our attention through cousin Lynette being asked to speak at their 95th anniversary banquet. Here's a picture from spring 1960 when young Lynette was exactly five years old. That's her great aunt Katie Reiss (my grandma Katie) showing Lynette how to weed tulips.

We know that Katie was an extra-miler on Grange work, memberships, service, meals, projects, and fun. She died on 10/17/1986 at age 96.5 so obviously Grange work was part of her longevity. She was a wonderful person and a terrific role model for those of us who are now grandparents ourselves. I'm sure on 9/20/2013 that Grandma Katie was looking down from heaven with pride and pleasure to watch Lynette become president of the Illinois State Grange.

Love, Granddad

George Basler at the Battle of Stones River

Dear Will, Kayla, Ava, and Blake,   December 26, 2016

Maybe you remember my story of 2/2/2015 about George Basler's Civil War history. As the younger brother of my great great grandmother Margaret Basler Reiss Ebert, he was my great great great uncle. Add two more "greats" for your generation. My earlier story was pretty comprehensive about Uncle George. This story today is just about how the Battle of Stones River developed where Uncle George was wounded in the foot and thereby disengaged from the rest of the Civil War. Grand DD and I visited the **Stones River National Battlefield** on 6/20/2004. That visit and several downloads from the internet are how I learned the battle details which follow.

The Union commander was Major General William Rosecrans (at right) commanding the XIV Corps which was also called the Army of the Cumberland. The Confederate commander was Major General Braxton Bragg commanding the Army of Tennessee. Both were West Point graduates, Bragg in 1837 and Rosecrans in 1842.

Under Rosecrans commanding the Right Wing was Major General Alexander McCook, then Brigadier General Phillip Sheridan commanding the Third Division, then Colonel George Roberts (killed and replaced by Colonel Luther Bradley) commanding the Third Brigade, then Lieutenant Colonel Francis Swanwick (wounded, captured, and replaced by Captain Samuel Johnson) commanding the 22nd Illinois Infantry Regiment which included Uncle George Basler. Here is that chain of command in chart form.

Division	Brigade	Regiments and Others
Third Division BG Philip Sheridan	3rd Brigade Col George W. Roberts (**k**) Col Luther P. Bradley	• 22nd Illinois: Ltc Francis Swanwick (**w&c**), Cpt Samuel Johnson • 27th Illinois: Col Fazilo Harrington (**k**), Maj William A. Schmitt • 42nd Illinois: Ltc Nathan H. Walworth • 51st Illinois: Col Luther P. Bradley, Cpt Henry F. Wescott

The Union Army arrived in Nashville on 9/11/1862 and set up camp for the winter, but with a watchful eye on what the Confederates might be planning. We know their camp was 12 miles southeast of a large race horse plantation called Belle Meade. Uncle George mentions on 12/5/1862 in his 90-day journal that he was part of a foraging party that "acquired" 900 wagon loads of hay from Belle Meade for their own needs. Foraging is a military term for stealing. Below is a map showing Nashville and Murfreesboro which are 36 miles apart.

Murfreesboro was a small town in the Stones River Valley, a former state capital named for a colonel in the Revolutionary War, Hardy Murfree. All through the Civil War it was a center for strong Confederate sentiment, and Bragg and his men were warmly welcomed and entertained during the month of December. It was located in a rich agricultural region from which Bragg planned to provision his army and a position that he intended to use to block a potential Union advance on Chattanooga. Hardee noted afterward that "The field of battle offered no particular advantages for defense." Despite this, Bragg was reluctant to move farther south, say to the arguably more defensible Duck River Valley, or farther north, to Stewart's Creek, where Rosecrans thought Bragg would defend. Sensitive to the political requirements that almost no Tennessee ground be yielded to Union control, he chose the relatively flat area northwest of the politically influential city, straddling the Stones River. None of his troops were ordered to construct field fortifications.

By the time Rosecrans had arrived in Murfreesboro on the evening of December 29, Bragg's Army of Tennessee had been encamped in the area for a month. By nightfall, two thirds of Rosecrans's army was in position along the Nashville Turnpike, and by the next day Rosecrans's army numbered about 41,000 to Bragg's 35,000. The odds were closer than those figures would indicate. Bragg had the advantage of the detached, but cooperating, cavalry commands under Forrest and Morgan, who raided deeply behind Union lines while Wheeler's cavalry slowed the Union forces with hit-and-run skirmishes. **On December 29**, Wheeler and 2,500 of his men rode completely around the Union army, destroying supply wagons and capturing reserve ammunition in Rosecrans's trains. They captured four wagon trains and 1,000 Union prisoners.

On December 30, the Union force moved into line two miles northwest of Murfreesboro. The two armies were in parallel lines, about four miles long, oriented from southwest to northeast. Bragg's left flank was weak at the start, and Rosecrans could have attacked there when he arrived and wheeled left, around the flank and directly into the town of Murfreesboro, but he did not know the full disposition of Bragg's forces because of the skillful screening of the Confederate cavalry during the Union march. In a manner similar to the previous year's First Battle of Bull Run, both commanders devised similar plans for the following day: envelop the enemy's right, get into his rear, and cut him off from his base. Since both plans were the same, the victory would probably go to the side that was able to attack first. Rosecrans ordered his men to be ready to attack after breakfast, but Bragg ordered an attack at dawn.

==You can see Uncle George's 22nd Illinois Infantry Regiment== under Generals Sheridan and McCook in the middle of the Union lines in blue on the west side of Stones River. Note the east/west Wilkinson Turnpike which bisects both armies. Watch troop movement totally to the north of that road as the battle progresses.

Bragg's forces were situated with Polk's corps on the west side of the river and Hardee's men on the east. He had expected Rosecrans to attack on December 30, but when that attack did not come, his plan was to drive Hardee's corps and the cavalry under Wharton deep into the Union rear. He began moving the bulk of Hardee's corps across the river to his left flank in preparation for the next morning's attack. This left Breckinridge's division in reserve on the east side of the river on the high ground.

Rosecrans planned to have Crittenden cross the river and attack the heights east of the river, which would be an excellent artillery platform from which to bombard the entire Confederate line. Crittenden—facing Breckinridge on the Union left—failed to notify McCook (on the Union right) of these troop movements. McCook, anticipating that the next day would start with a major attack by Crittenden, planted numerous campfires in his area, hoping to deceive the Confederates as to his strength on that flank, and to disguise the fact that his flank was not anchored on an obstacle (the nearby Overall Creek). Thomas, in the center, was ordered to make a limited attack and act as the pivot for Crittenden's wheel.

The armies bivouacked only 700 yards from each other, and their bands started a <mark>musical battle</mark> that became a non-lethal preview of the next day's events. Northern musicians played "Yankee Doodle" and "Hail, Columbia" and they were answered by "Dixie" and "The Bonnie Blue Flag." Finally, one band started playing "Home! Sweet Home!" and the others joined in. Thousands of Northern and Southern soldiers sang the sentimental song together across the lines.

By 8:00 a.m. December 31, Confederate General Hardee is crossing Stones River on a left flank maneuver to engage the Union right wing. <mark>Sheridan and Uncle George</mark> stay in the middle facing east. The Union begins their own left flank under Crittenden with that blue arrow near the top by crossing Stones River.

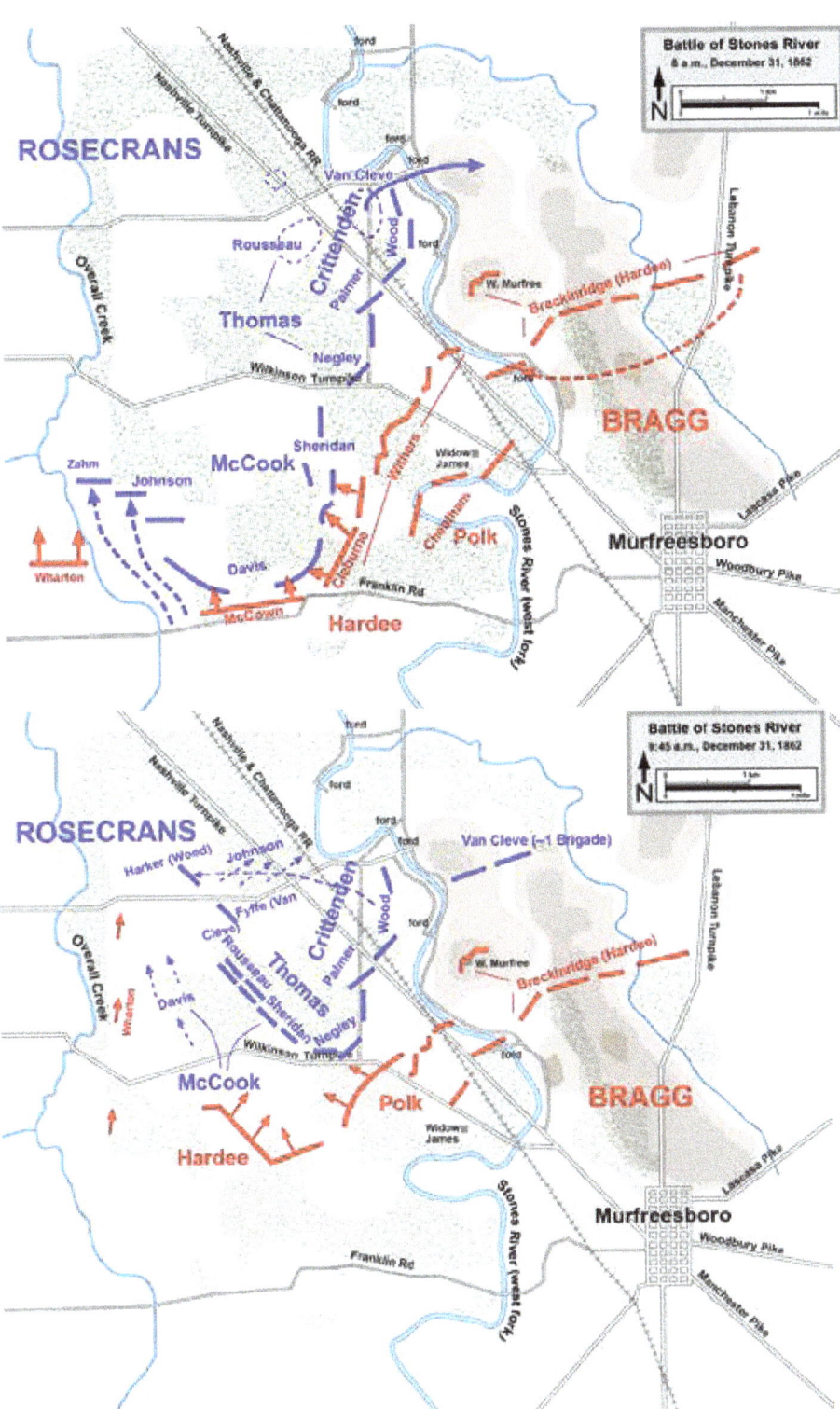

By 9:45 a.m. December 31, the Union is getting boxed in. <mark>Sheridan and Uncle George</mark> have turned 135 degrees and now face the Confederates approaching from the southwest. The Union is now totally north of Wilkinson Turnpike.

By 11:00 a.m. December 31, Sheridan and Uncle George are still in the middle but getting squeezed. Both armies are north of Wilkinson Turnpike.

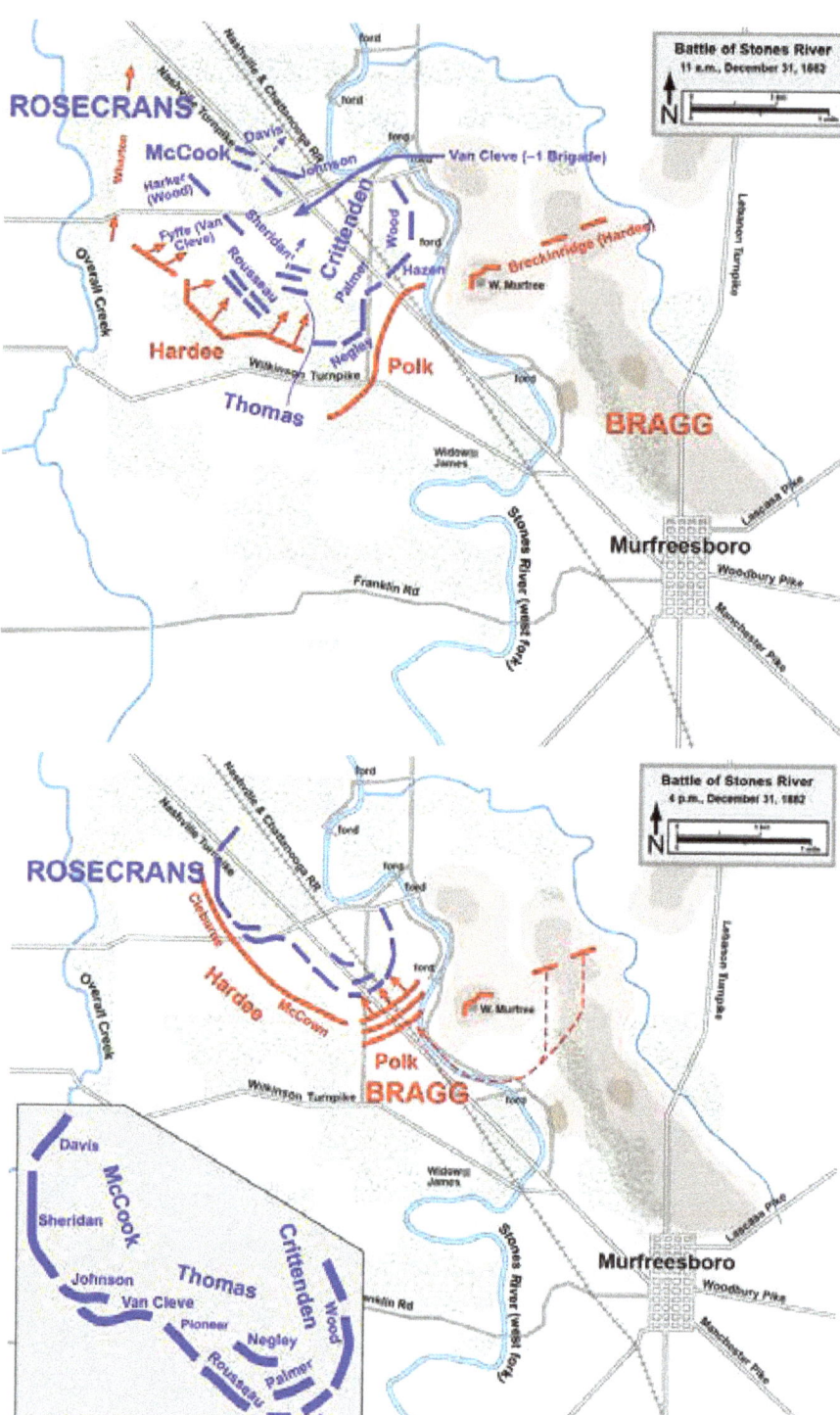

By 4:00 p.m. December 31, both armies are on the west side of Stones River and are much more consolidated. Sunset on 12/31/1862 was at 4:43 p.m. Sheridan and Uncle George are facing west.

Sometime today Uncle George was wounded and taken prisoner. Below are the medical words from his official record but they don't say in which foot he was wounded. George was returned to the Union three days later on 1/3/1863 in a prisoner exchange.

"Gun shot ball entering at joint of 4th toe passing diagonally through the foot emerging at tarso-metatarsal joint of the great toe and resulting in partial loss of use of foot. Disability one-third."

January 1, 1863 – very limited fighting.
Fighting resumed on January 2, 1863, when Bragg ordered Breckinridge to assault the well-fortified Union position on a hill to the east of the Stones River. Faced with overwhelming

artillery, the Confederates were repulsed with heavy losses. Falsely believing that Rosecrans was receiving reinforcements, Bragg chose to withdraw his army on 1/3/1863 to Tullahoma, Tennessee.

By 4:00 p.m. January 2, the Union is now on both sides of Stones River. Both armies are north of Wilkinson Turnpike. Sheridan's position is not shown but he's under McCook.

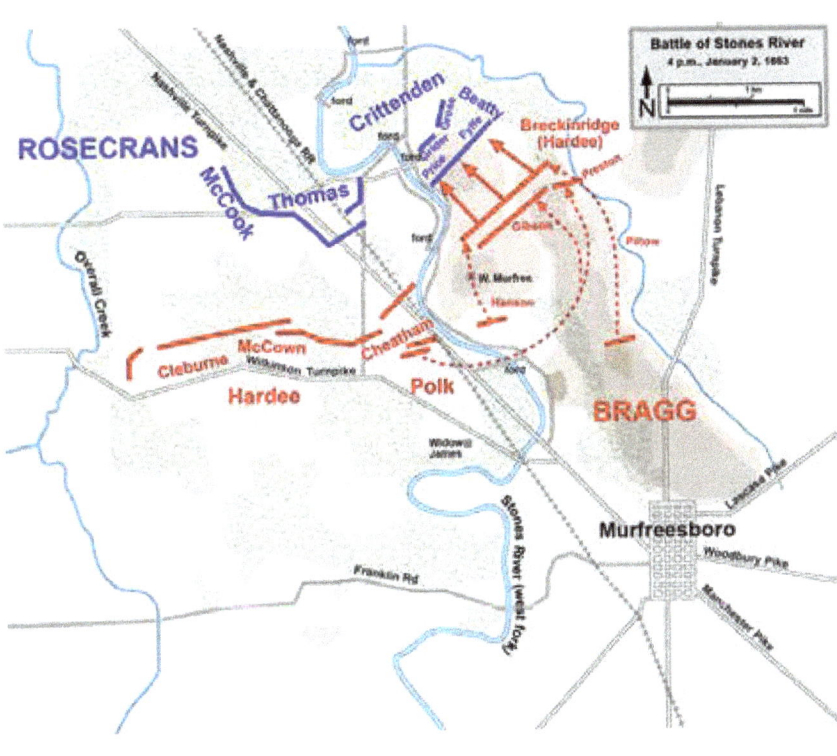

By 4:45 p.m. January 2, Sheridan's and McCook's positions are not shown but they have to be along the west side.

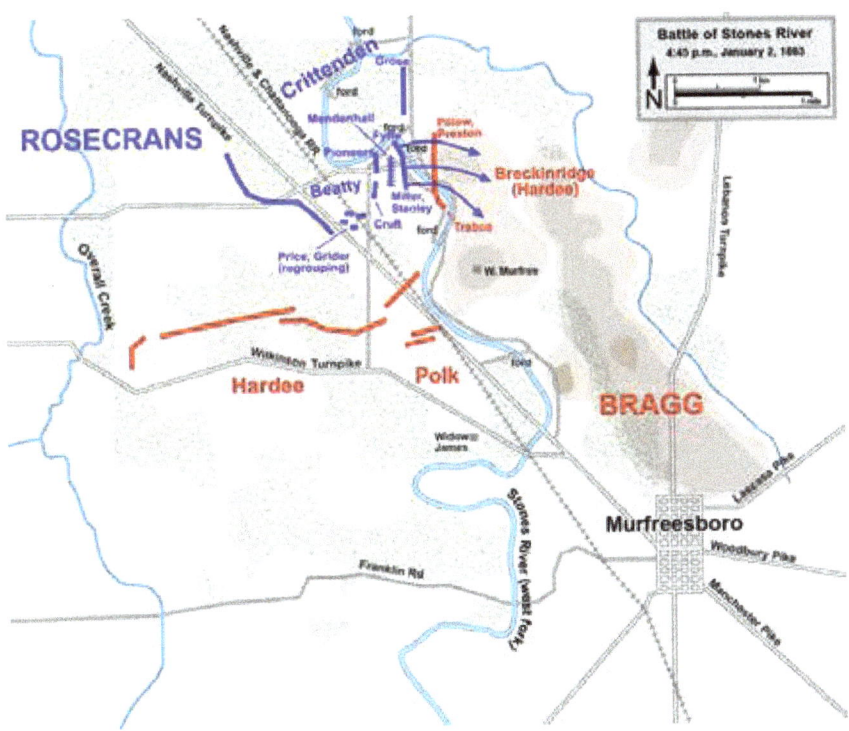

Will, Kayla, Ava, and Blake, here's a summary of the significant points of the Battle of Stones River and your Uncle George Basler.

The **Battle of Stones River** was fought from December 31, 1862, to January 2, 1863, in Middle Tennessee, as the culmination of the **Stones River Campaign** in the Western Theater of the Civil War. Of the major battles of the Civil War, Stones River had the highest percentage of casualties on both sides. Although the battle itself was inconclusive, the Union Army's repulse of two Confederate attacks and the subsequent Confederate withdrawal were a much-needed boost to Union morale after the defeat at the Battle of Fredericksburg, and it dashed Confederate aspirations for control of Middle Tennessee.

On December 31, each army commander planned to attack his opponent's right flank, but Bragg struck first. A massive assault by the corps of Confederate Generals Hardee and Polk overran the wing commanded by Union General McCook. A stout defense by the division of Union General Sheridan in the right center of the line prevented a total collapse and the Union assumed a tight defensive position backing up to the Nashville Turnpike. Repeated Confederate attacks were repulsed from this concentrated line.

I think we can conclude that Uncle George Basler was another of our long line of family heroes.

Love, Granddad

My Dear Son

Dear Will, Kayla, Ava, and Blake,   July 4, 2016

Happy Independence Day!!! Here's a letter my dad wrote to me 72 years ago today which was shortly after I was born on 6/12/1944. He learned about my birth ten days later on 6/22/1944 via a telegram from the American Red Cross because he was away serving in India with the US Army during World War II. Dad's words were poignant and still apply for the next three and ongoing generations of both sons and daughters.

What the next generation will value most is not what we owned, but the evidence of who we were and the tales of how we lived. In the end, it's the family stories that are worth the storage.

Love, Granddad

Ramgarh, India
July 4, 1944

My dear Son,

How are you? I have never seen you. I don't even know how you look. All that I know is what the cablegram said – you arrived safely (on June 12) and you and Mother are doing fine.

I am very sorry that I wasn't there with your mommie to help welcome you into this world. But right now I am in the far away land of India doing a job which society has presumed upon me. But I want you to know that spiritually I was right there with you when you were born. I am very proud of you, Son, and your mother and I love you very much.

Sometime soon I am coming back home, Son, to make a happy home for you and Mommie. Your mother and I will give you the best of care. We will try and give you very good education. In return I want you to do something for us. Wherever you are and whatever you do, I want you to do it so that your mother and I can say with pride, "that is our son." In other words, Son, I always want you to be a man.

Every day here in India, I see thousands of boys and girls who don't have a chance in life. They have no food to eat or a place to sleep. They don't have an opportunity to get an education. They don't have the privilege of worshiping in Christian churches. You have every opportunity in the world to do some good for society. I want you to make the most of that opportunity.

One more thing, Son – when you were born, you made your mother and myself very happy. I want you to continue to make us happy the rest of our lives. Will you do that for us, Son?

Your affectionate father,

Irwin H. Reiss

333

The Old Barn Is Demolished in 2015

Dear Will, Kayla, Ava, and Blake,   December 28, 2015

Here's a picture from the heydays of hay days at the barn on our Reiss family farm. You may remember it from my Granddad's Mondays story of 6/8/2015 titled "Hoistin' Hay" which was about hay carriers or trolleys. Well, thanks to today's jumbo bales, two-story barns are now obsolete, all those people and horses are gone, all that technology is gone, and now after about 95 years this barn is gone. All that remains are a few photographs, memories, stories, and the original foundation stones. This story which follows is not only the last one of 2015, it will be the last story in my next book called 200 Stories for My Grandchildren about the Reiss Family and Farm, St. Clair County, IL from 1833 to Present. So pay attention. There may be a quiz.

My grandfather George Reiss built this barn about 1920. In the next photo you can see pegged post and beam construction and a few mud dauber nests. You can also see circular sawblade marks on the timbers indicating they were not hand hewn like those in the adjacent log granary built 80 years earlier in 1838. The original roof was shingles and there was a cupola for ventilation. In later years the cupola was removed and the roof was covered with galvanized sheet metal. The original exterior board and batten siding is pretty much still there but different layers of red paint have all but faded away.

Six months ago my generation of owners sadly agreed that salvaging this barn as a building was not practical, but we all quickly agreed that salvaging the timbers and siding was practical and highly desirable. That part of our history could then continue as someone's barn board project rather than as so much firewood. We found Aaron Bergmann in Belleville at 618 234 3630 who is in the barn recycling business to undertake a careful demolition in mid-October. His compensation was the wood that he salvaged. Aaron did a great job and supplied several pictures. He also salvaged the hay carrier and track from the top ridge of the second story haymow.

Your dad/uncle Adam, cousin Jesse, and I visited this barn last June and took pictures after attending the 150-year Luetzelschwab family reunion. It measured 30 by 36 feet. Some good junk that was stored in the first floor west half and later moved to a shed to the north. We also found a notice from 1971 where Lavern Lang had used stored soybeans as loan collateral.

Here's Aaron's picture after the volunteer tree was removed but before he tackled the building itself. You can see the foundation stones underneath. You can also see the raised floor on the near half which required a row of center stones for that support. The far side was for animals and had a dirt floor.

Here's the salvaged hay carrier with 12 feet of track which will soon find new life in our log cabin as a chandelier. Lights will be LED bulbs inside old fruit canning jars. It's the same Cloverleaf brand as the one I bought on eBay that was in my previous story. Now our log cabin will have hay carrier chandeliers in stereo. Notice the mud dauber nests in the drop pulley which will stay.

Will, Kayla, Ava, and Blake, you've seen the "before" pictures of our barn. An in-process picture is below. The "after" picture on the next page shows only the original foundation stones which remain. We wanted to keep that part of the old barn kinda like a cemetery of tombstones representing memories, people, events, and histories for what has been. I love this farm. It's very sad that your generation cannot experience what my generation did but that's just the way life is. You'll have to learn about it from our stories, books, and pictures. Now

only three old buildings remain on the homestead – the log granary above from 1838, a new home behind it from 1889, and a newer home off to the left from 1940. We need your help with ongoing preservation. Thank you,

Love, Granddad

You can shed tears that she is gone, or you can smile because she has lived. You can close your eyes and pray that she'll come back, or you can open your eyes and see all she's left. Your heart can be empty because you can't see her, or you can be full of the love you shared. You can turn your back on tomorrow and live yesterday, or you can be happy for tomorrow because of yesterday. You can remember her only that she is gone, or you can cherish her memory and let it live on. You can cry and close your mind, be empty and turn your back. Or you can do what she'd want: smile, open your eyes, love and go on.

The Old Barn Garden

Dear Will, Kayla, Ava, and Blake,   October 24, 2016

You'll remember my last story of last year dated 12/28/2015 about the old red barn being demolished on the Reiss family farm. Well, I'm thrilled to report that that demolition is not the end of the line for that unique family asset and history. The barn footprint is still contributing as a very productive vegetable and flower garden. It's the left, west, or animal side of the barn in this first picture from May 25. The garden project was the brainchild and hard work of our tenants, Mark and Beth Smith. Their other pictures are from June 11.

I'll send you another story next month about how the old barn boards and timbers from that barn were recycled by barn demolisher, Aaron Bergmann, into an awesome rustic man cave office.

The Smiths moved some of the smaller barn foundation stones to surround the old summer kitchen which had been transformed into their son's bedroom. That's like a "boy cave" of its own which dates from 1889 and has lots of unique history. If only the walls could speak.

Will, Kayla, Ava, and Blake. The Smiths have done a wonderful job preserving part of our old barn history by developing two applications which continue into the future. Sadly that structure was beyond restoration but at least now its memory lives on. That's a win/win.

Love, Granddad

The Old Barn is Recycled

Dear Will, Kayla, Ava, and Blake,   December 26, 2016

This is my fourth story about the old barn on the Reiss Family farmstead. The first was 6/8/2015 about loading hay into the second story mow or loft. The second was 12/28/2015 about Aaron Bergmann demolishing that barn in 2015 since it was beyond restoration. The third was 10/24/2016 about our tenants converting the old barn footprint into a very fertile family garden. And the fourth is this one about Aaron recycling some of our barn wood into a home office or man cave for one of his friends.

Will, Kayla, Ava, and Blake, my grandfather George Reiss built this barn about 1920 and used it daily for animals and storage until he retired from farming in 1948. The barn eventually became obsolete when farmers converted to jumbo hay bales which were stored outside rather than in two-story barns. Later farm tenants did not raise animals so the barn was simply abandoned and left to the forces of nature. That's the way the world normally works. I think my grandfather would be pleased that his wood is seeing new life and that we have documented his barn history in four stories to his great great grandchildren. This is the final story in your book of 2016 Granddad's Mondays. It is also be the final story in this two-volume set of books I compiled of 179 stories that deal with the Reiss family and farm in St. Clair County, Illinois.

Love, Granddad

MATRIARCH #2
Anna Sybilla Feder Reiss

MATRIARCH #3
Katie Luetzelschwab Reiss